NAOMI

SEASON ONE

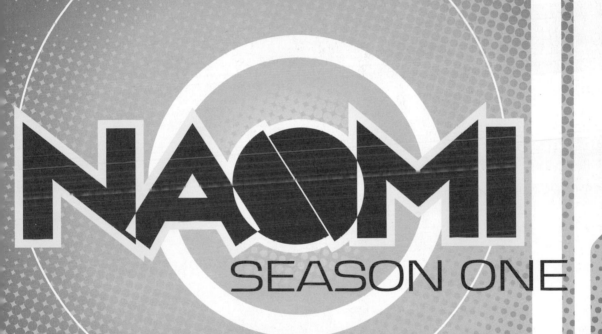

NAOMI
SEASON ONE

BRIAN MICHAEL BENDIS
DAVID F. WALKER
writers

JAMAL CAMPBELL
artist

JOSH REED
CARLOS M. MANGUAL
letterers

JAMAL CAMPBELL
collection and original series cover artist

NAOMI created by BENDIS, WALKER, and CAMPBELL

SUPERMAN created by JERRY SIEGEL and JOE SHUSTER
By special arrangement with the Jerry Siegel family

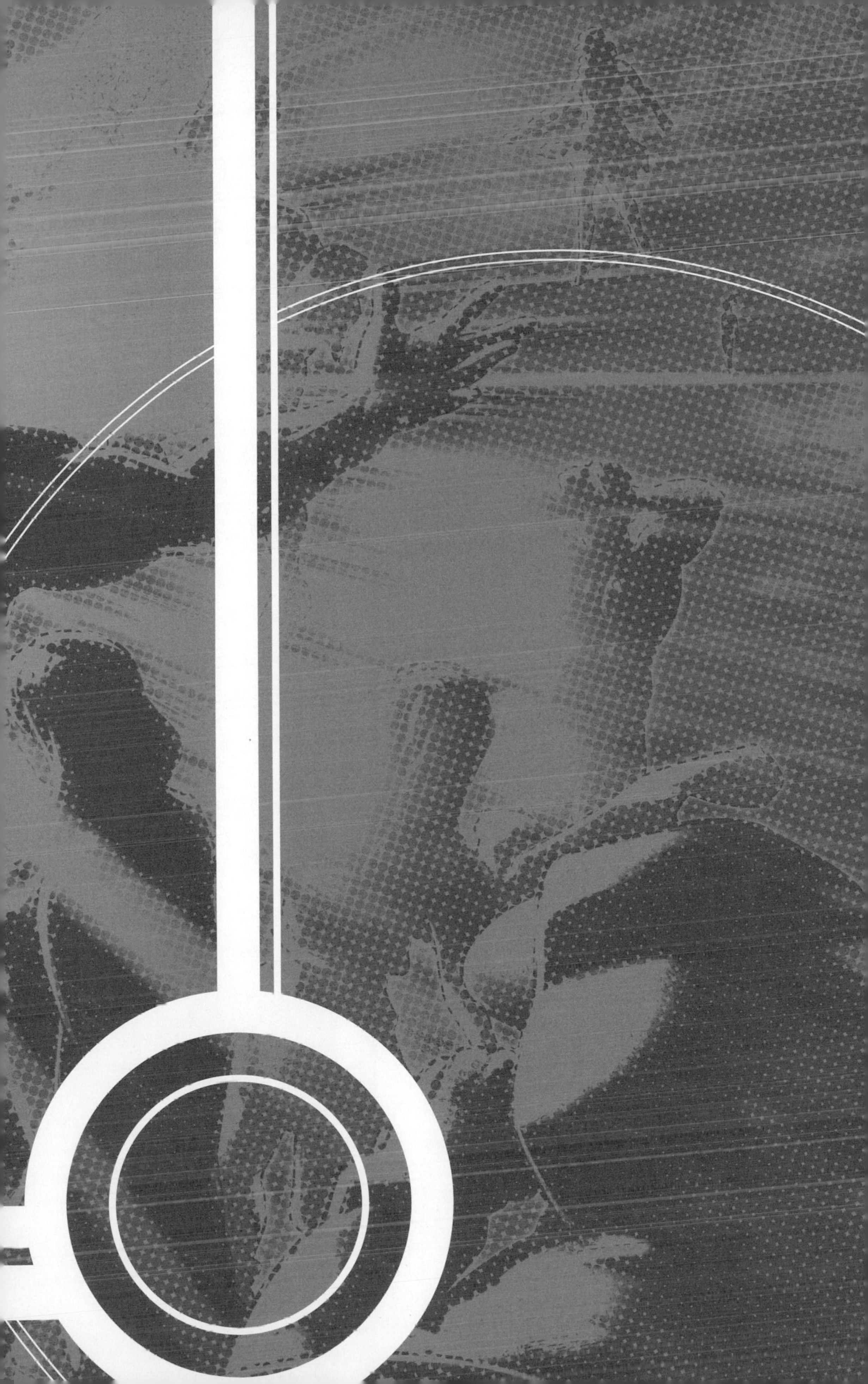

MIKE COTTON, ANDY KHOURI Editors – Original Series
JESSICA CHEN Associate Editor – Original Series
JEB WOODARD Group Editor – Collected Editions
SCOTT NYBAKKEN Editor – Collected Edition
STEVE COOK Design Director – Books
CURTIS KING JR. Publication Design
ERIN VANOVER Publication Production

BOB HARRAS Senior VP – Editor-in-Chief, DC Comics
PAT McCALLUM Executive Editor, DC Comics

DAN DiDIO Publisher
JIM LEE Publisher & Chief Creative Officer
BOBBIE CHASE VP – New Publishing Initiatives & Talent Development
DON FALLETTI VP – Manufacturing Operations & Workflow Management
LAWRENCE GANEM VP – Talent Services
ALISON GILL Senior VP – Manufacturing & Operations
HANK KANALZ Senior VP – Publishing Strategy & Support Services
DAN MIRON VP – Publishing Operations
NICK J. NAPOLITANO VP – Manufacturing Administration & Design
NANCY SPEARS VP – Sales
MICHELE R. WELLS VP & Executive Editor, Young Reader

NAOMI: SEASON ONE

DC Comics, 2900 West Alameda Ave., Burbank, CA 91505
Printed by LSC Communications, Kendallville, IN, USA. 9/20/19.
First Printing. ISBN: 978-1-4012-9495-3

Library of Congress
Cataloging-in-Publication Data is available.

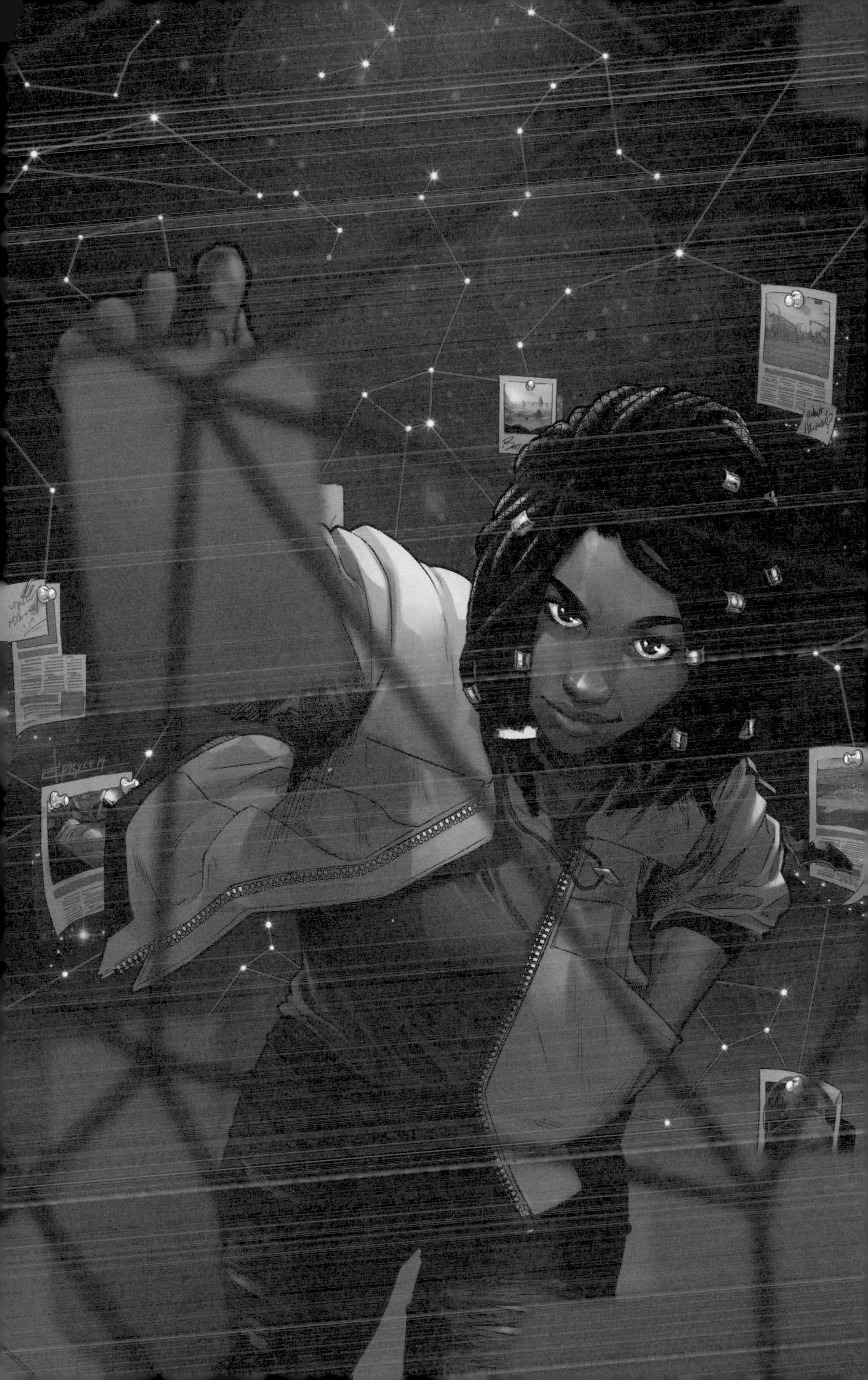

ONE

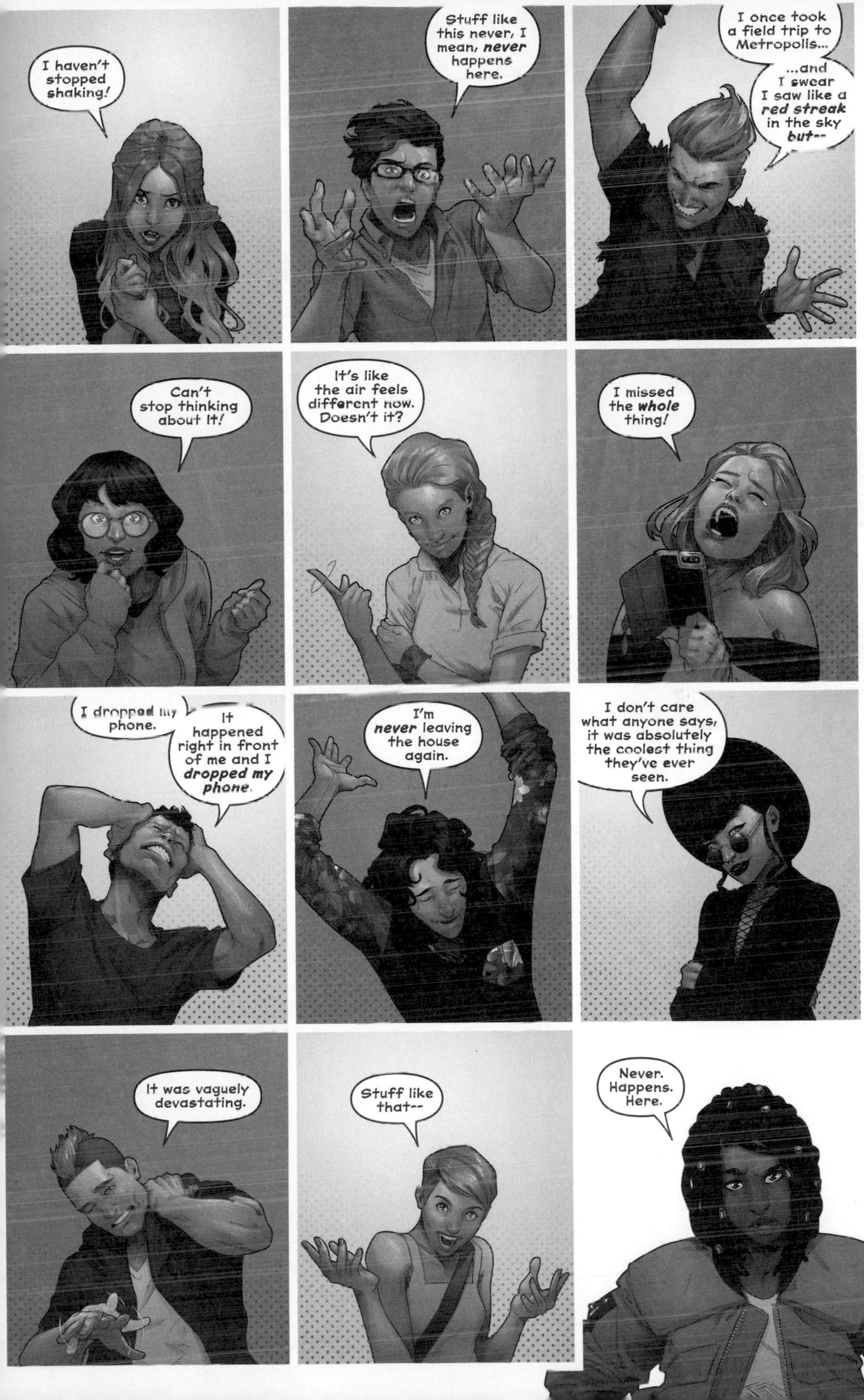
I haven't stopped shaking!
Stuff like this never, I mean, *never* happens here.
I once took a field trip to Metropolis...
...and I swear I saw like a *red streak* in the sky *but--*
Can't stop thinking about it!
It's like the air feels different now. Doesn't it?
I missed the *whole* thing!
I dropped my phone.
It happened right in front of me and I *dropped my phone*.
I'm *never* leaving the house again.
I don't care what anyone says, it was absolutely the coolest thing they've ever seen.
It was vaguely devastating.
Stuff like that--
Never. Happens. Here.

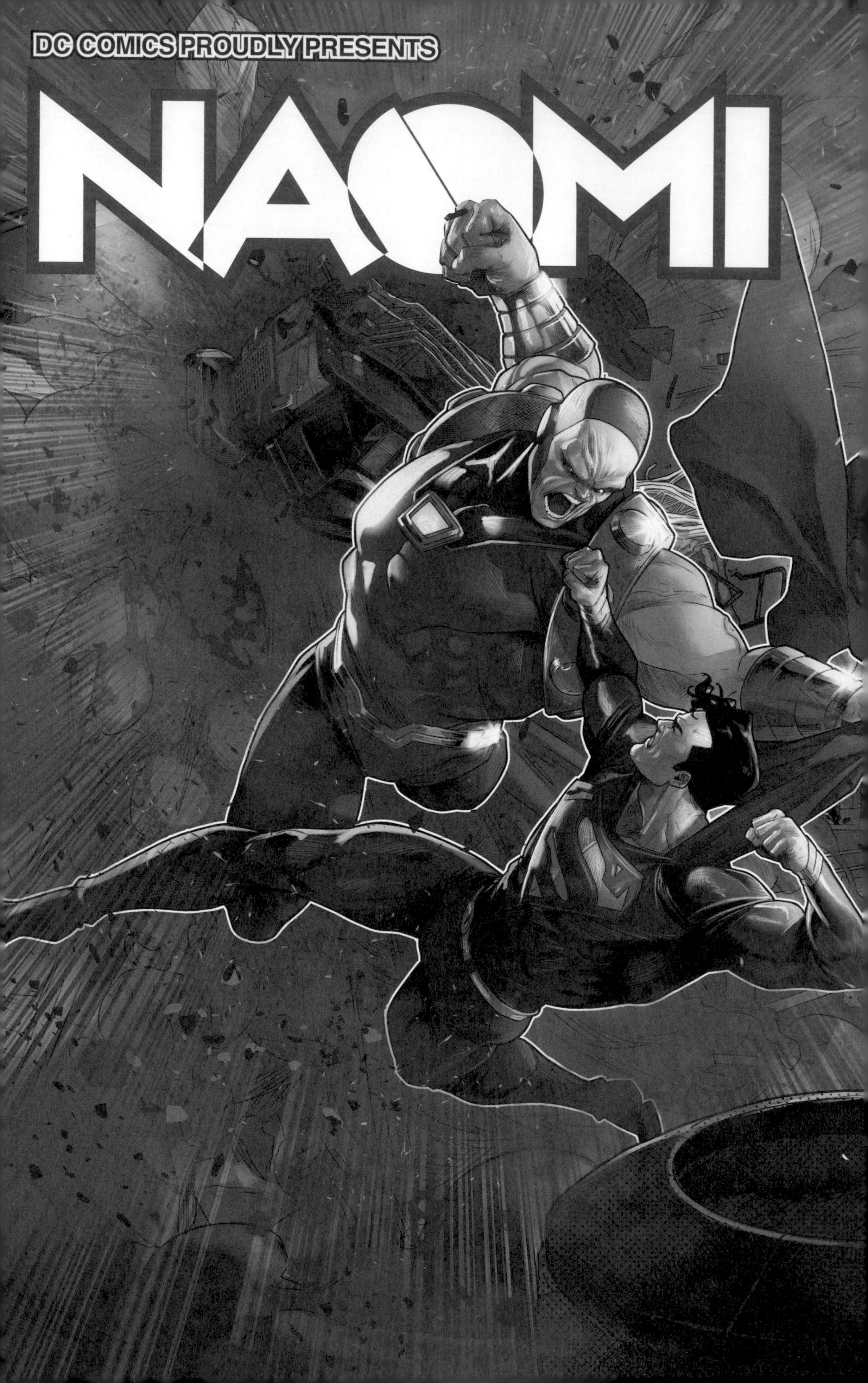
DC COMICS PROUDLY PRESENTS
NAOMI

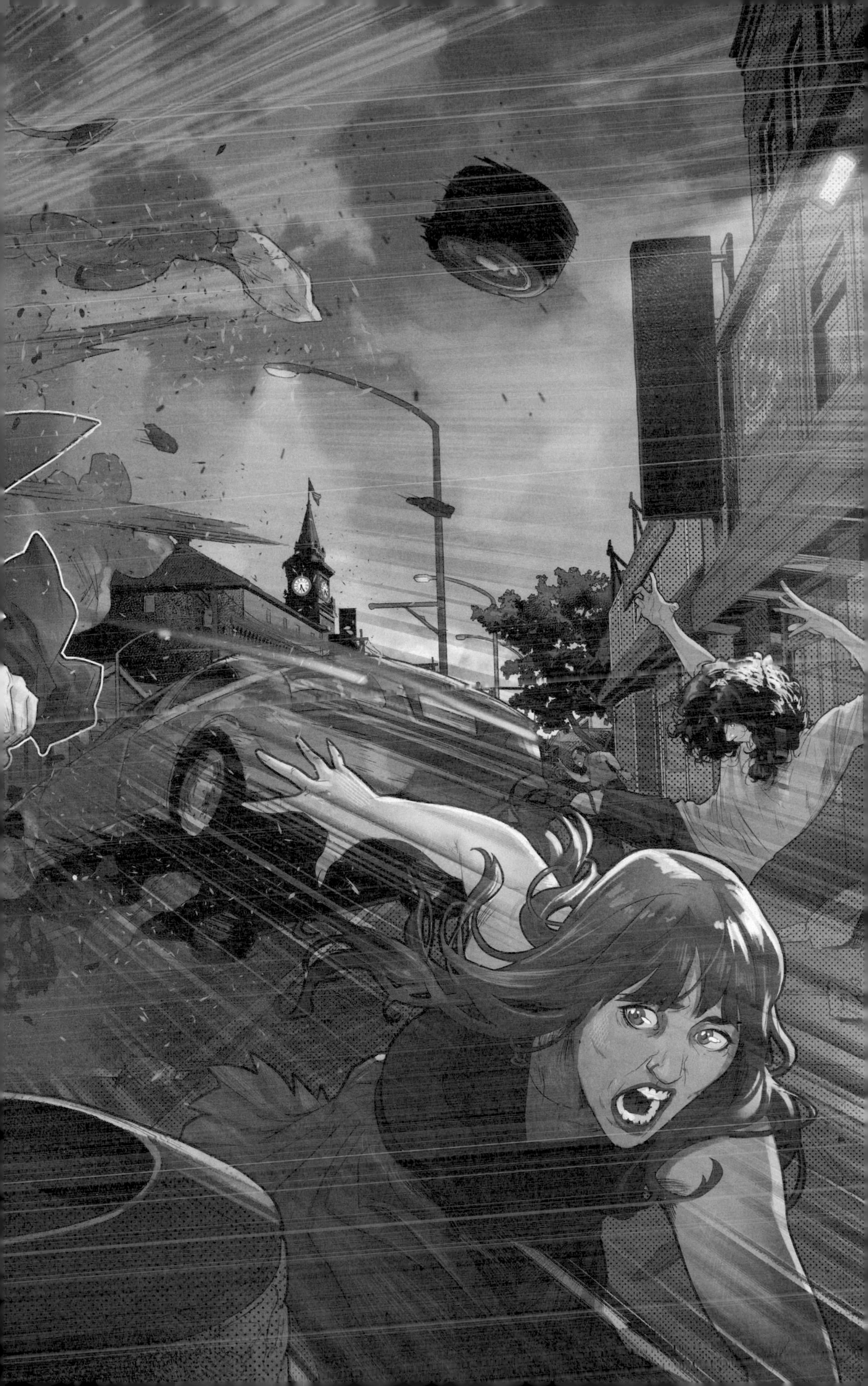

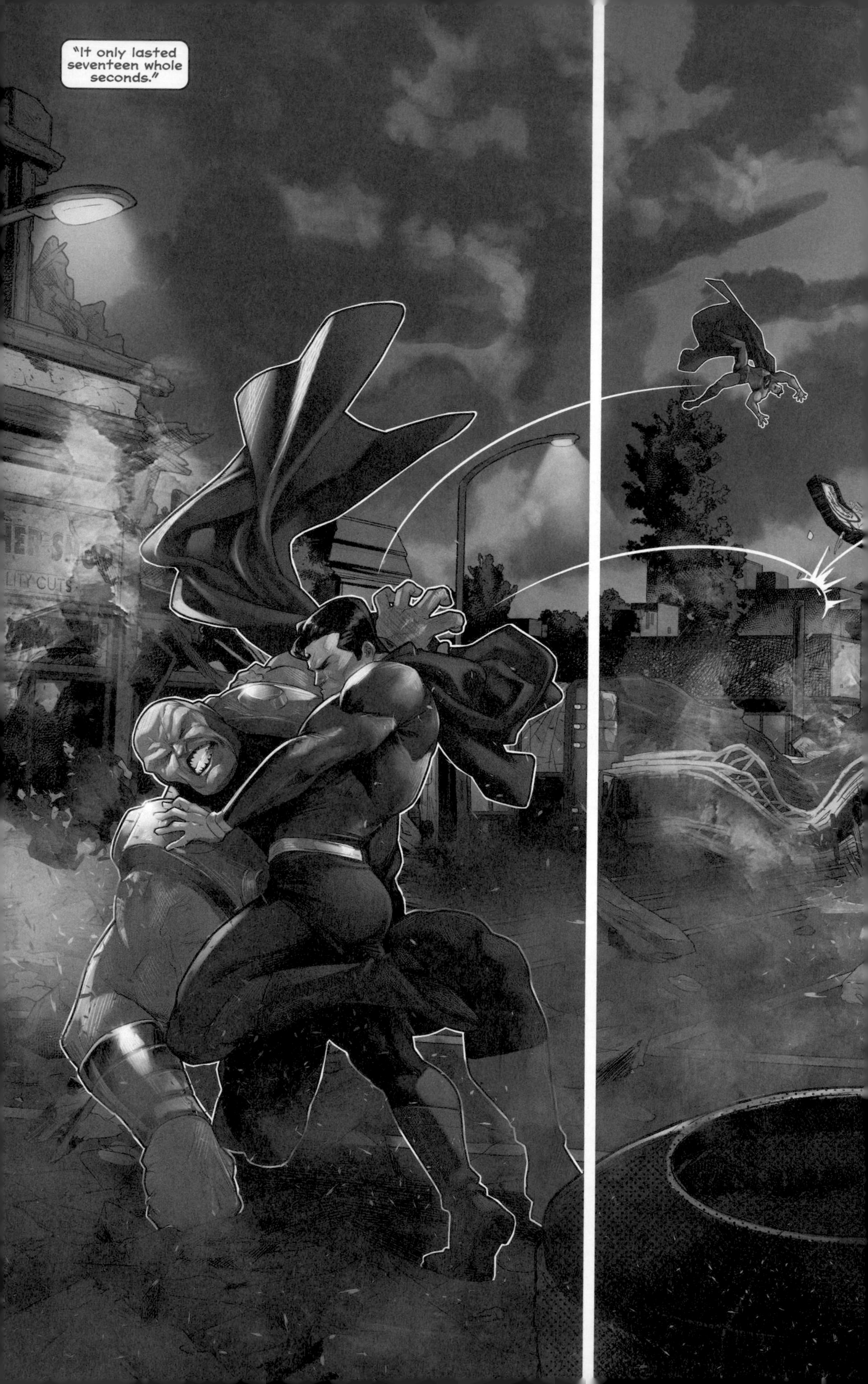
"It only lasted seventeen whole seconds."
LITY CUTS

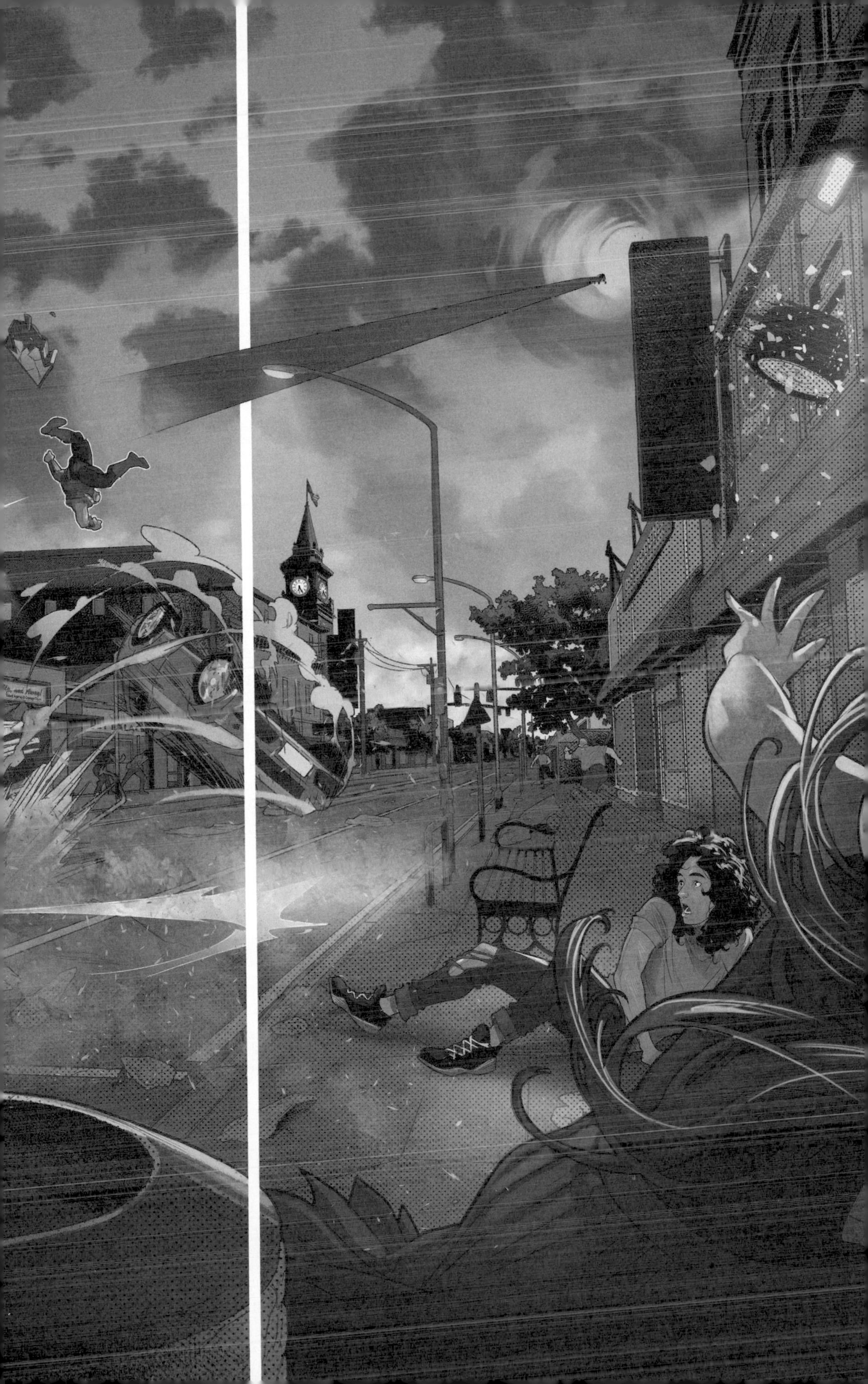

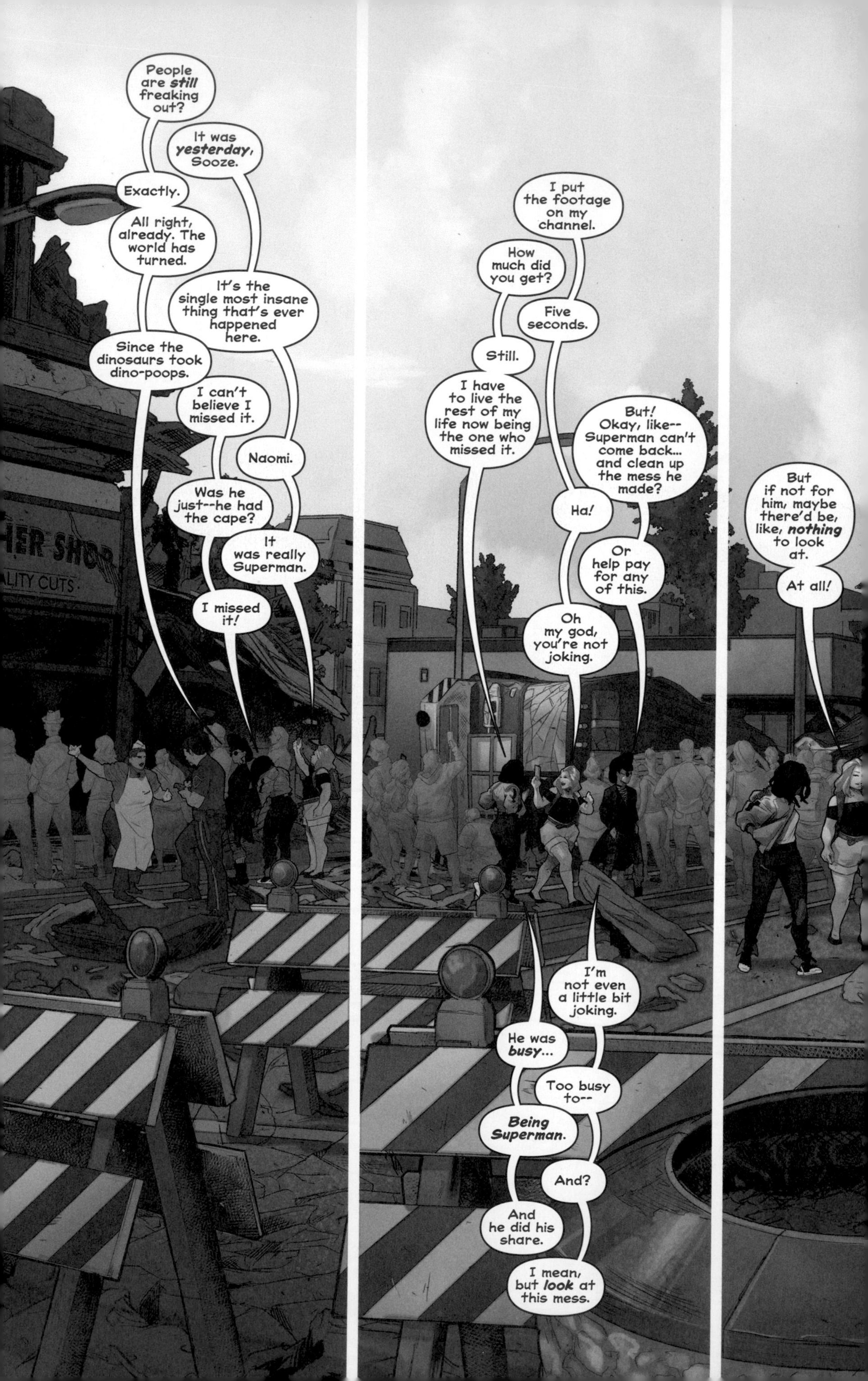

People are *still* freaking out?
It was *yesterday*, Sooze.
Exactly.
All right, already. The world has turned.
It's the single most insane thing that's ever happened here.
Since the dinosaurs took dino-poops.
I can't believe I missed it.
Naomi.
Was he just--he had the cape?
It was really Superman.
I missed it!
IER SHOP
ALITY CUTS
I put the footage on my channel.
How much did you get?
Five seconds.
Still.
I have to live the rest of my life now being the one who missed it.
Ha!
But! Okay, like-- Superman can't come back... and clean up the mess he made?
Or help pay for any of this.
Oh my god, you're not joking.
I'm not even a little bit joking.
He was *busy*...
Too busy to--
Being Superman.
And?
And he did his share.
I mean, but *look* at this mess.
But if not for him, maybe there'd be, like, *nothing* to look at.
At all!

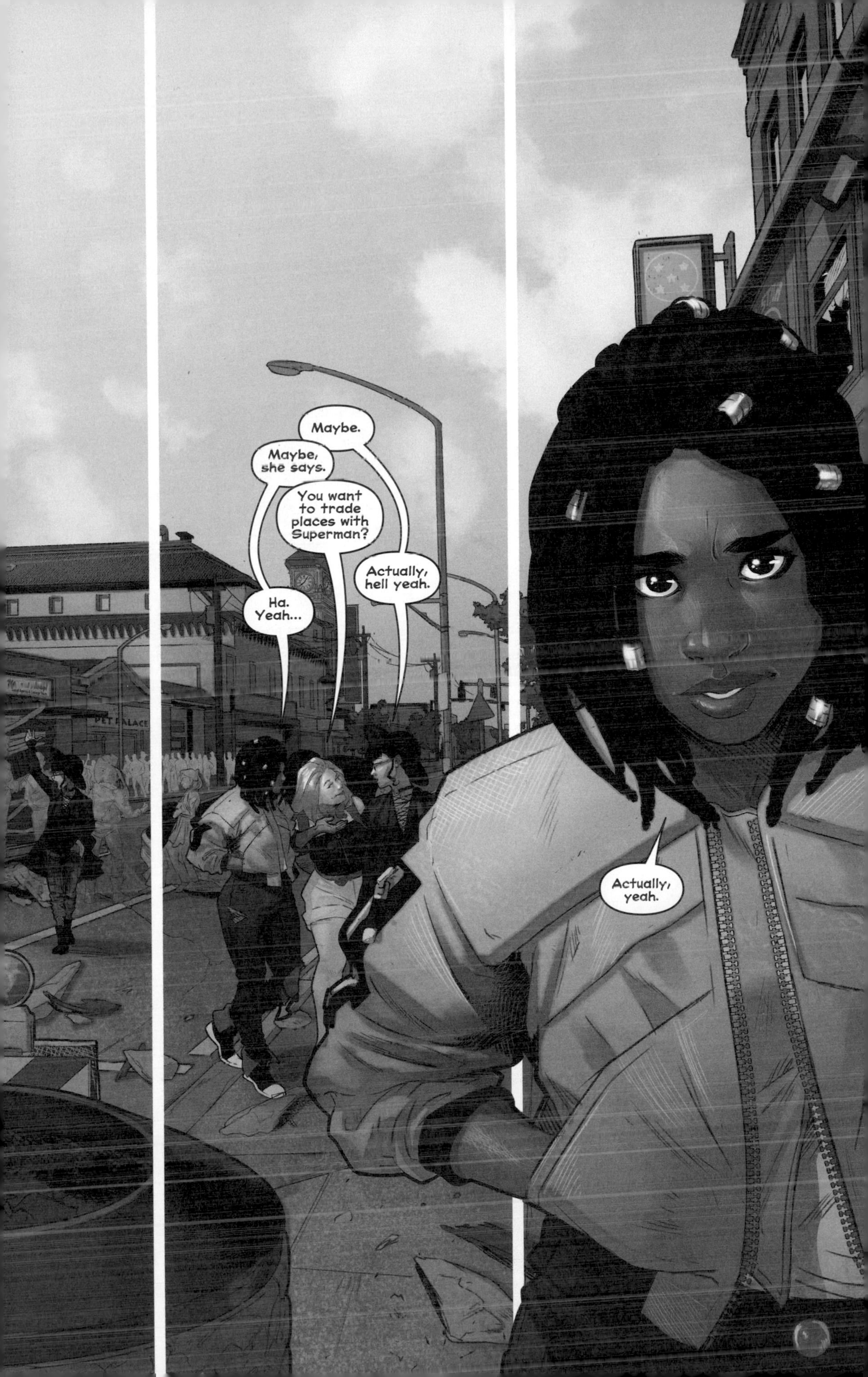
Maybe.
Maybe, she says.
You want to trade places with Superman?
Actually, hell yeah.
Ha. Yeah...
Actually, yeah.
PET PALACE

EXCLUSIVE! SUPERMAN SAVES ME!
IS REAL! THIS HAPPENED TODAY!
3 views
#superman #portoswego #yellowalienm
👍 👎
AnnaBab
59 subscribe

COLLEEN
OPEN
Colle

lighthous
searc
Superman Port Oswego
images   news   vide

0 results
Did you mean...
Superman Metropolis?
Superman New York?
Superman Gotham?
Superman Coast City?

video results
EXCLUSIVE! SUPERMAN S
ME! THIS IS REAL
AnnaB

lighthous
se
Superman
Superman Metro
Superman trunk
Superman v Ba
Who is Super
What is Super
Does Superm
Is there mo

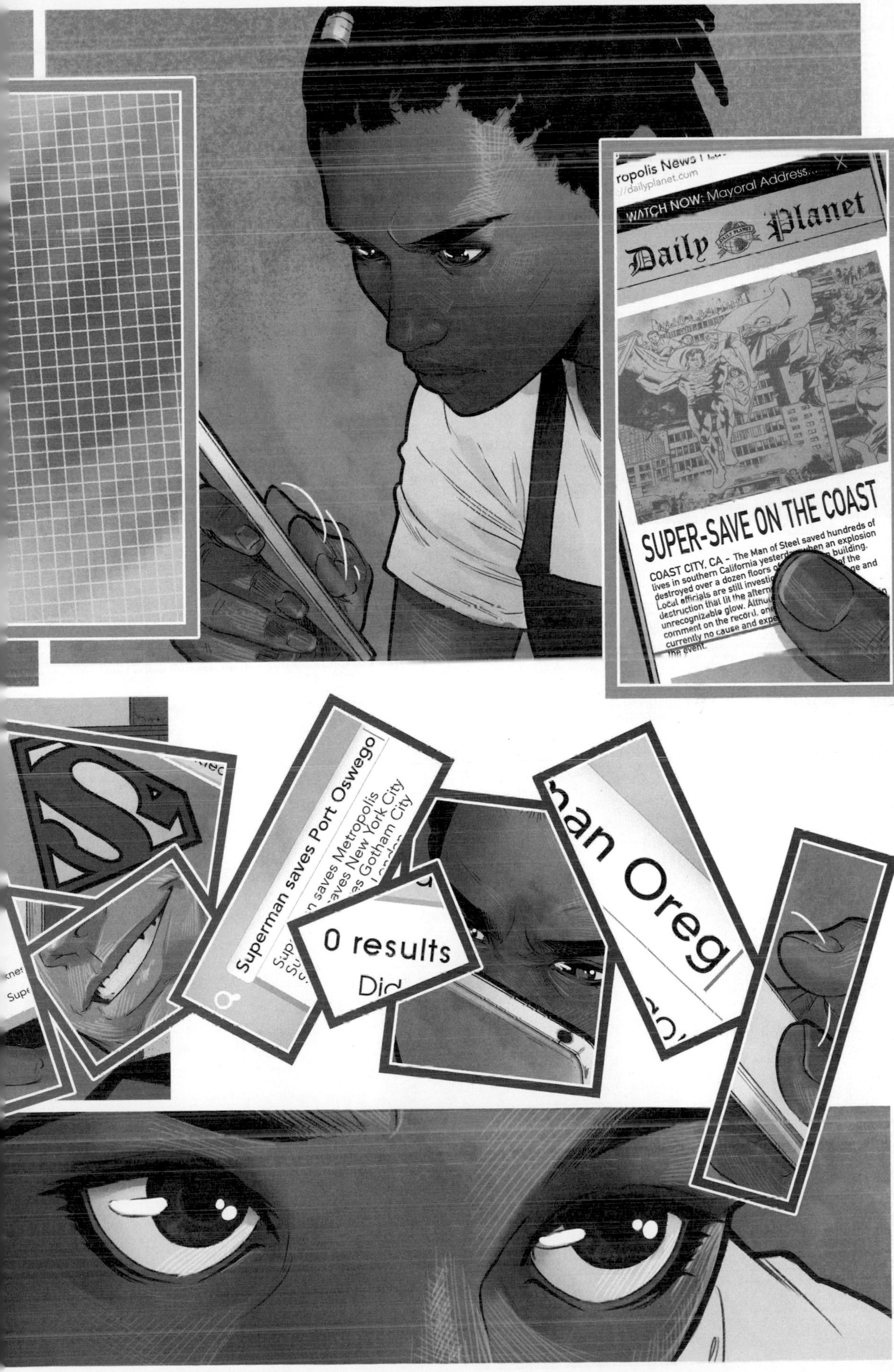

ropolis News
://dailyplanet.com
WATCH NOW: Mayoral Address...
Daily Planet
SUPER-SAVE ON THE COAST
COAST CITY, CA - The Man of Steel saved hundreds of lives in southern California yesterd destroyed over a dozen floors o Local officials are still investi destruction that lit the aftern unrecognizable glow. Althou comment on the record, one currently no cause and expe the event.
Superman saves Port Oswego
Superman saves Metropolis
New York City
Gotham City
0 results
Did
an Oreg

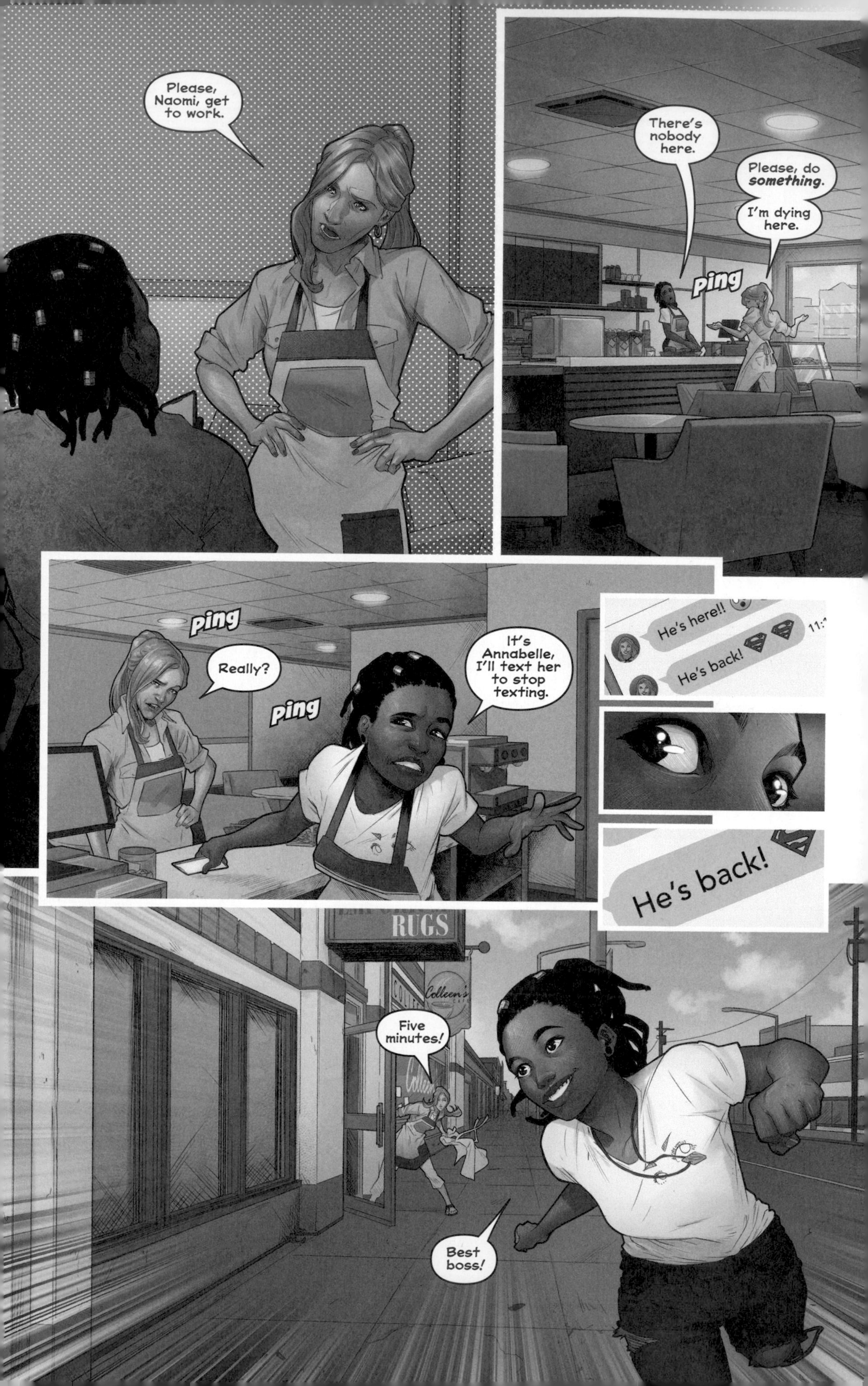
Please, Naomi, get to work.
There's nobody here.
Please, do *something*.
I'm dying here.
Ping
Ping
Really?
Ping
It's Annabelle, I'll text her to stop texting.
He's here!!
He's back!
He's back!
RUGS
Five minutes!
Best boss!

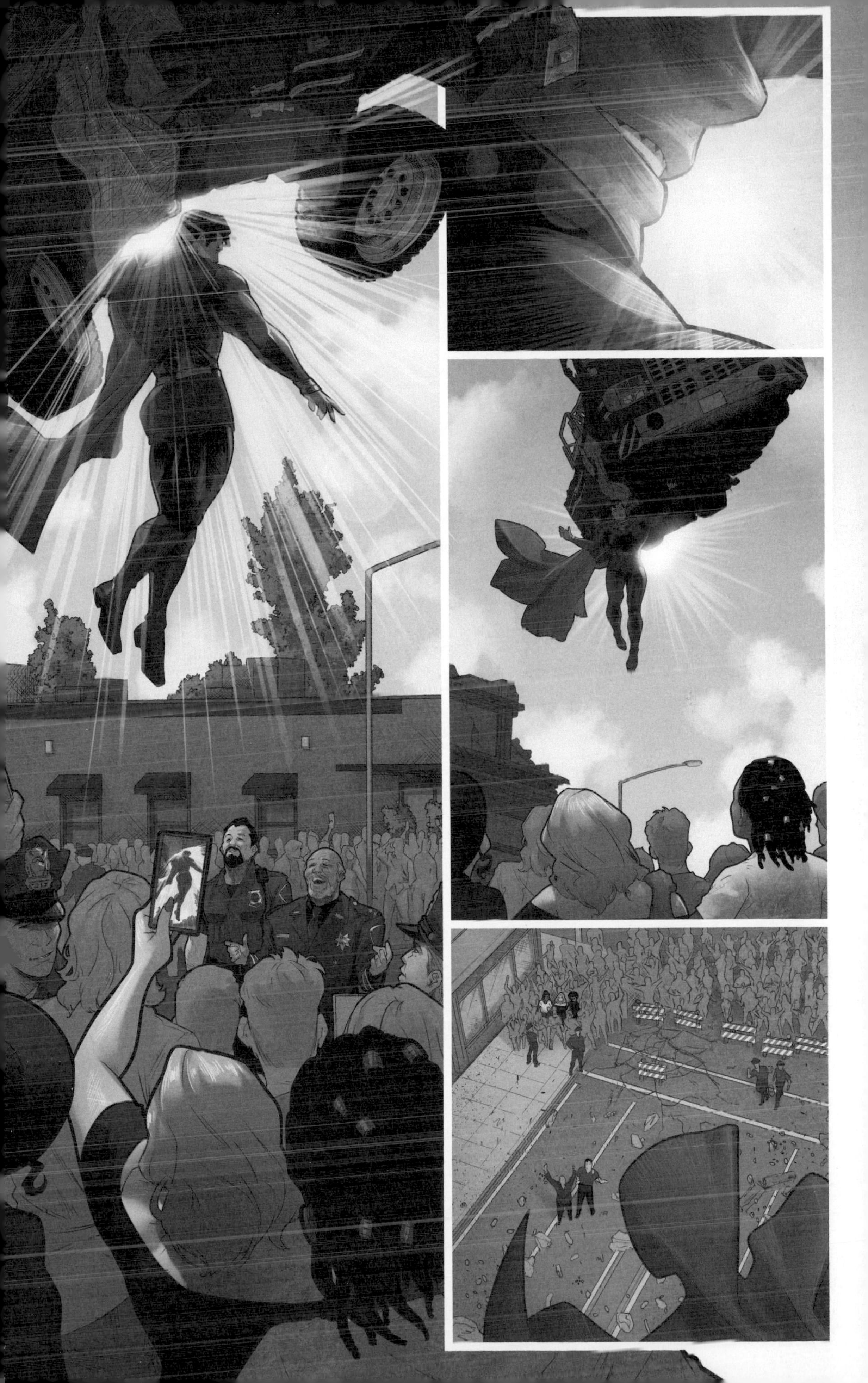

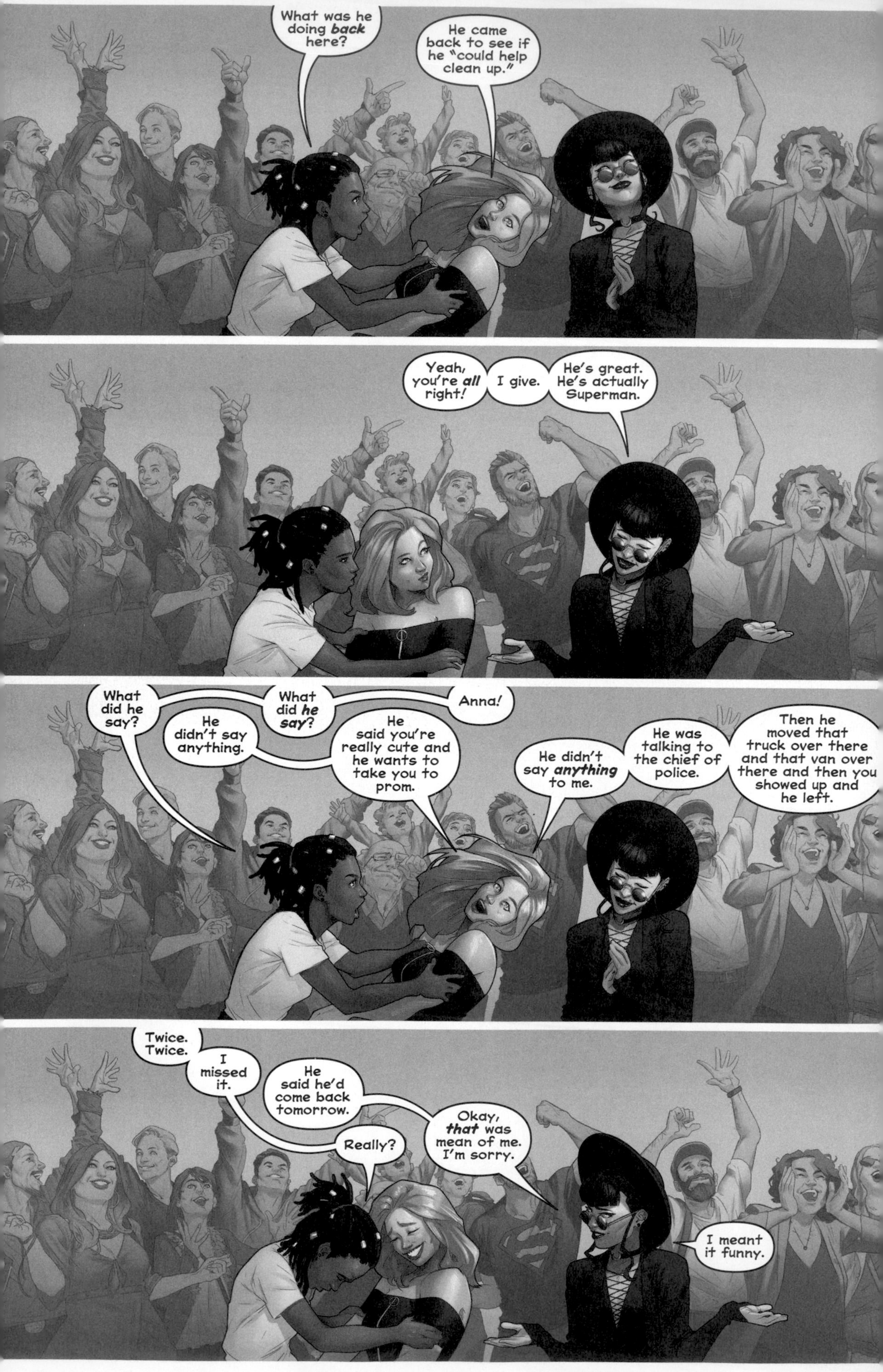
What was he doing *back* here?
He came back to see if he "could help clean up."
Yeah, you're *all* right!
I give.
He's great. He's actually Superman.
What did he say?
What did *he say*?
Anna!
He didn't say anything.
He said you're really cute and he wants to take you to prom.
He didn't say *anything* to me.
He was talking to the chief of police.
Then he moved that truck over there and that van over there and then you showed up and he left.
Twice. Twice.
I missed it.
He said he'd come back tomorrow.
Really?
Okay, *that* was mean of me. I'm sorry.
I meant it funny.

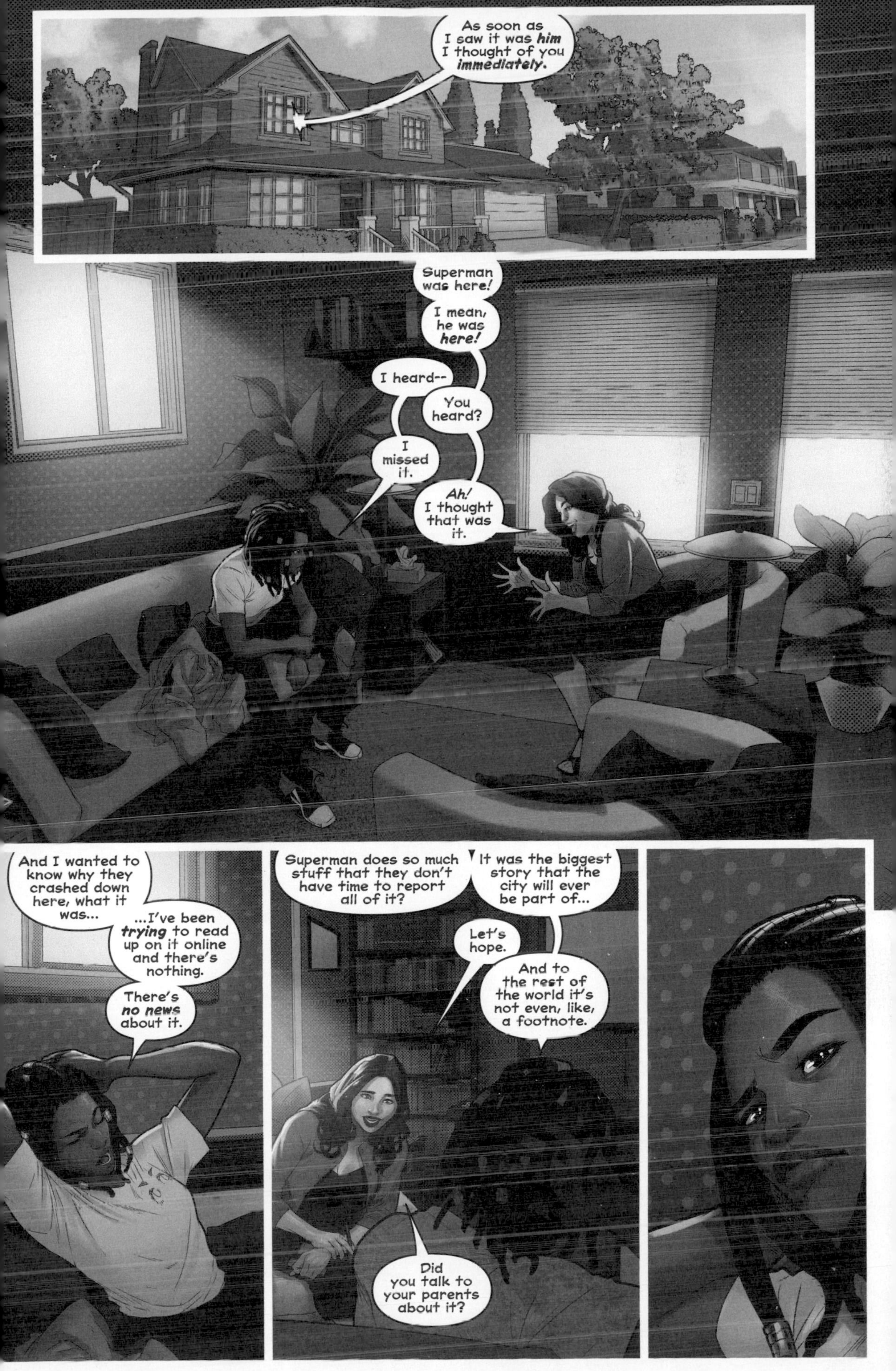
As soon as I saw it was *him* I thought of you *immediately.*
Superman was here!
I mean, he was *here!*
I heard--
You heard?
I missed it.
Ah! I thought that was it.
And I wanted to know why they crashed down here, what it was...
...I've been *trying* to read up on it online and there's nothing.
There's *no news* about it.
Superman does so much stuff that they don't have time to report all of it?
It was the biggest story that the city will ever be part of...
Let's hope.
And to the rest of the world it's not even, like, a footnote.
Did you talk to your parents about it?

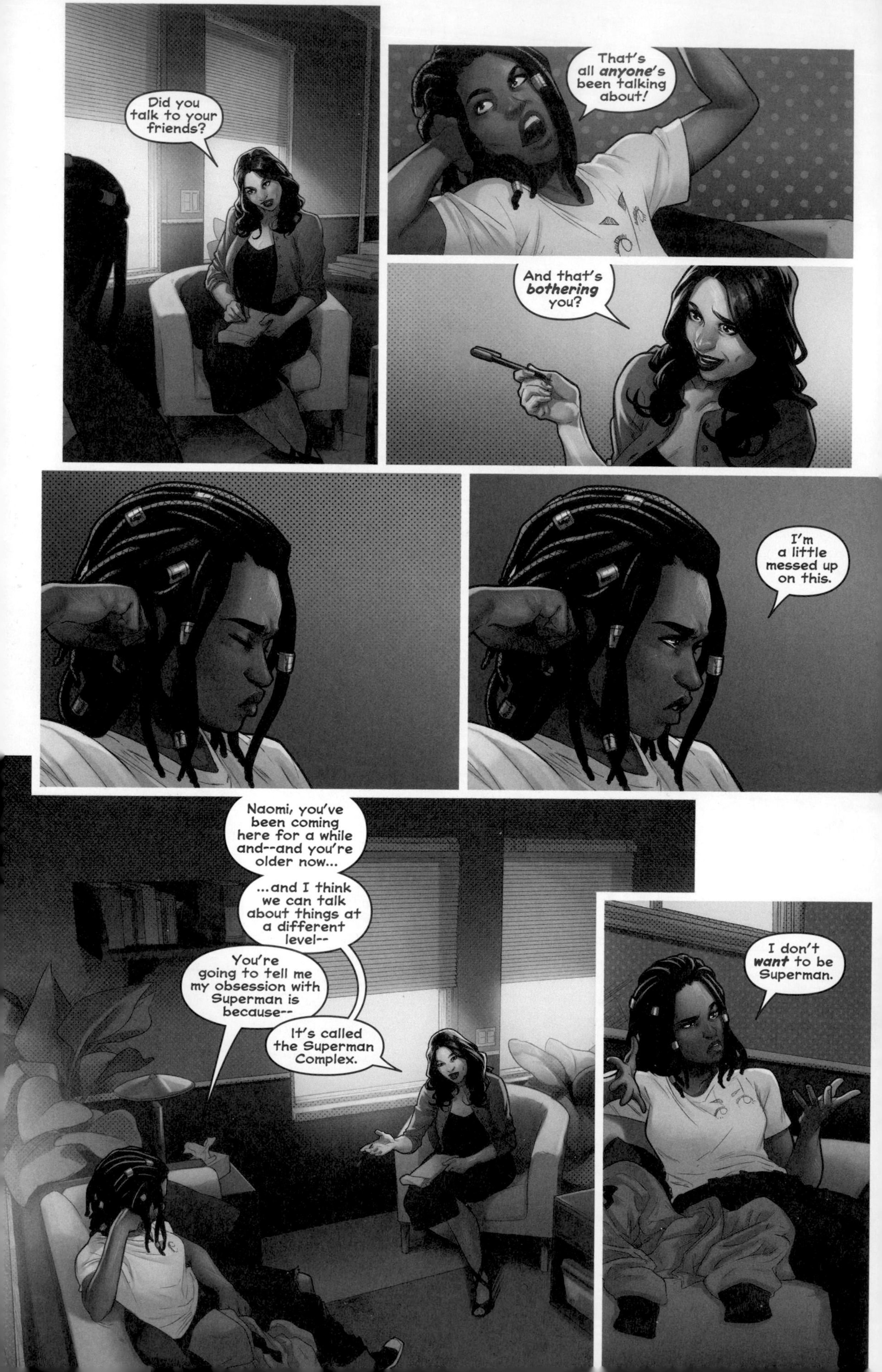

Did you talk to your friends?
That's all *anyone*'s been talking about!
And that's *bothering* you?
I'm a little messed up on this.
Naomi, you've been coming here for a while and--and you're older now...
...and I think we can talk about things at a different level--
You're going to tell me my obsession with Superman is because--
It's called the Superman Complex.
I don't *want* to be Superman.

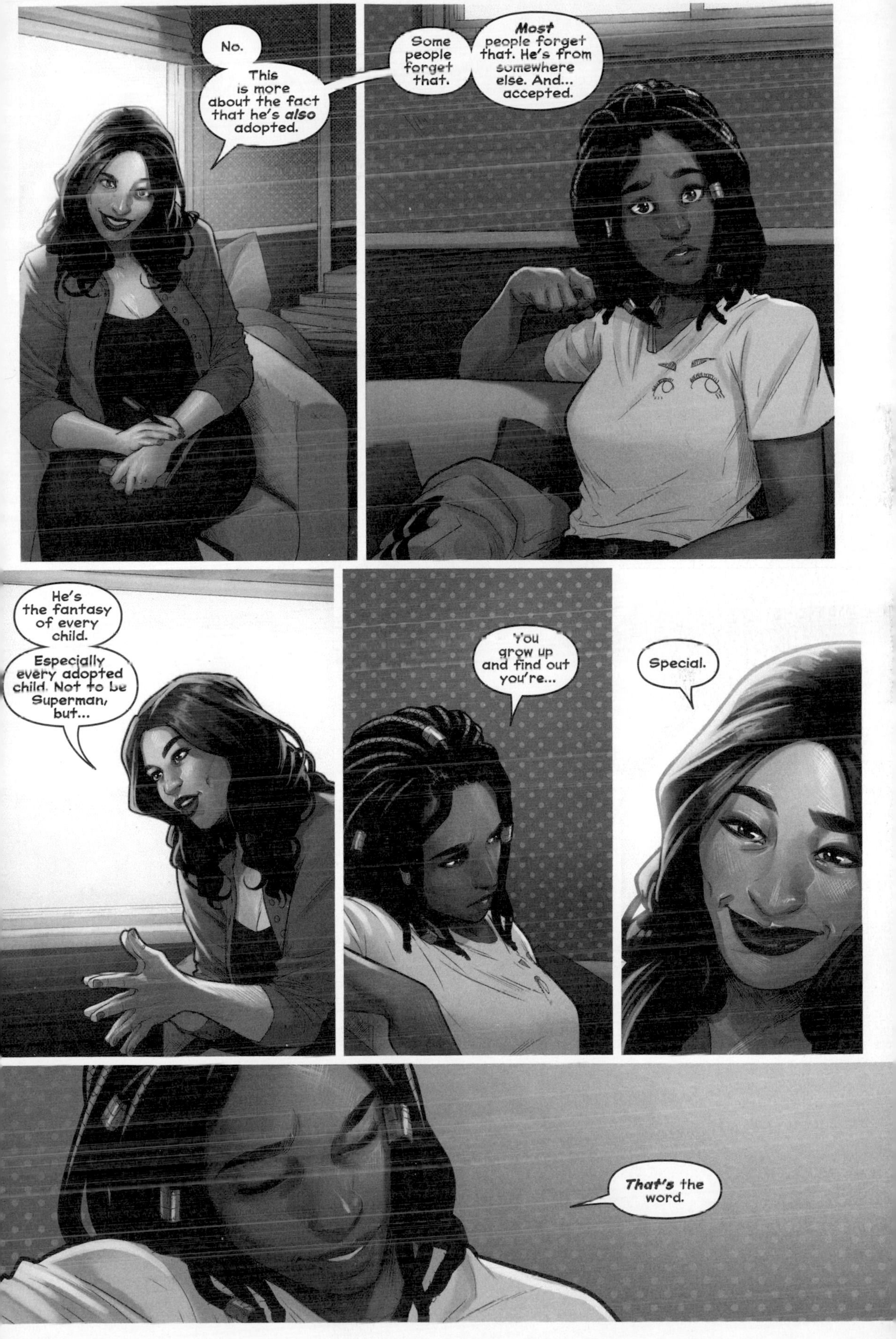
No.
This is more about the fact that he's *also* adopted.
Some people forget that.
Most people forget that. He's from somewhere else. And... accepted.
He's the fantasy of every child.
Especially every adopted child. Not to be Superman, but...
You grow up and find out you're...
Special.
That's the word.

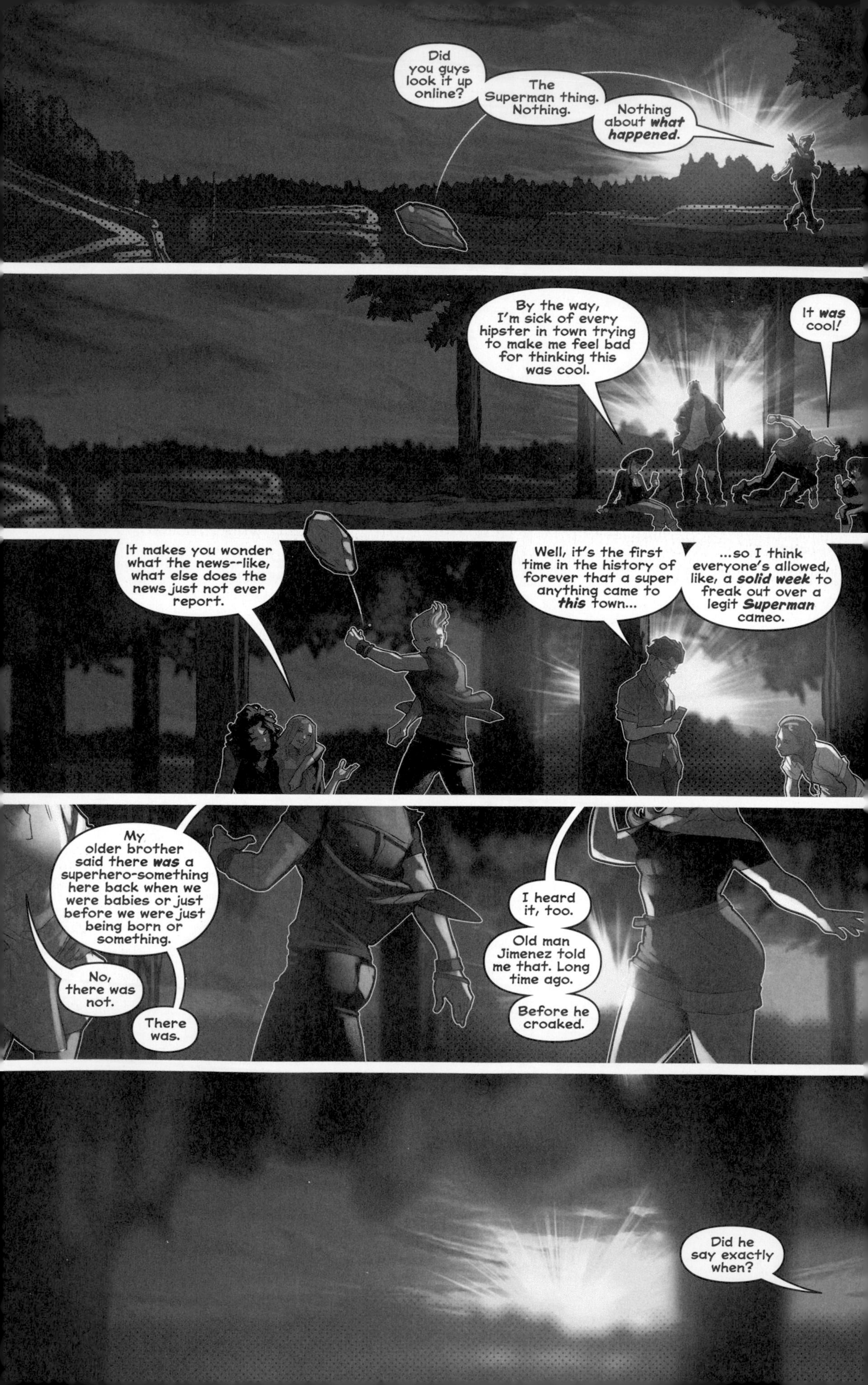
Did you guys look it up online?
The Superman thing. Nothing.
Nothing about *what happened*.
By the way, I'm sick of every hipster in town trying to make me feel bad for thinking this was cool.
It *was* cool!
It makes you wonder what the news--like, what else does the news just not ever report.
Well, it's the first time in the history of forever that a super anything came to *this* town...
...so I think everyone's allowed, like, a *solid week* to freak out over a legit *Superman* cameo.
My older brother said there *was* a superhero-something here back when we were babies or just before we were just being born or something.
No, there was not.
There was.
I heard it, too.
Old man Jimenez told me that. Long time ago.
Before he croaked.
Did he say exactly when?

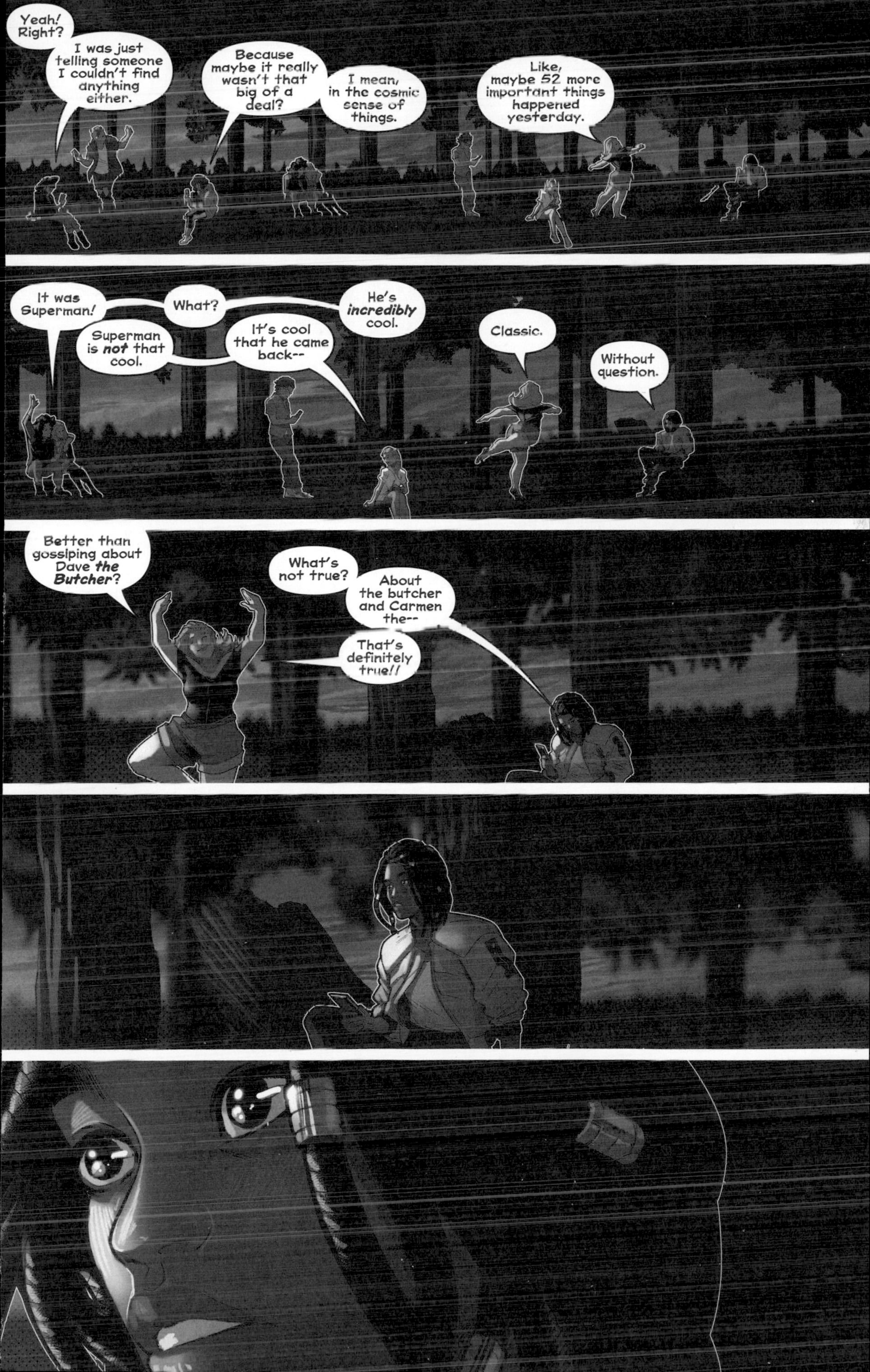

Yeah! Right?
I was just telling someone I couldn't find anything either.
Because maybe it really wasn't that big of a deal?
I mean, in the cosmic sense of things.
Like, maybe 52 more important things happened yesterday.
It was Superman!
What?
He's *incredibly* cool.
Superman is ***not*** that cool.
It's cool that he came back--
Classic.
Without question.
Better than gossiping about Dave ***the Butcher***?
What's not true?
About the butcher and Carmen the--
That's definitely ***true!!***

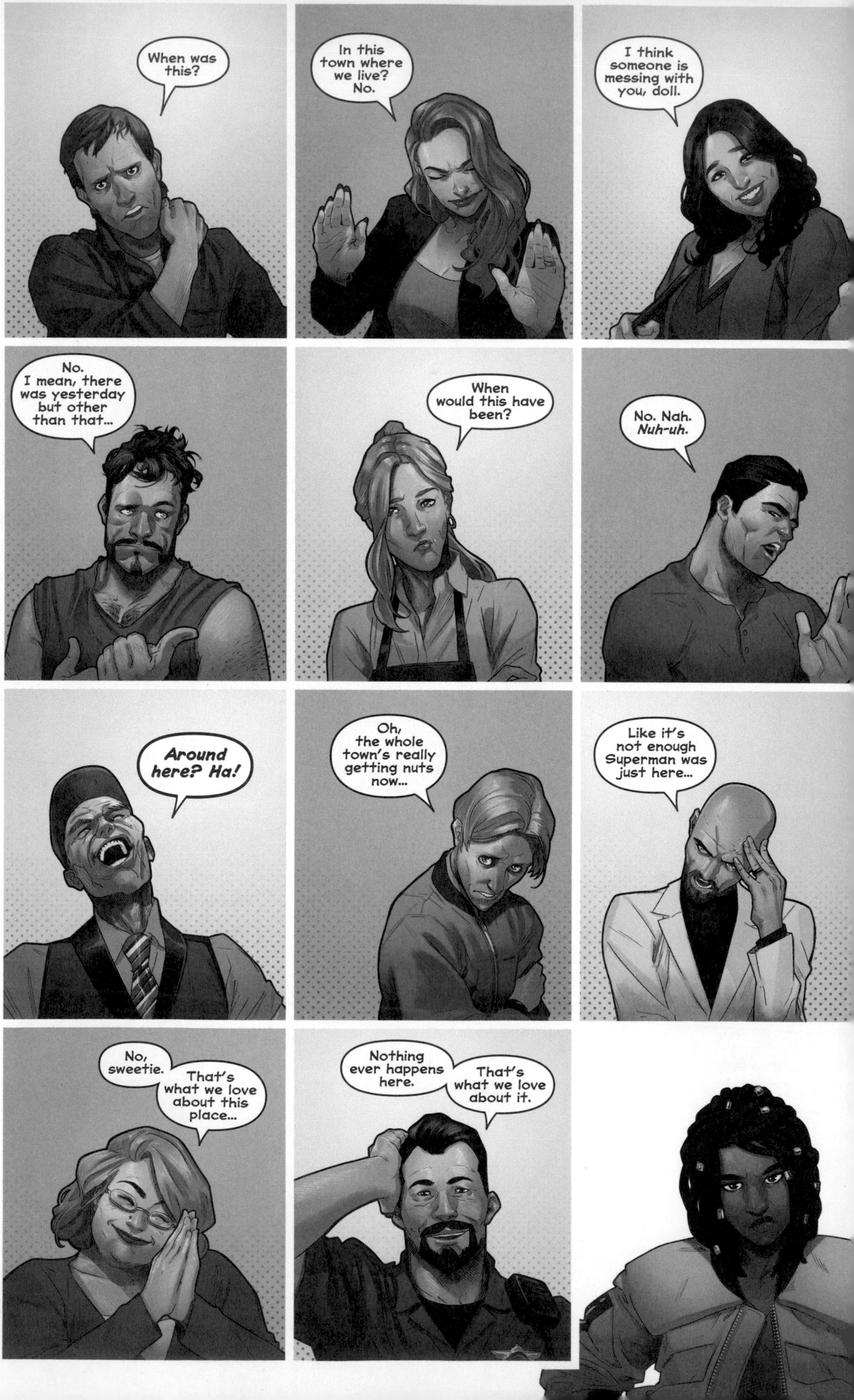
When was this?
In this town where we live? No.
I think someone is messing with you, doll.
No. I mean, there was yesterday but other than that...
When would this have been?
No. Nah. *Nuh-uh.*
Around here? Ha!
Oh, the whole town's really getting nuts now...
Like it's not enough Superman was just here...
No, sweetie.
That's what we love about this place...
Nothing ever happens here.
That's what we love about it.

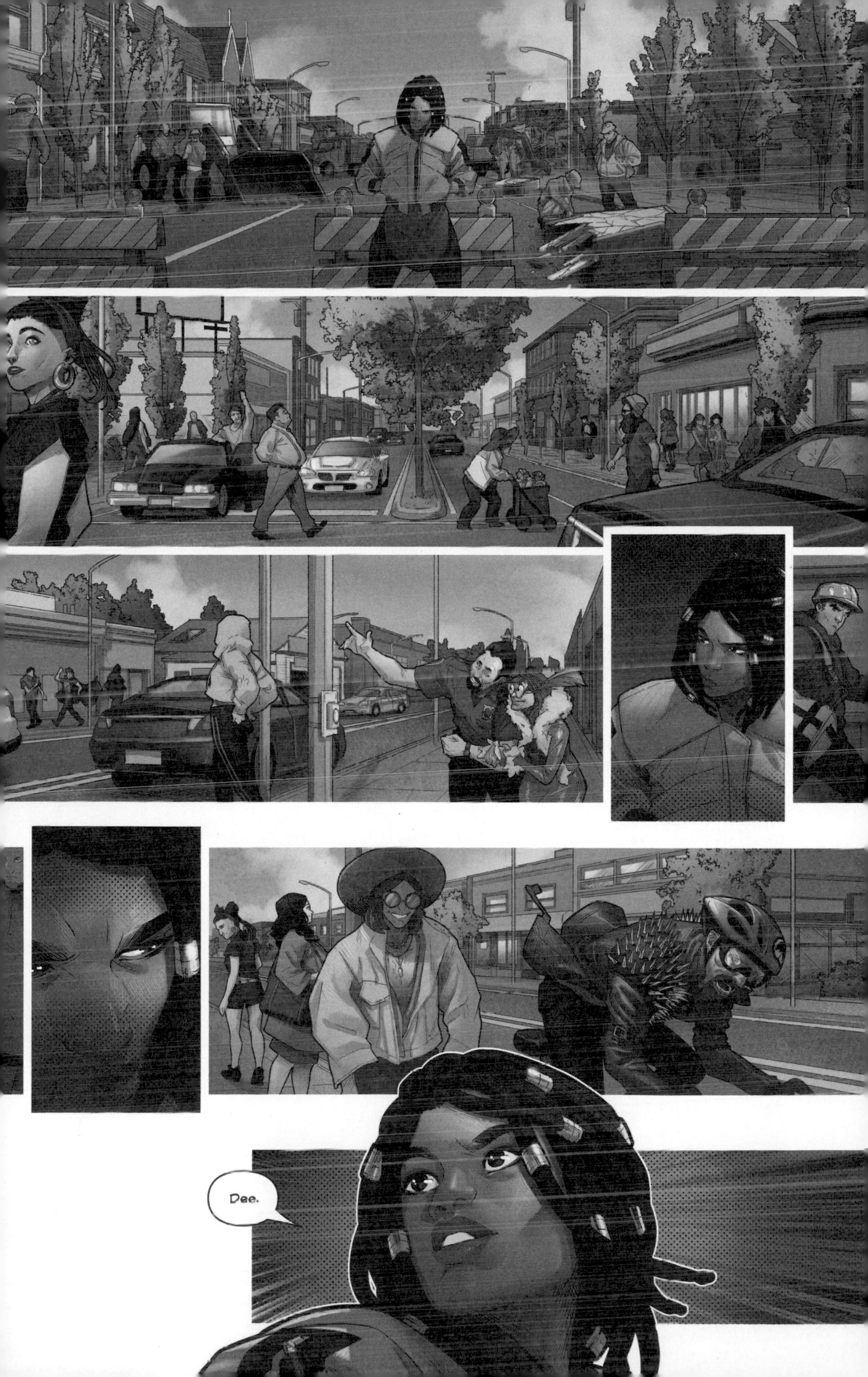
Dee.

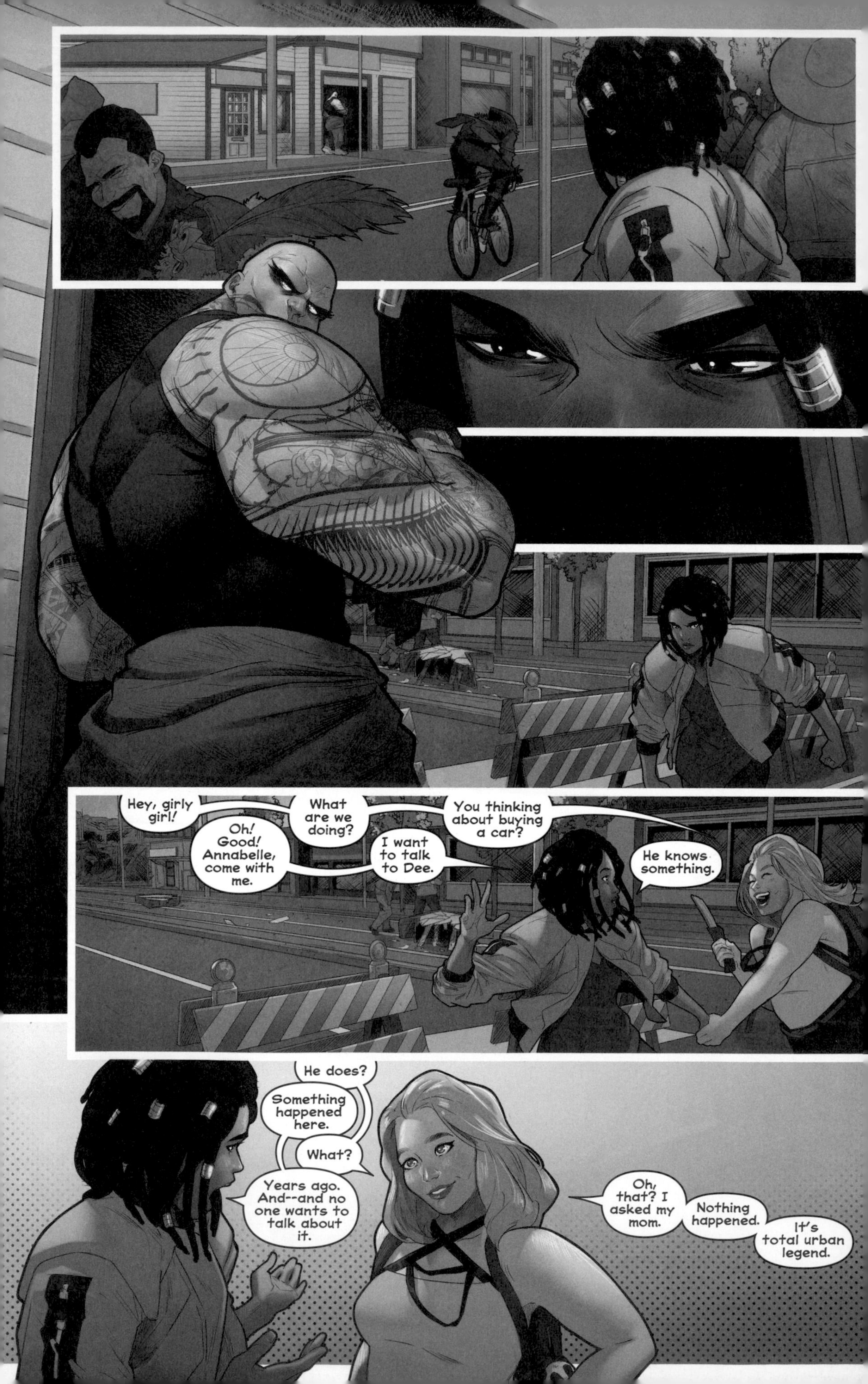

Hey, girly girl!
What are we doing?
You thinking about buying a car?
Oh! Good! Annabelle, come with me.
I want to talk to Dee.
He knows something.
He does?
Something happened here.
What?
Years ago. And--and no one wants to talk about it.
Oh, that? I asked my mom.
Nothing happened.
It's total urban legend.

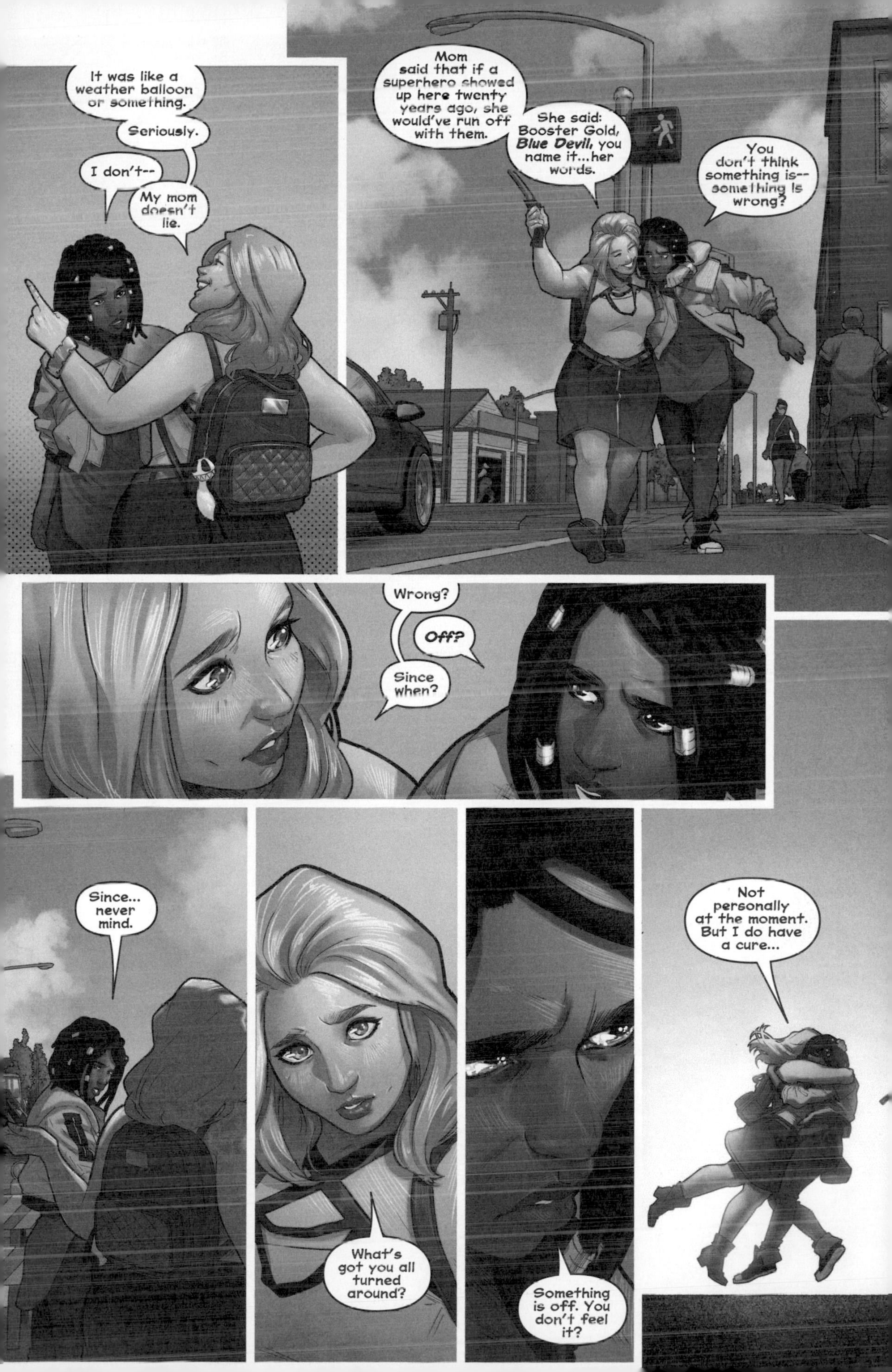
It was like a weather balloon or something.
Seriously.
I don't--
My mom doesn't lie.
Mom said that if a superhero showed up here twenty years ago, she would've run off with them.
She said: Booster Gold, *Blue Devil*, you name it...her words.
You don't think something is--something is wrong?
Wrong?
Off?
Since when?
Since... never mind.
What's got you all turned around?
Something is off. You don't feel it?
Not personally at the moment. But I do have a cure...

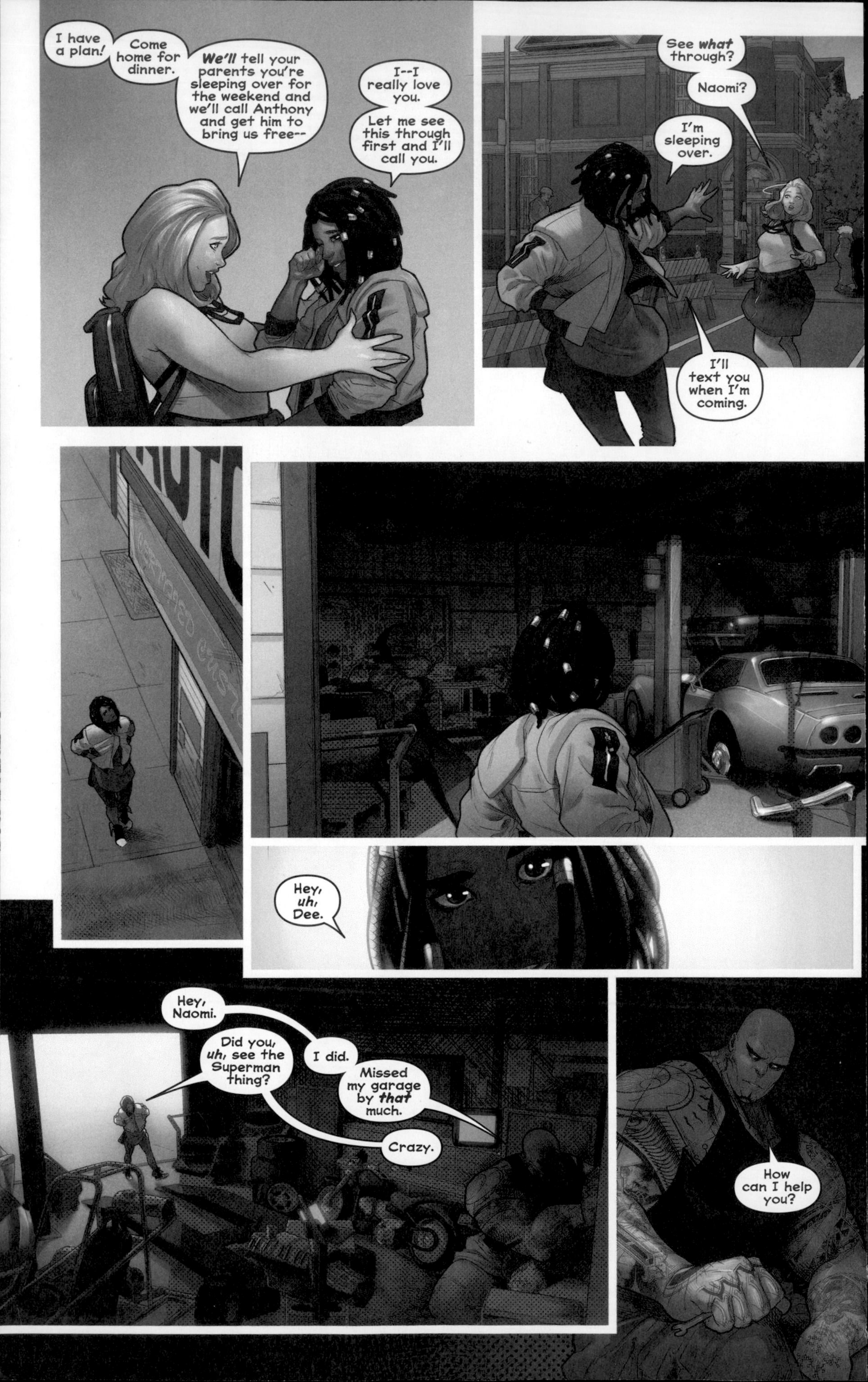

I have a plan!
Come home for dinner.
We'll tell your parents you're sleeping over for the weekend and we'll call Anthony and get him to bring us free--
I--I really love you.
Let me see this through first and I'll call you.
See what through?
Naomi?
I'm sleeping over.
I'll text you when I'm coming.
Hey, uh, Dee.
Hey, Naomi.
Did you, uh, see the Superman thing?
I did.
Missed my garage by that much.
Crazy.
How can I help you?

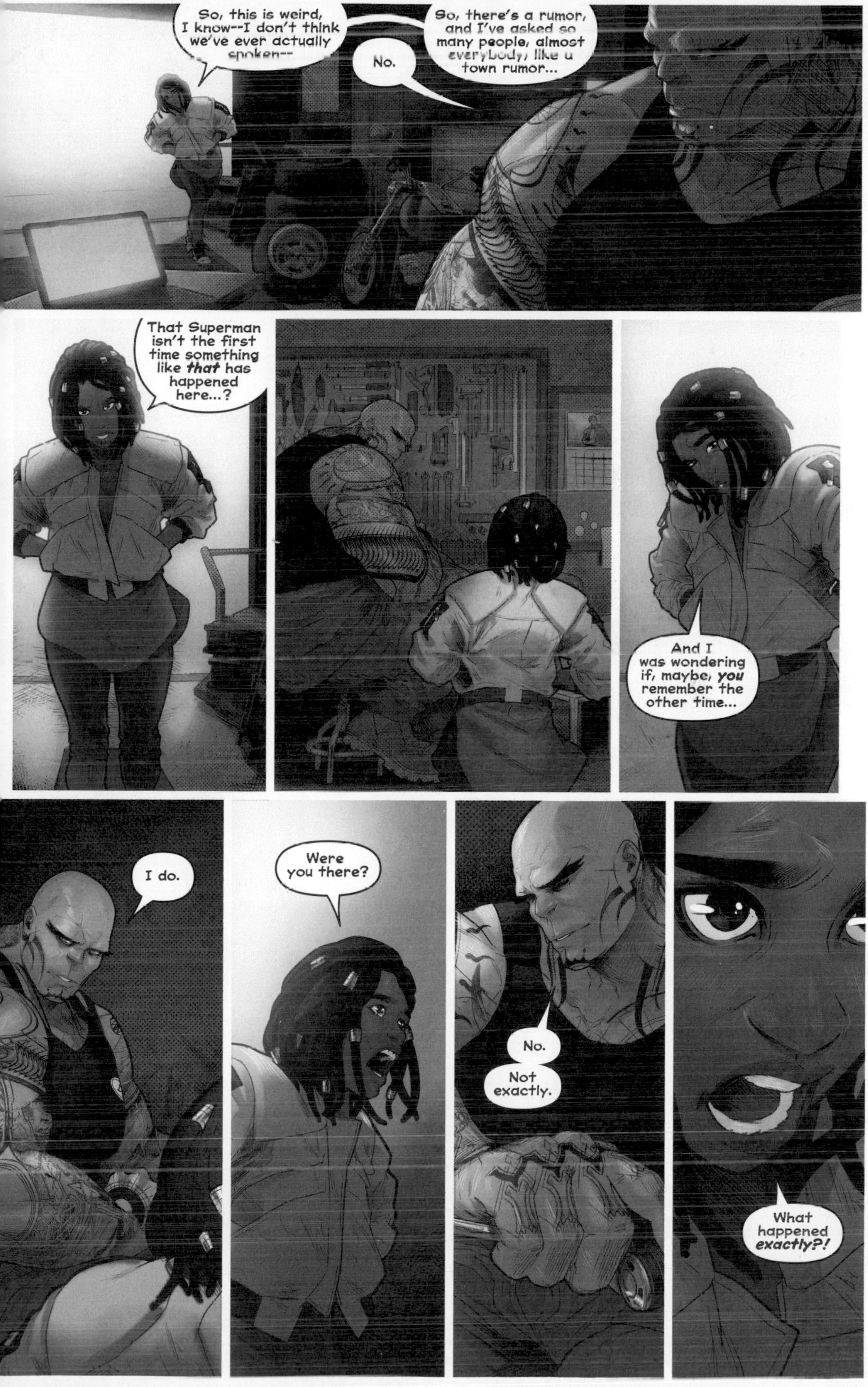

So, this is weird, I know--I don't think we've ever actually spoken--
No.
So, there's a rumor, and I've asked so many people, almost everybody, like a town rumor...
That Superman isn't the first time something like *that* has happened here...?
And I was wondering if, maybe, *you* remember the other time...
I do.
Were you there?
No.
Not exactly.
What happened *exactly?!*

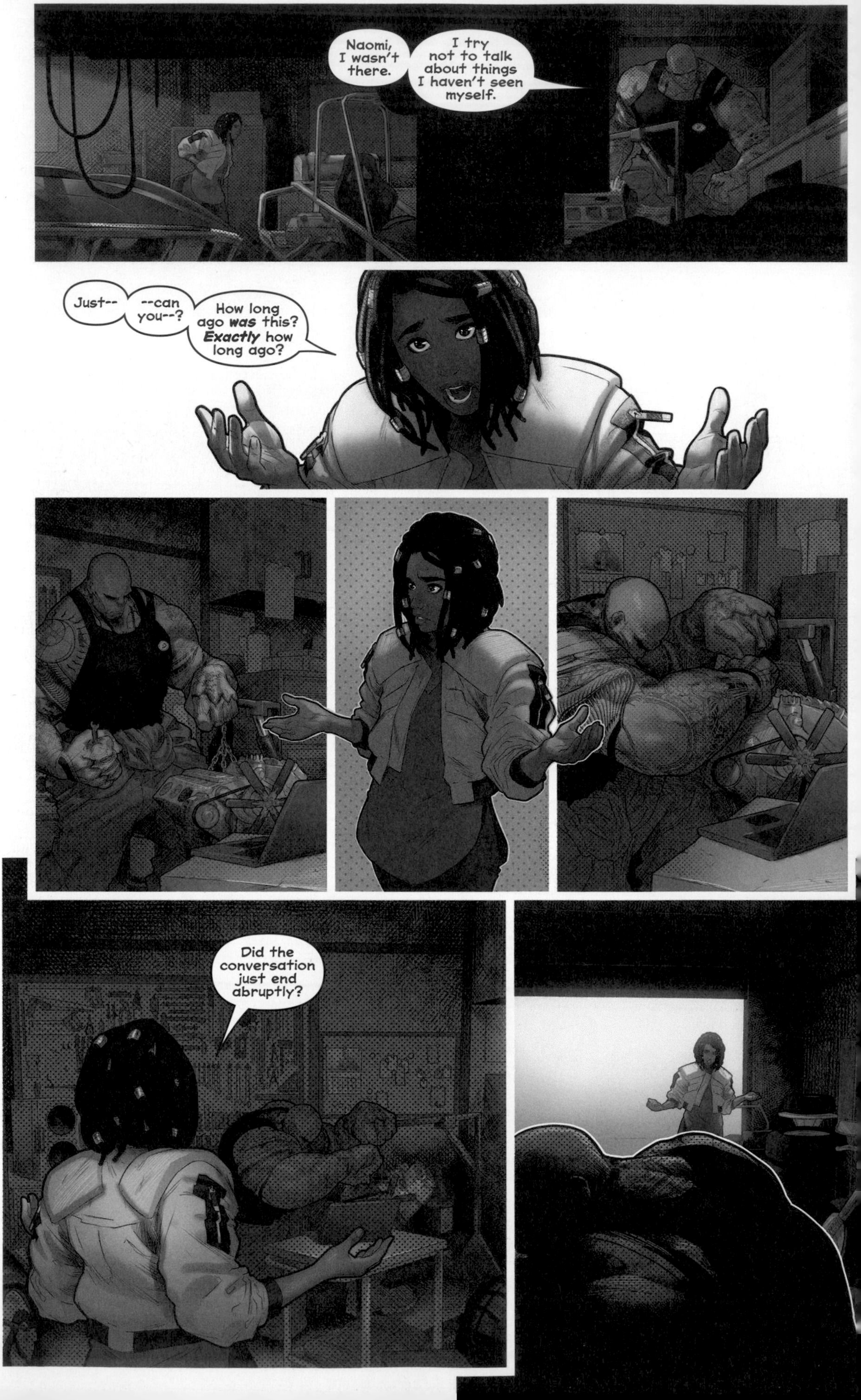
Naomi, I wasn't there.
I try not to talk about things I haven't seen myself.
Just--
--can you--?
How long ago **was** this? ***Exactly*** how long ago?
Did the conversation just end abruptly?

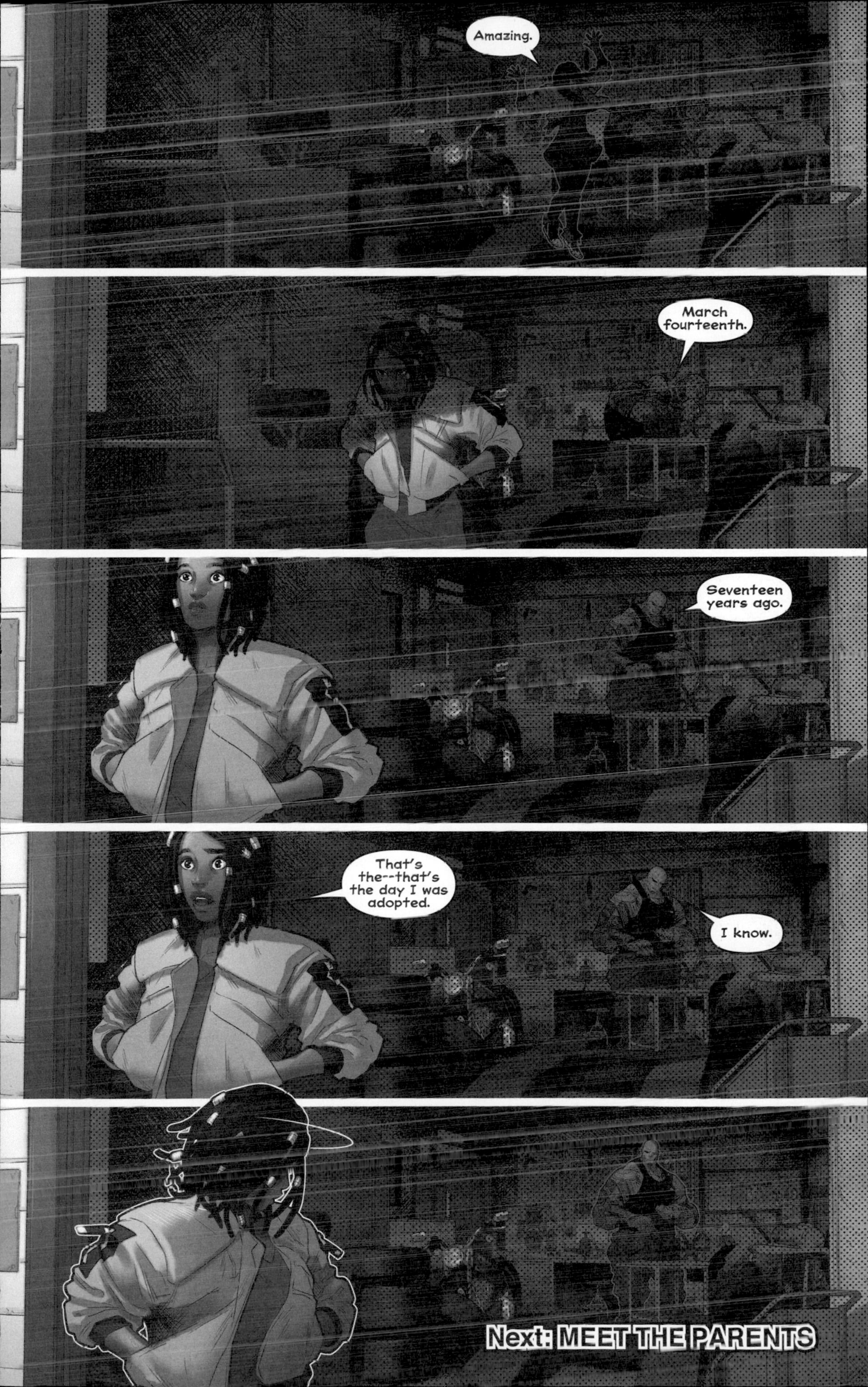
Amazing.
March fourteenth.
Seventeen years ago.
That's the--that's the day I was adopted.
I know.
Next: MEET THE PARENTS

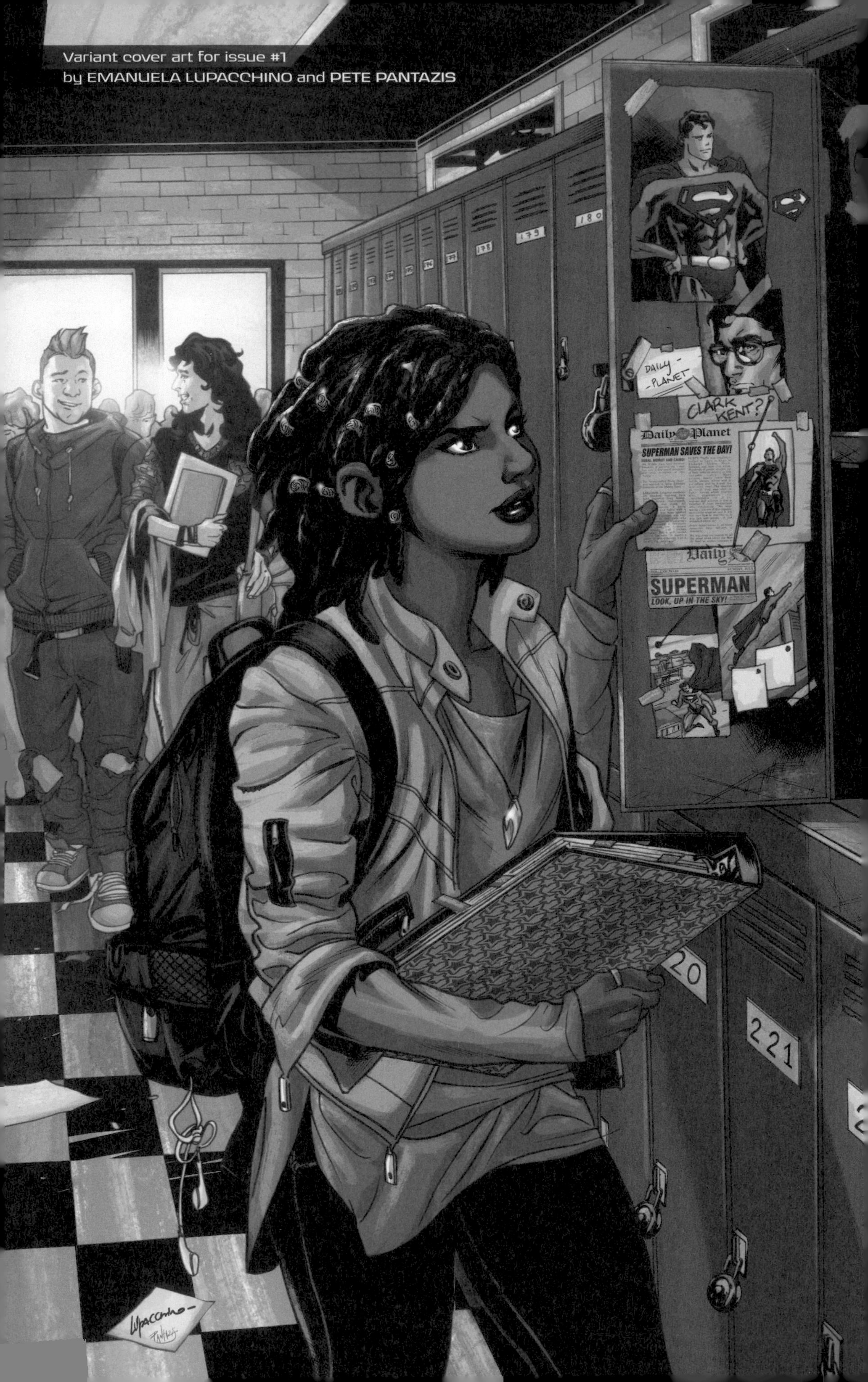
180
179
178
DAILY -PLANET
CLARK KENT?
Daily Planet
SUPERMAN SAVES THE DAY!
SUPERMAN
LOOK, UP IN THE SKY!
20
221
Variant cover art for issue #1
by EMANUELA LUPACCHINO and PETE PANTAZIS

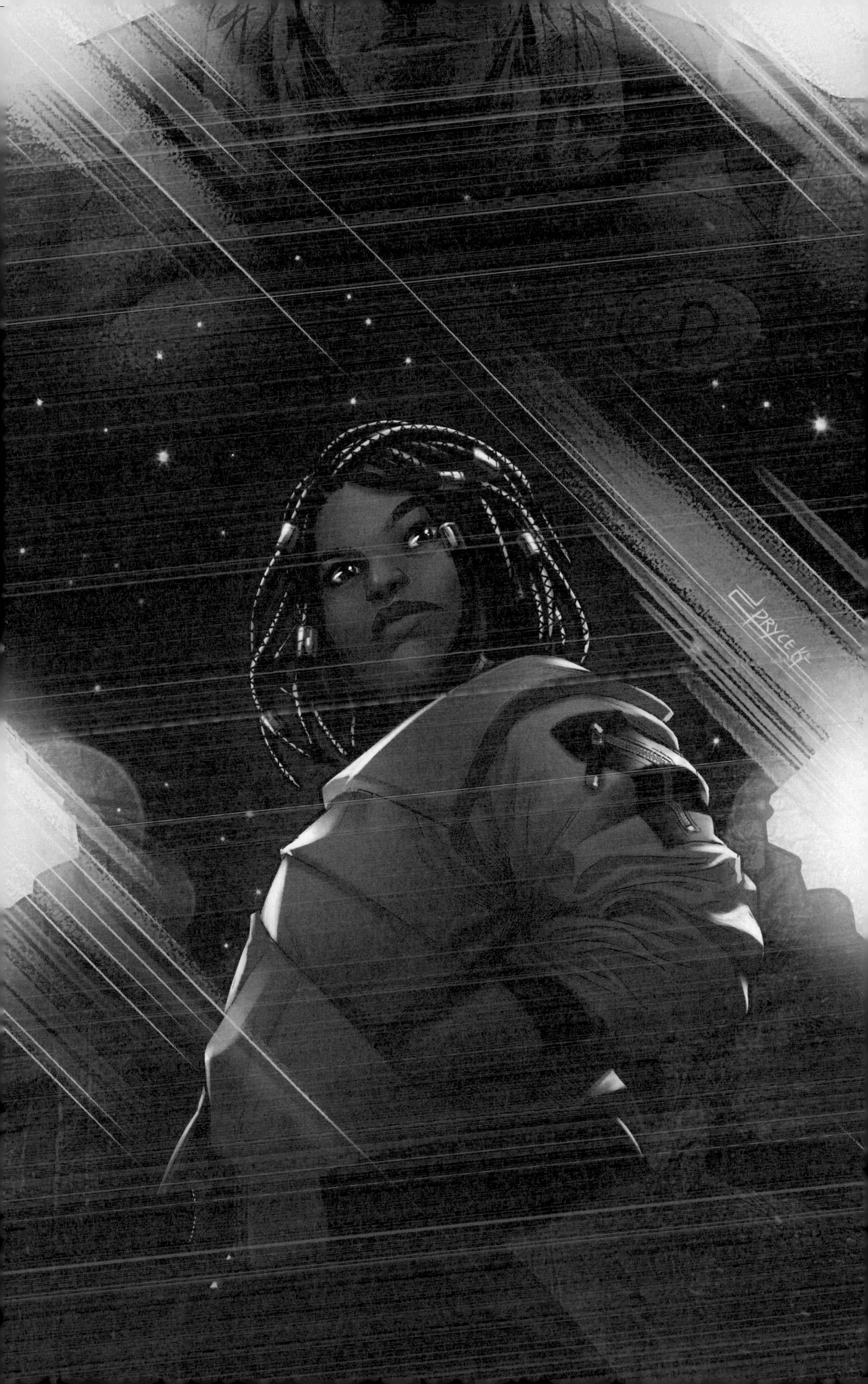
PRYCE

TWO

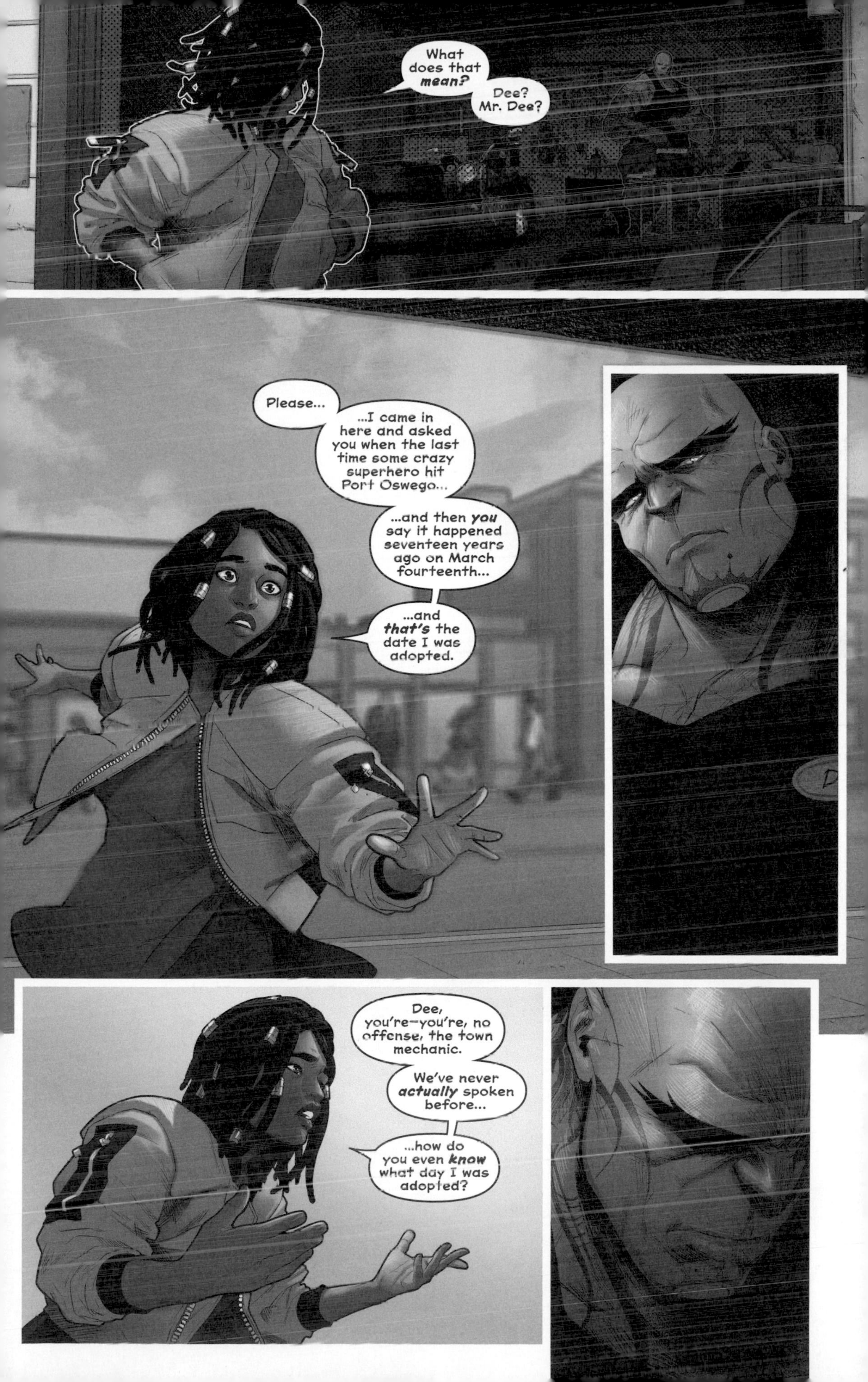
What does that *mean?*
Dee? Mr. Dee?
Please...
...I came in here and asked you when the last time some crazy superhero hit Port Oswego...
...and then *you* say it happened seventeen years ago on March fourteenth...
...and *that's* the date I was adopted.
Dee, you're—you're, no offense, the town mechanic.
We've never *actually* spoken before...
...how do you even *know* what day I was adopted?

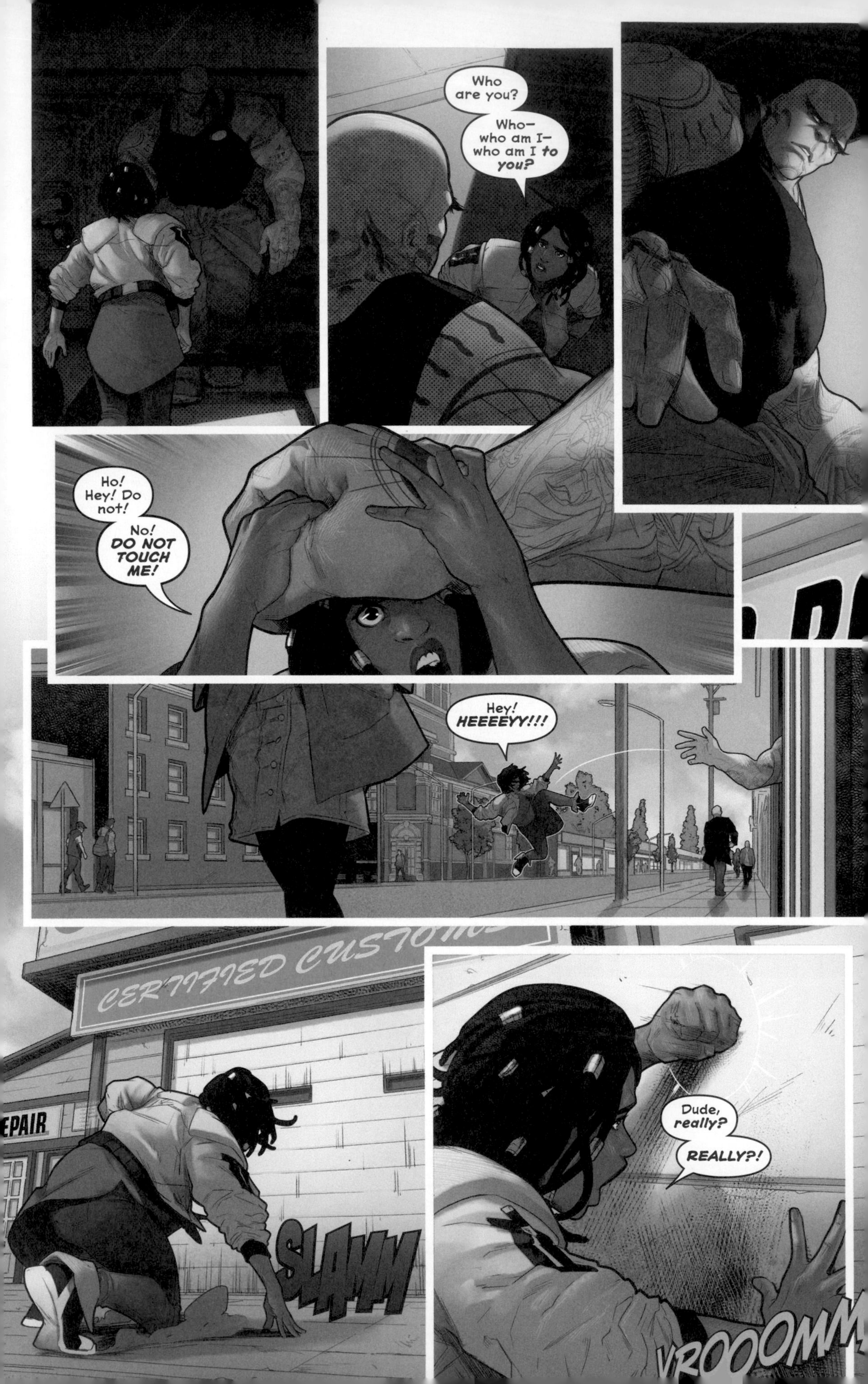
Who are you?
Who— who am I— who am I to you?
Ho! Hey! Do not!
No! DO NOT TOUCH ME!
Hey! HEEEEYY!!!
CERTIFIED CUSTOMS
EPAIR
SLAMM
Dude, really?
REALLY?!
VROOOMM

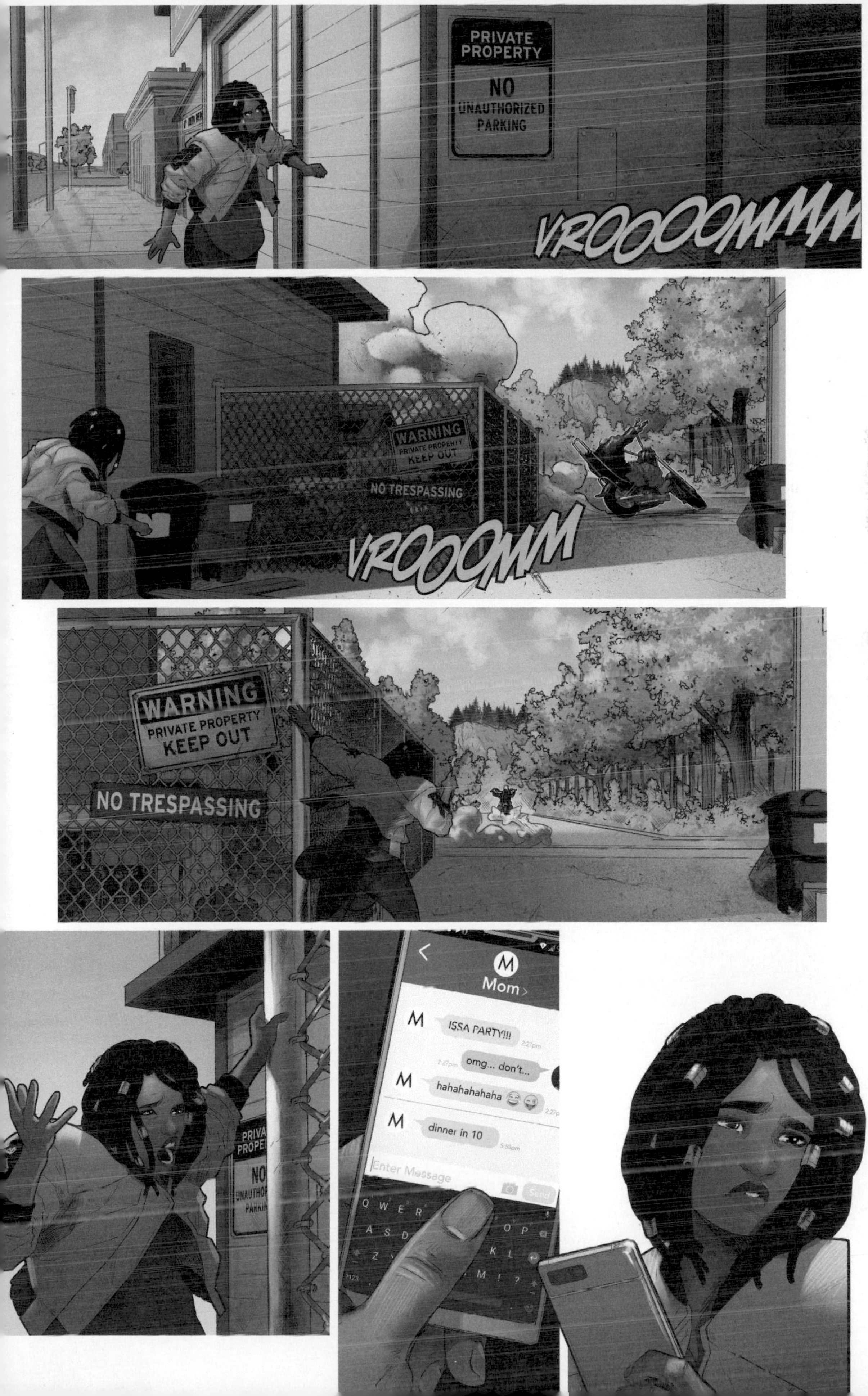
PRIVATE PROPERTY
NO UNAUTHORIZED PARKING
VROOOOMMM
WARNING PRIVATE PROPERTY KEEP OUT
NO TRESPASSING
VROOOMM
WARNING PRIVATE PROPERTY KEEP OUT
NO TRESPASSING
Mom
ISSA PARTY!!!
2:27pm
omg... don't...
2:27pm
hahahahahaha
2:27pm
dinner in 10
5:58pm
Enter Message
Send

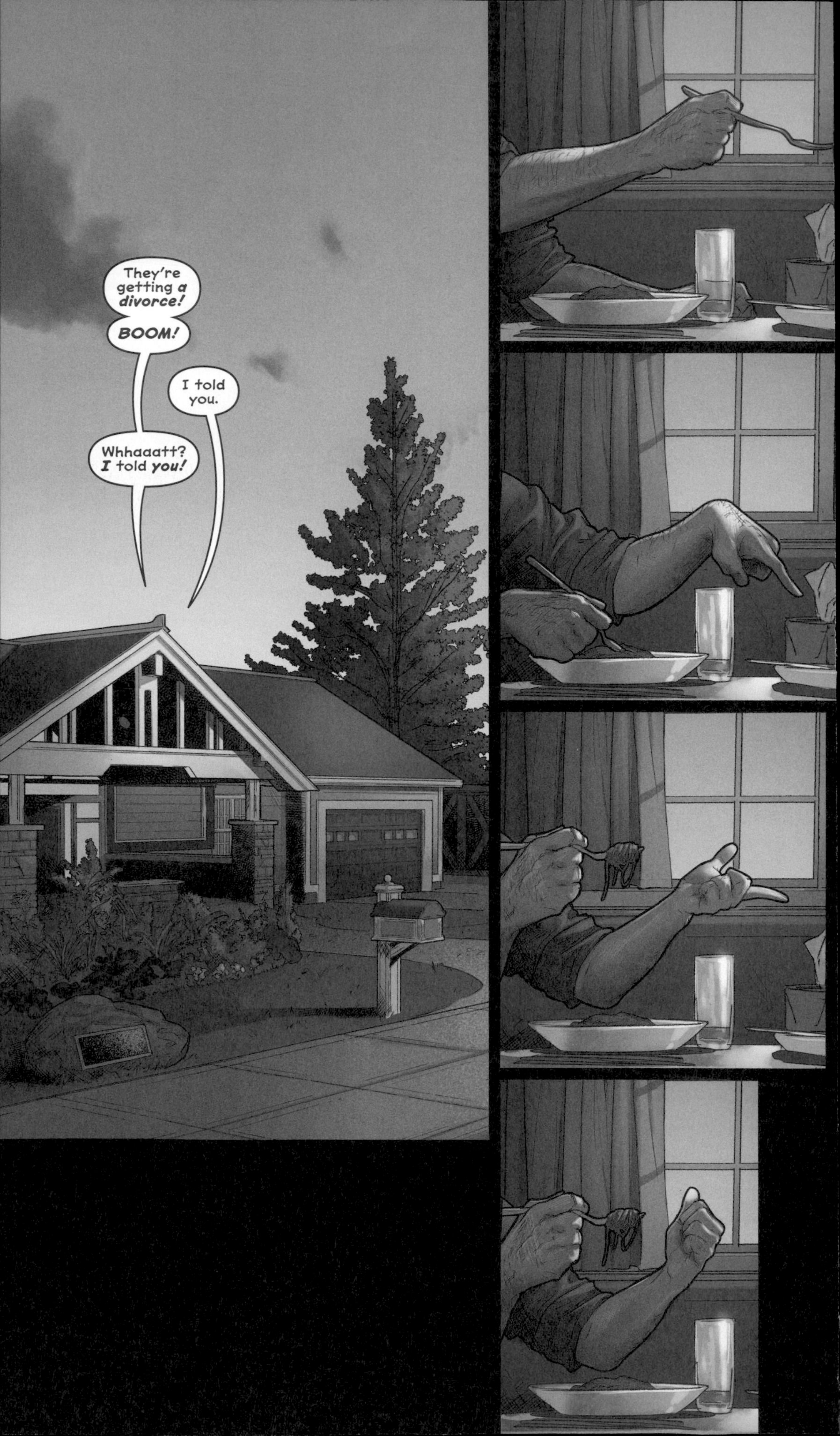
They're getting a *divorce!*
BOOM!
I told you.
Whhaaatt? ***I*** told ***you!***

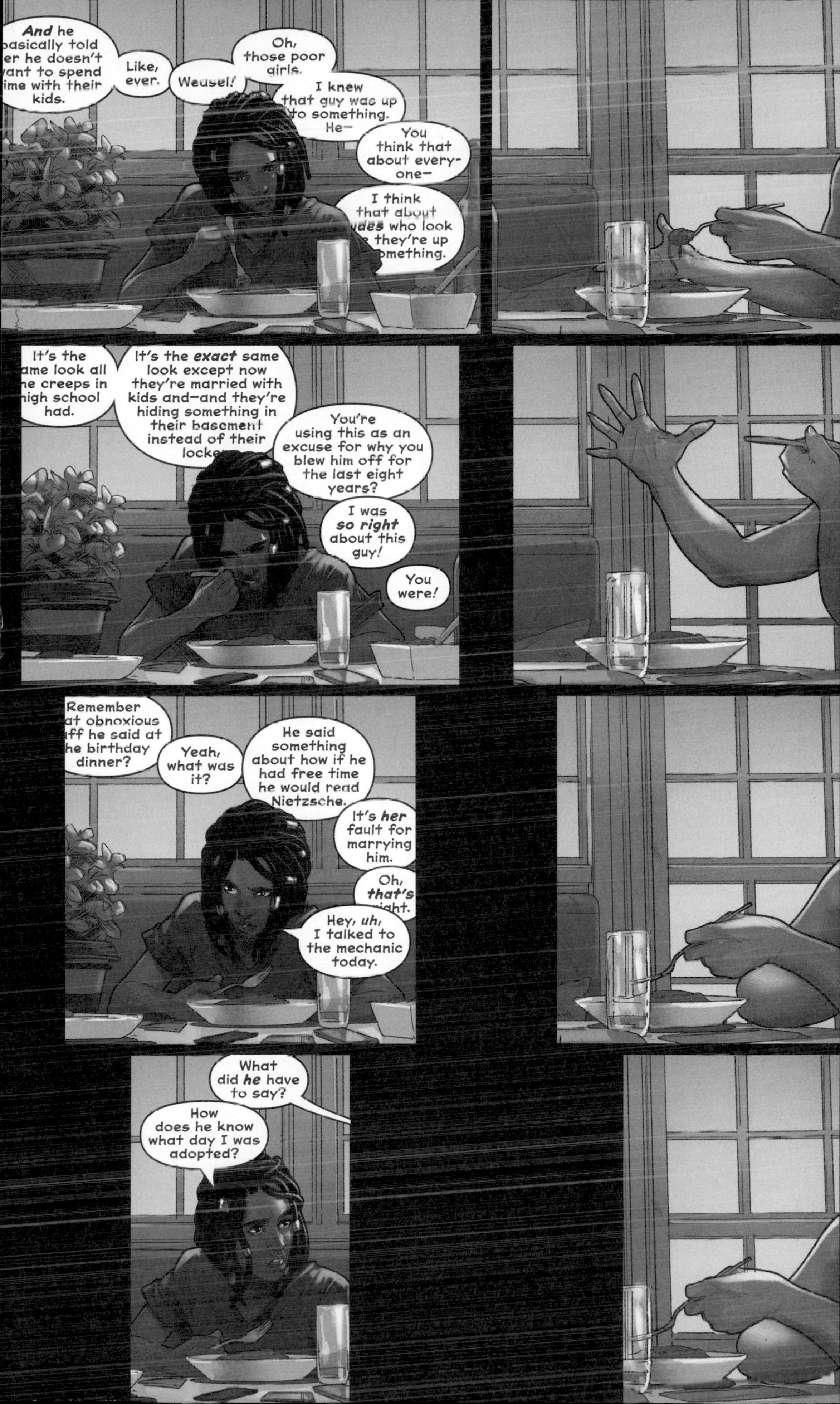

And he basically told her he doesn't want to spend time with their kids.
Like, ever.
Oh, those poor girls.
Weasel!
I knew that guy was up to something. He—
You think that about every-one—
I think that about dudes who look like they're up to something.
It's the same look all the creeps in high school had.
It's the exact same look except now they're married with kids and—and they're hiding something in their basement instead of their locker.
You're using this as an excuse for why you blew him off for the last eight years?
I was so right about this guy!
You were!
Remember that obnoxious stuff he said at the birthday dinner?
Yeah, what was it?
He said something about how if he had free time he would read Nietzsche.
It's her fault for marrying him.
Oh, that's right.
Hey, uh, I talked to the mechanic today.
What did he have to say?
How does he know what day I was adopted?

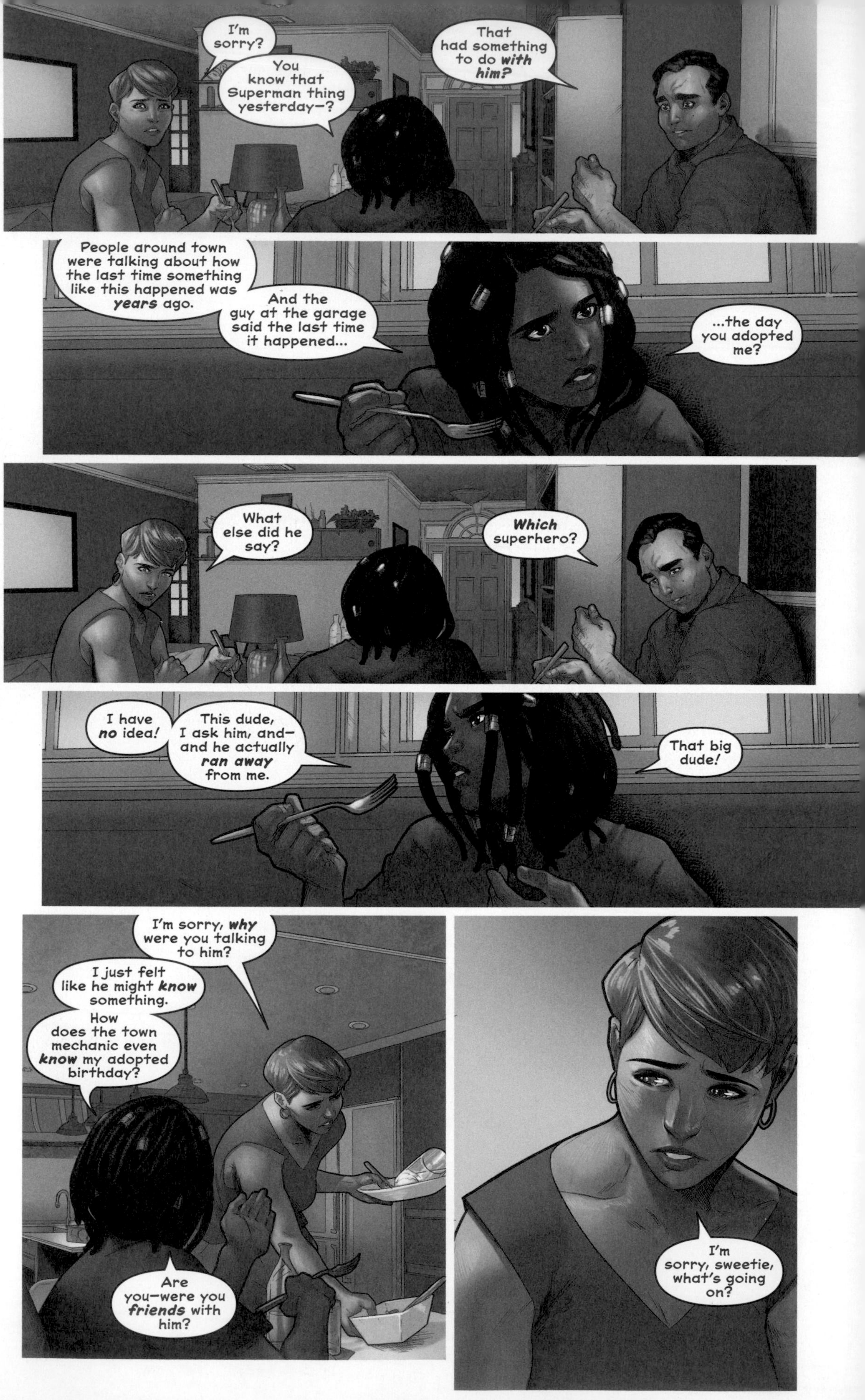

I'm sorry?
You know that Superman thing yesterday—?
That had something to do with him?
People around town were talking about how the last time something like this happened was years ago.
And the guy at the garage said the last time it happened...
...the day you adopted me?
What else did he say?
Which superhero?
I have no idea!
This dude, I ask him, and—and he actually ran away from me.
That big dude!
I'm sorry, why were you talking to him?
I just felt like he might know something.
How does the town mechanic even know my adopted birthday?
Are you—were you friends with him?
I'm sorry, sweetie, what's going on?

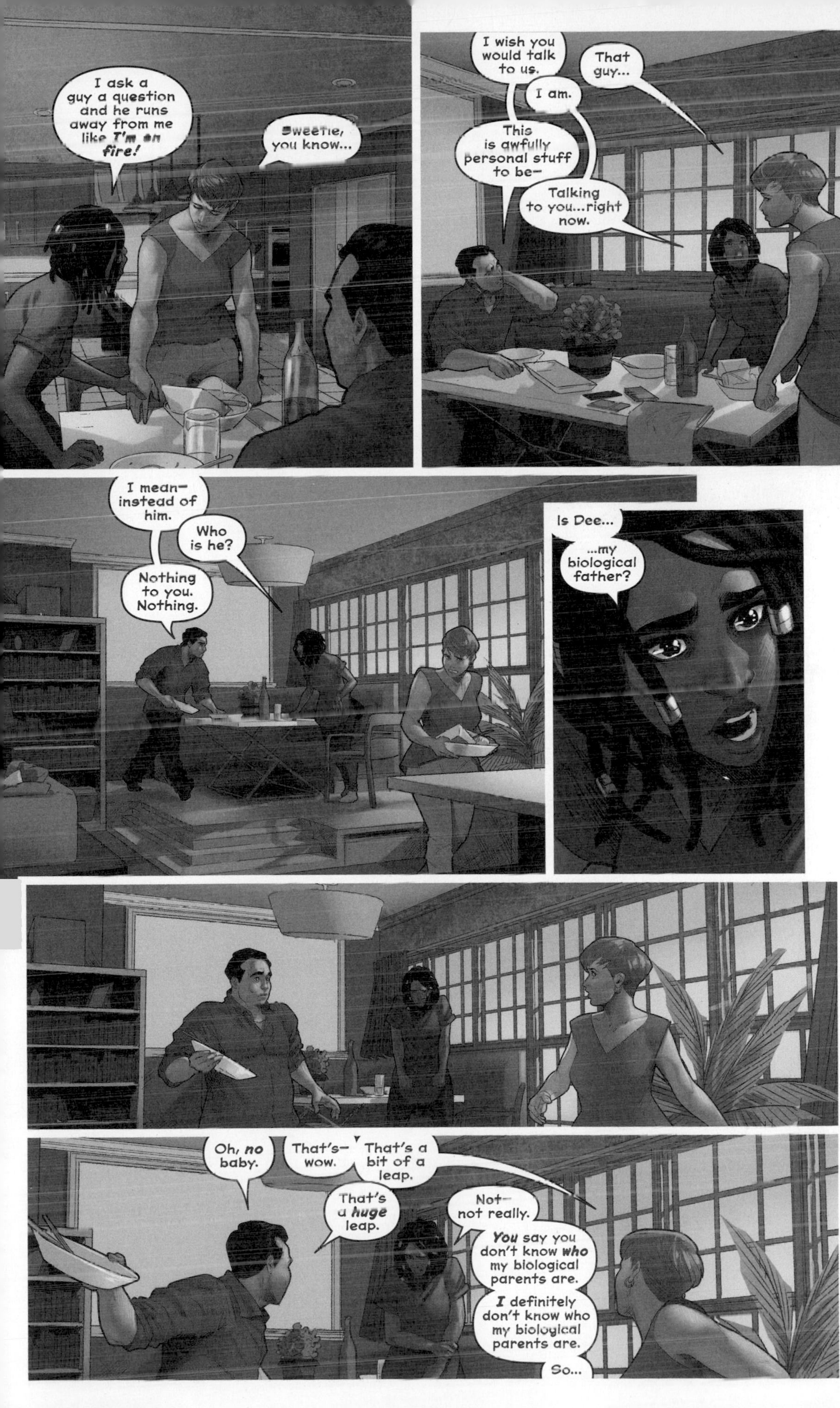
I ask a guy a question and he runs away from me like *I'm on fire!*
Sweetie, you know...
I wish you would talk to us.
That guy...
I am.
This is awfully personal stuff to be—
Talking to you...right now.
I mean— instead of him.
Who is he?
Nothing to you. Nothing.
Is Dee...
...my biological father?
Oh, **no** baby.
That's— wow.
That's a bit of a leap.
That's a *huge* leap.
Not— not really.
You say you don't know *who* my biological parents are.
I definitely don't know who my biological parents are.
So...

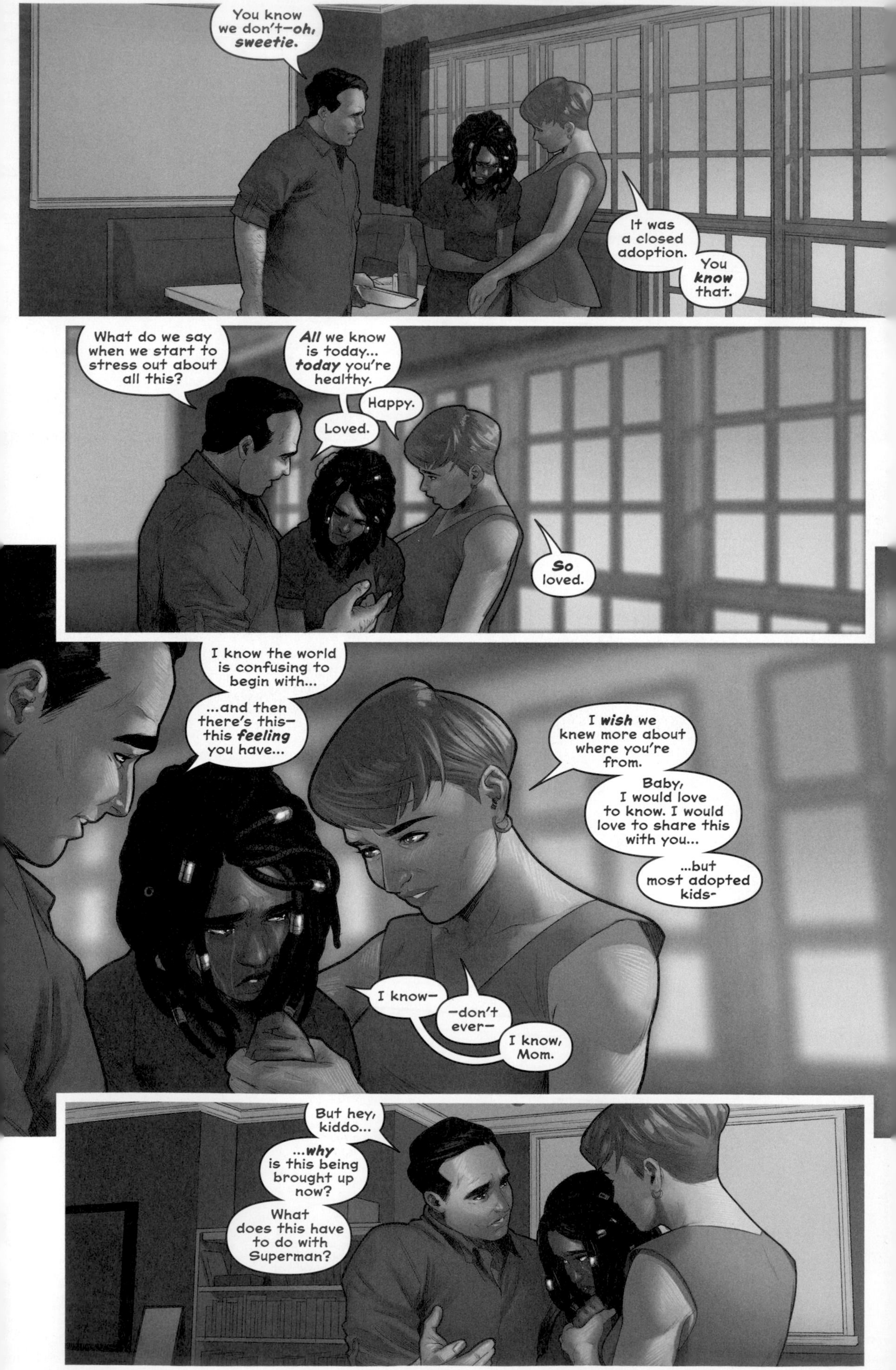
You know we don't—*oh, sweetie.*
It was a closed adoption.
You *know* that.
What do we say when we start to stress out about all this?
All we know is today... *today* you're healthy.
Happy.
Loved.
So loved.
I know the world is confusing to begin with...
...and then there's this— this *feeling* you have...
I *wish* we knew more about where you're from.
Baby, I would love to know. I would love to share this with you...
...but most adopted kids-
I know—
—don't ever—
I know, Mom.
But hey, kiddo...
...*why* is this being brought up now?
What does this have to do with Superman?

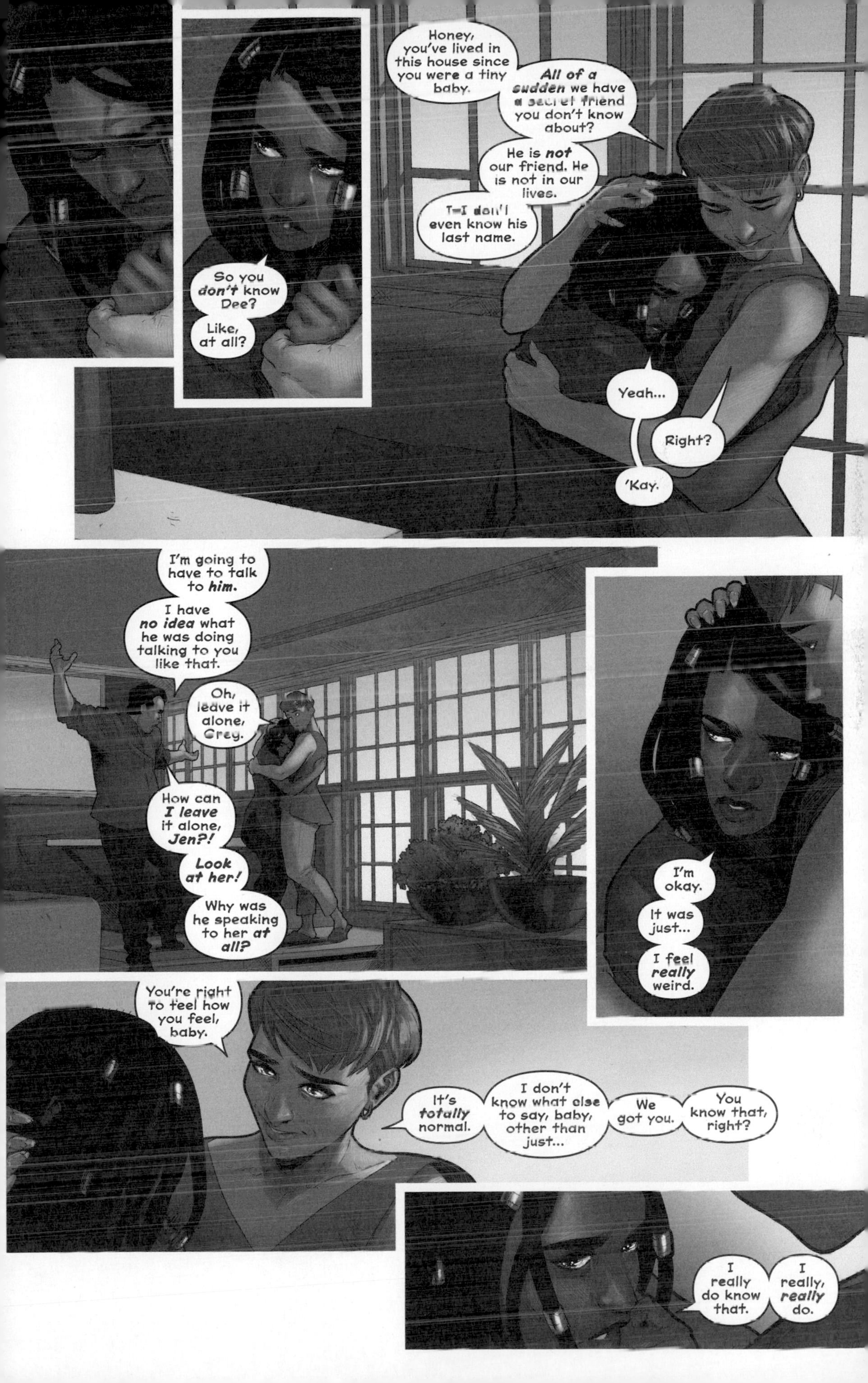

So you *don't* know Dee?
Like, at all?
Honey, you've lived in this house since you were a tiny baby.
All of a sudden we have a secret friend you don't know about?
He is *not* our friend. He is not in our lives.
T-I don't even know his last name.
Yeah...
Right?
'Kay.
I'm going to have to talk to *him.*
I have *no idea* what he was doing talking to you like that.
Oh, leave it alone, Greg.
How can *I leave* it alone, *Jen?!*
Look at her!
Why was he speaking to her *at all?*
I'm okay.
It was just...
I feel *really* weird.
You're right to feel how you feel, baby.
It's *totally* normal.
I don't know what else to say, baby, other than just...
We got you.
You know that, right?
I really do know that.
I really, *really* do.

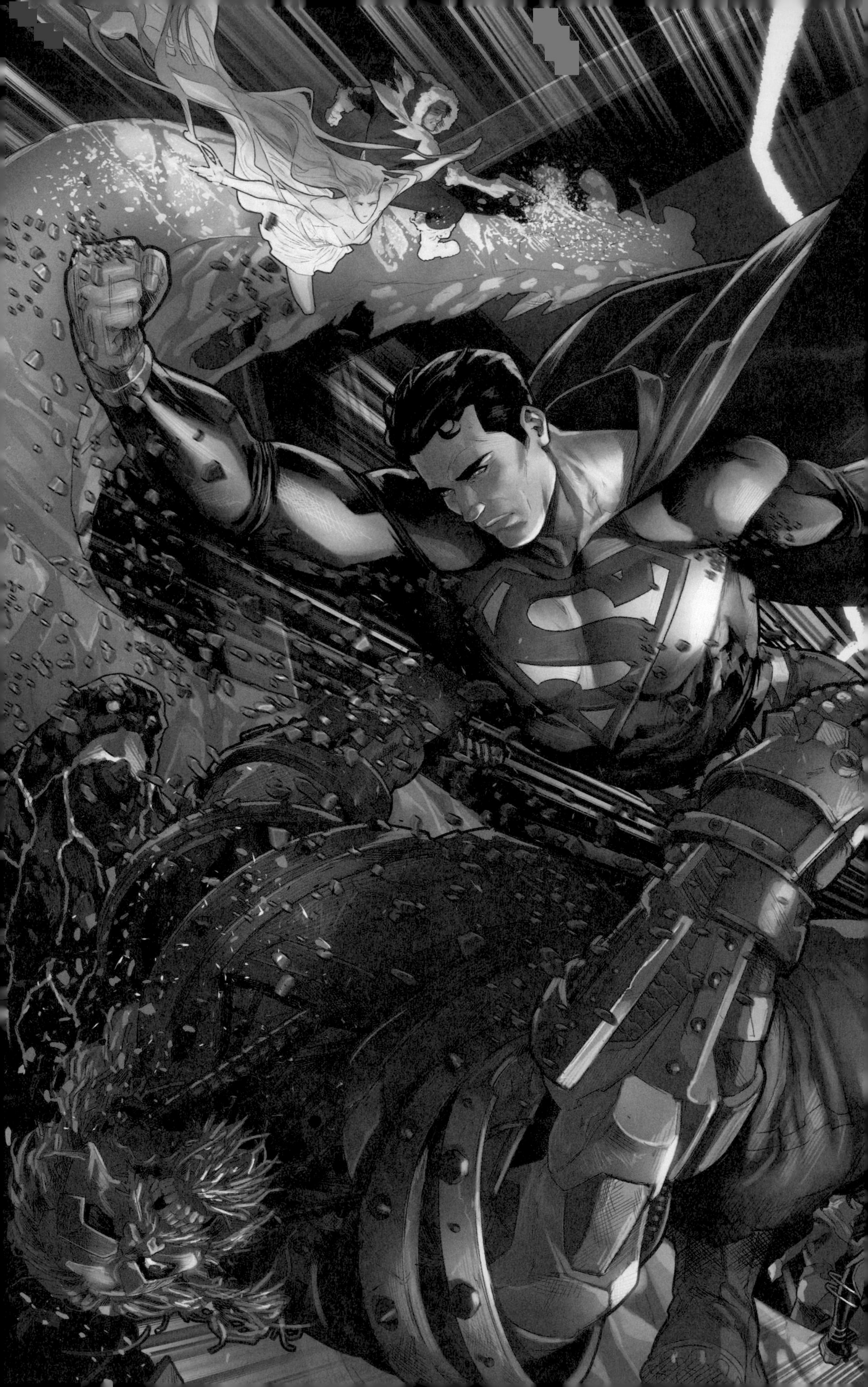

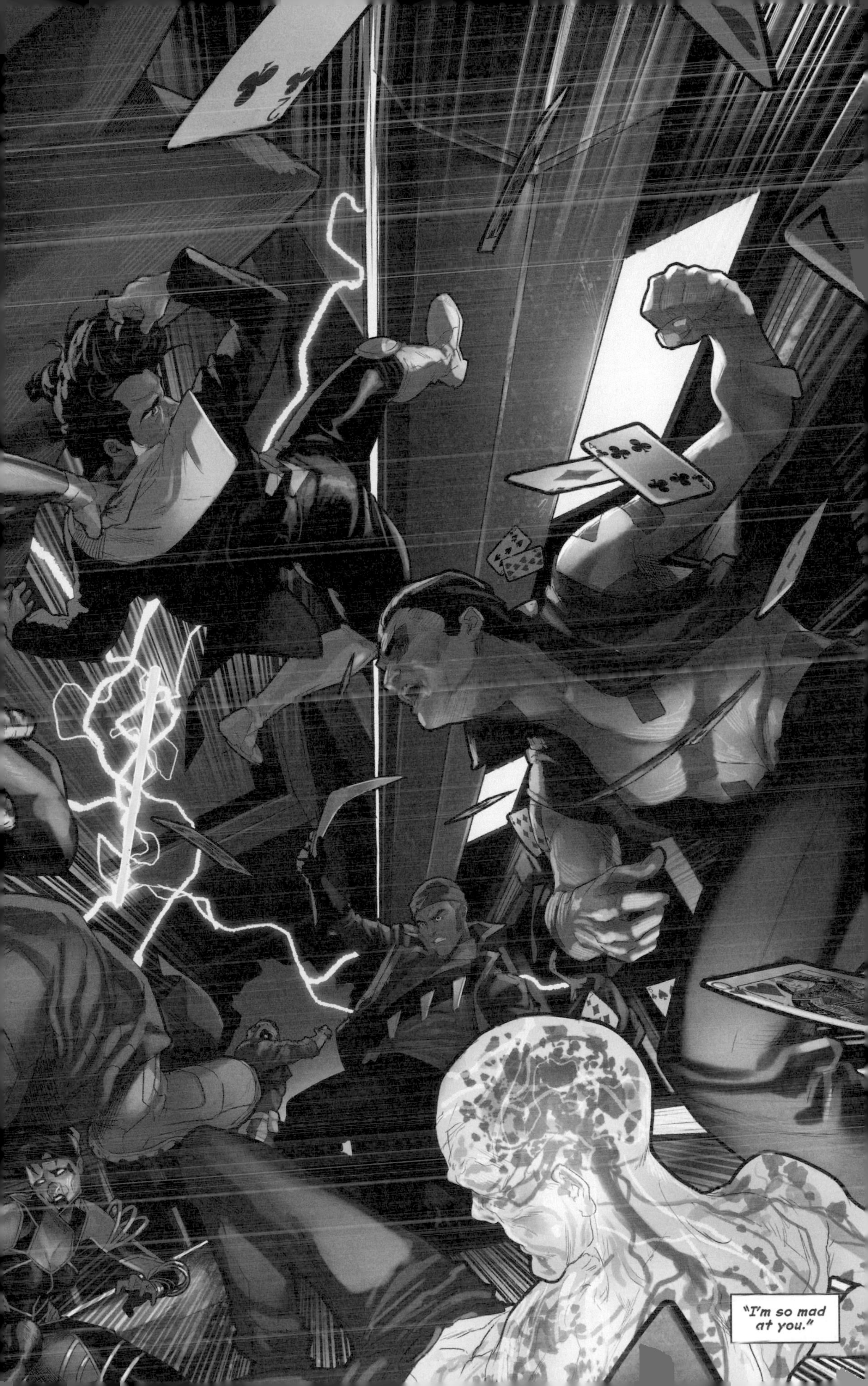
"I'm so mad at you."

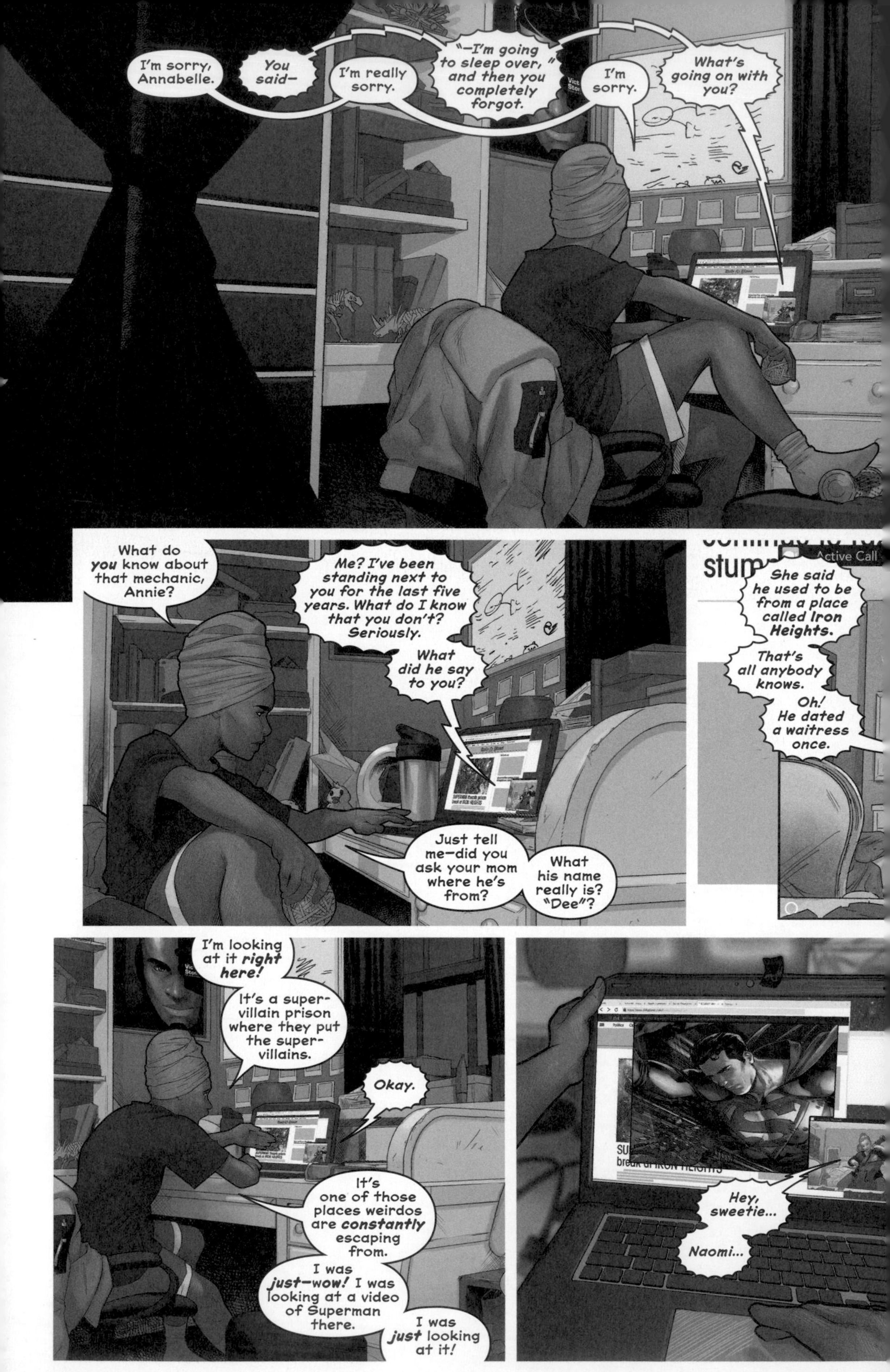
I'm sorry, Annabelle.
You said—
I'm really sorry.
"—I'm going to sleep over," and then you completely forgot.
I'm sorry.
What's going on with you?
What do *you* know about that mechanic, Annie?
Me? I've been standing next to you for the last five years. What do I know that you don't? Seriously.
What did he say to you?
Active Call
She said he used to be from a place called **Iron Heights.**
That's all anybody knows.
Oh! He dated a waitress once.
Just tell me—did you ask your mom where he's from?
What his name really is? "Dee"?
I'm looking at it ***right here!***
It's a super-villain prison where they put the super-villains.
Okay.
It's one of those places weirdos are ***constantly*** escaping from.
I was ***just—wow!*** I was looking at a video of Superman there.
I was ***just*** looking at it!
Hey, sweetie...
Naomi...

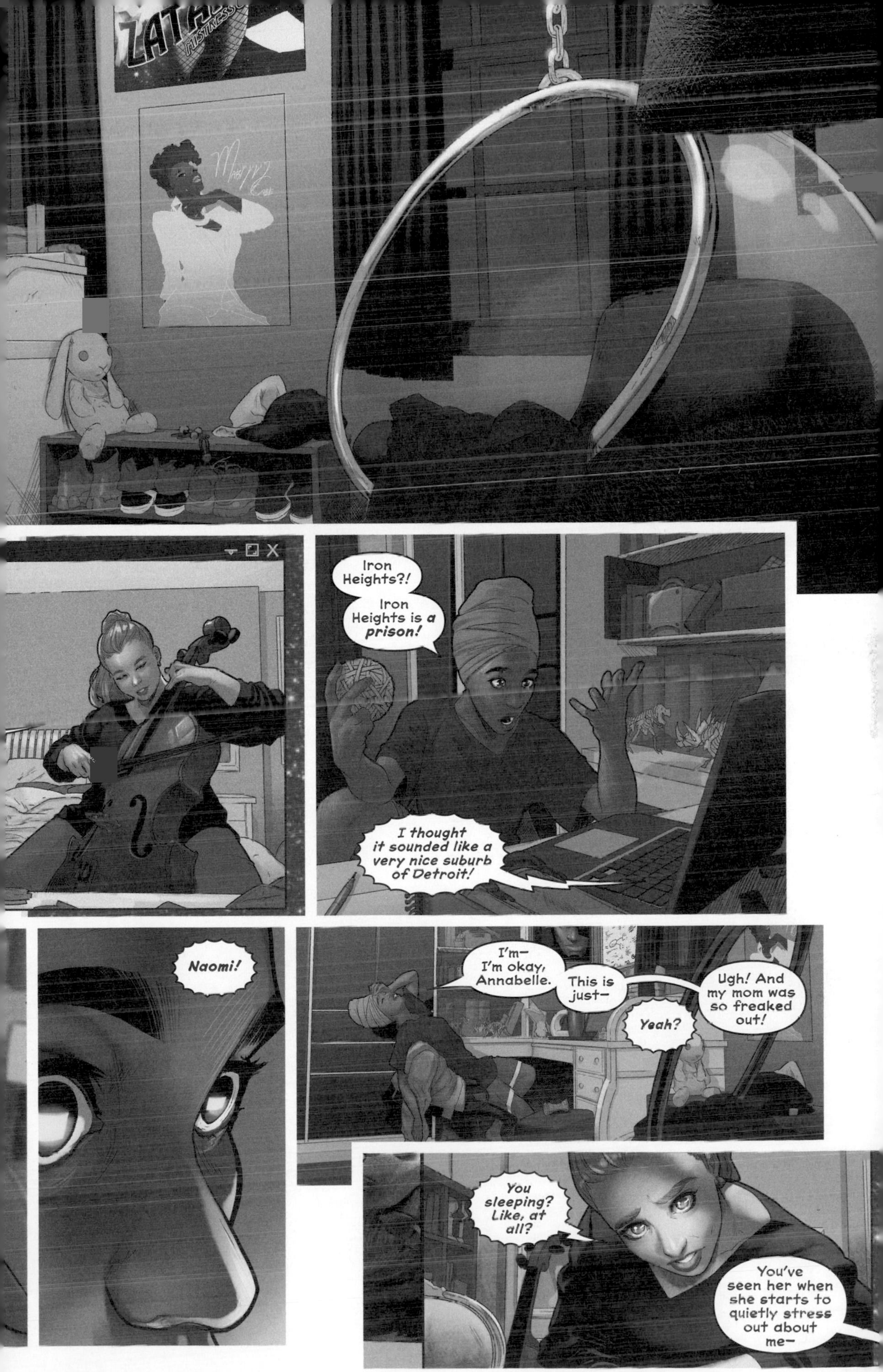
Iron Heights?!
Iron Heights is a *prison!*
I thought it sounded like a very nice suburb of Detroit!
Naomi!
I'm— I'm okay, Annabelle.
This is just—
Yeah?
Ugh! And my mom was so freaked out!
You sleeping? Like, at all?
You've seen her when she starts to quietly stress out about me—

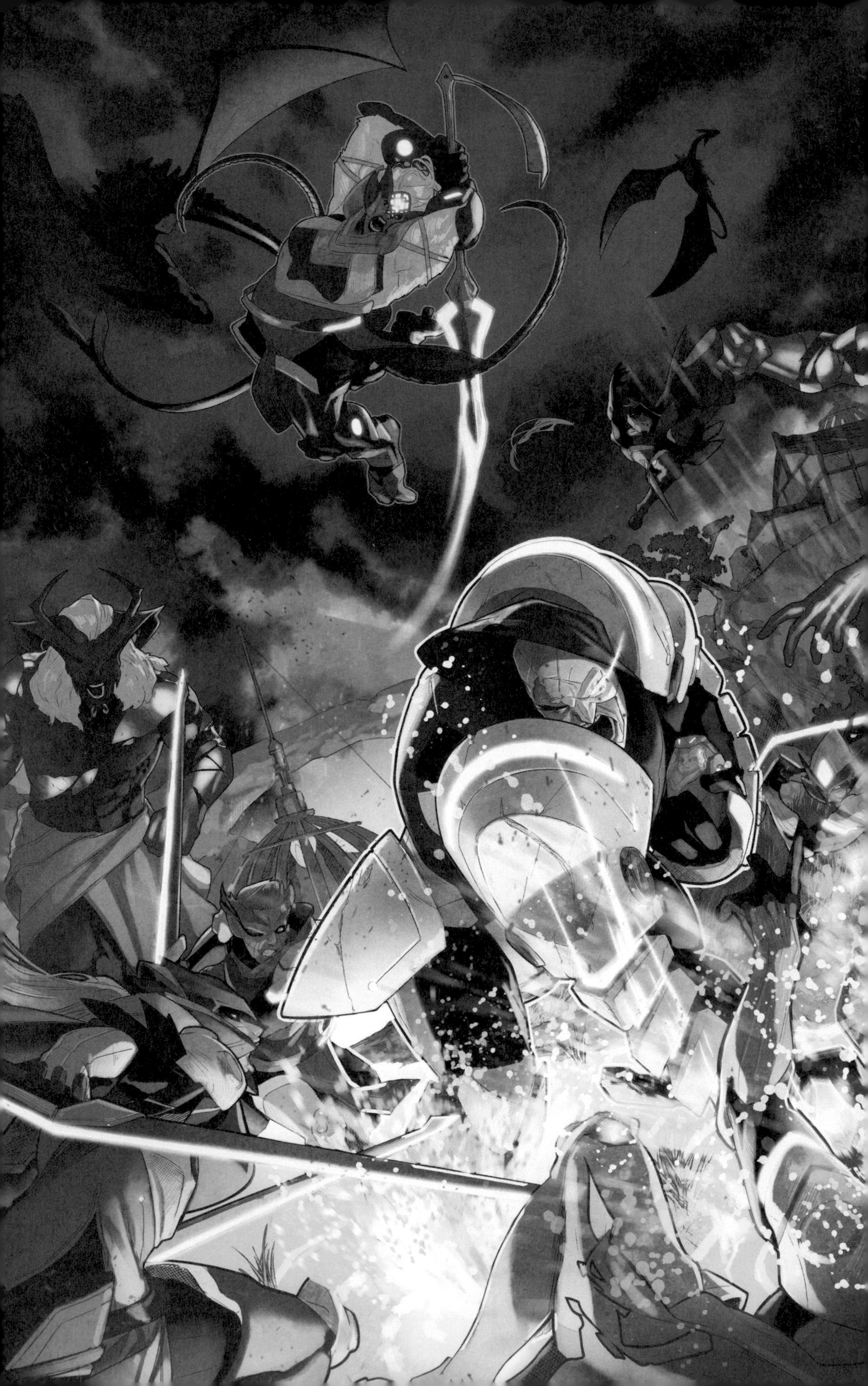

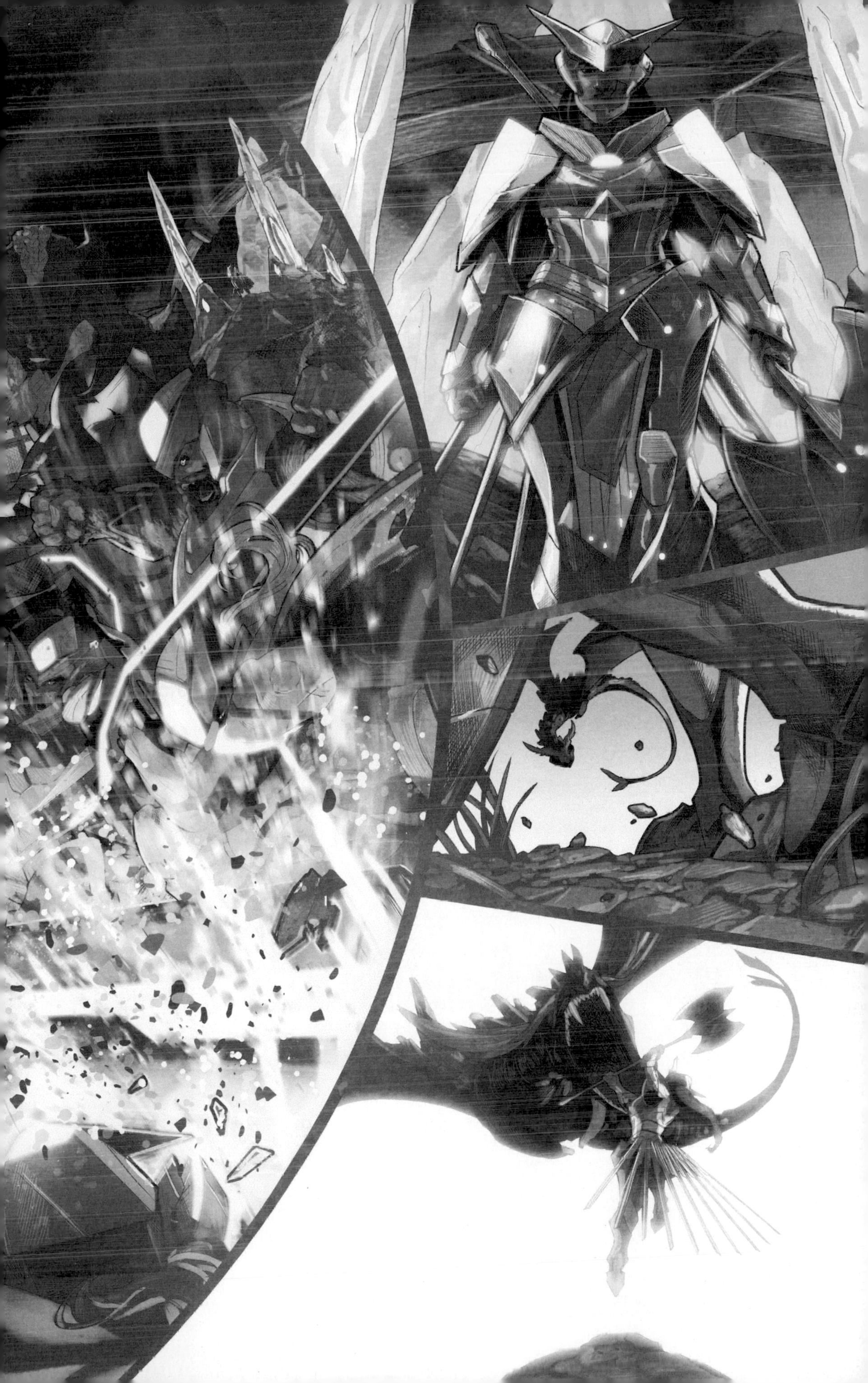

...No.

No, I'm not sleeping.

Damn it.

Well, funny thing, ever since *Superman* flew by, every time I close my eyes...

...I see that. So...

Wow.

I mean... *Pft!*

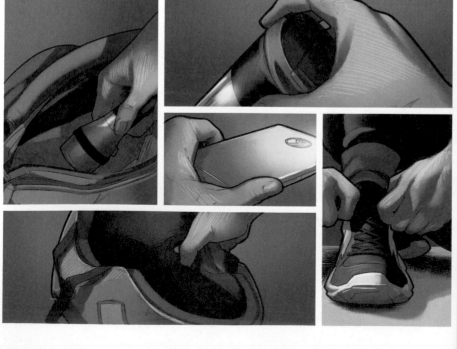

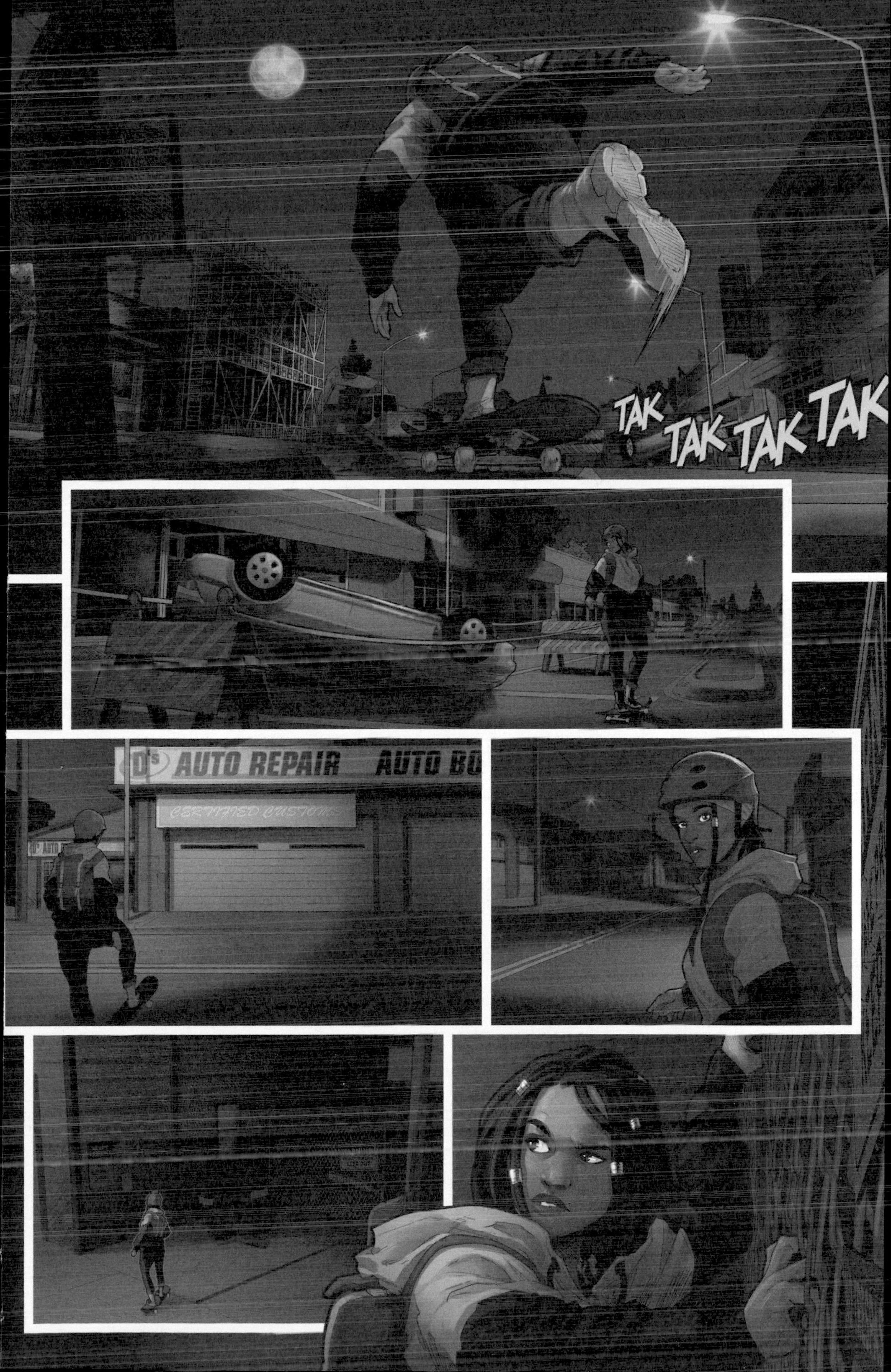
TAK
TAK TAK TAK
D's AUTO REPAIR

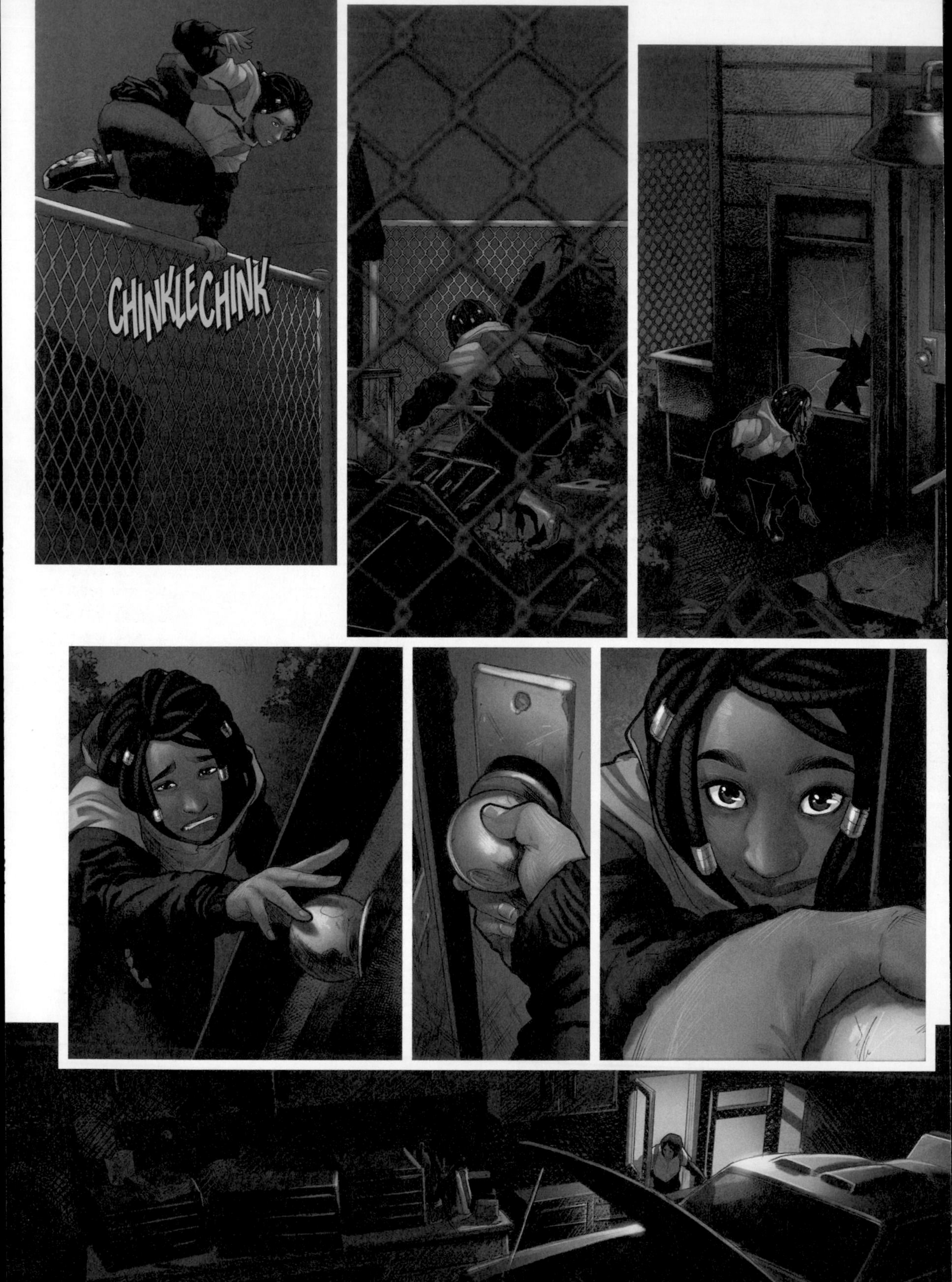
CHINKLECHINK

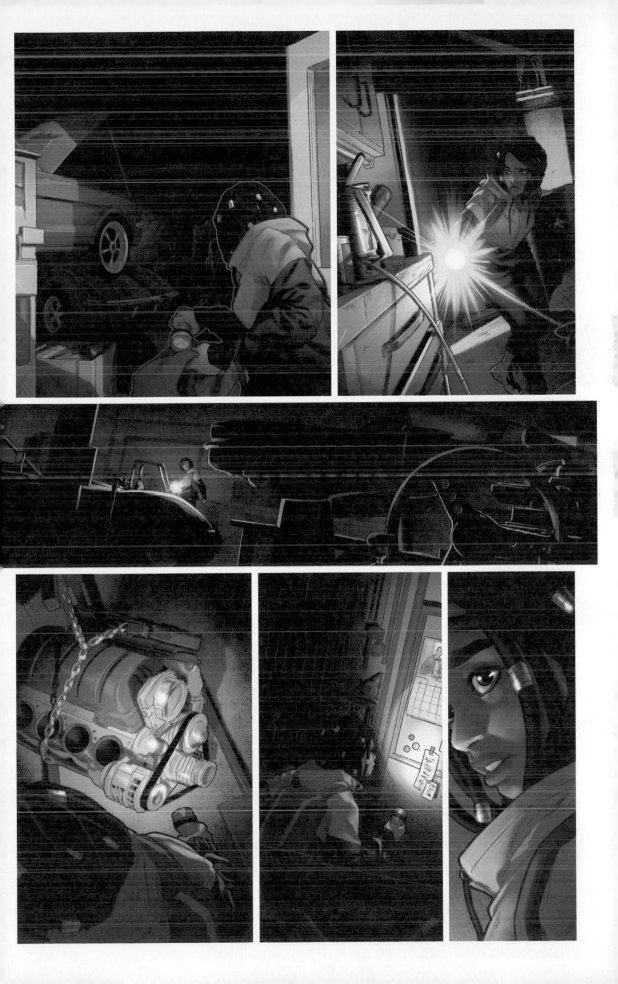

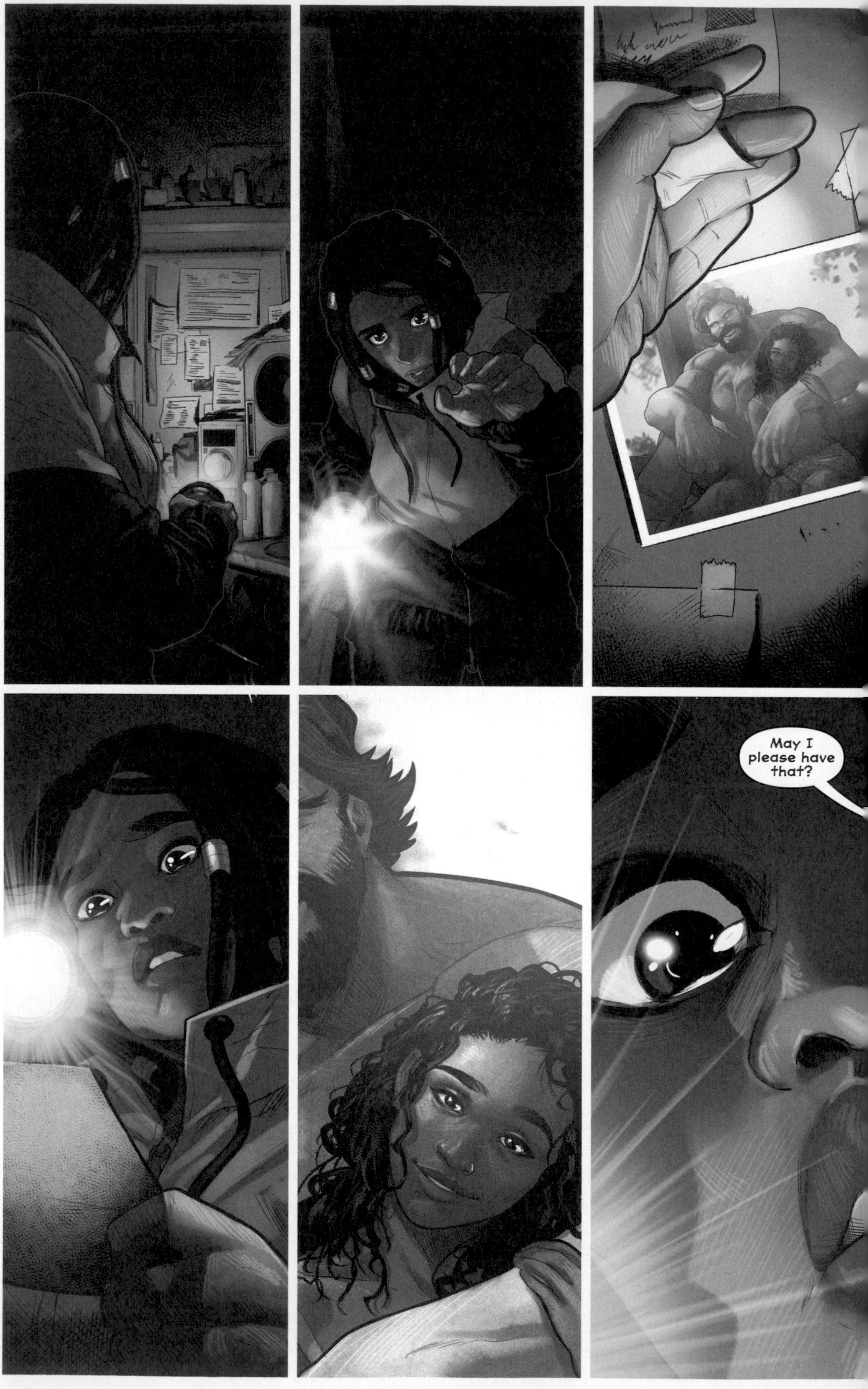
May I please have that?

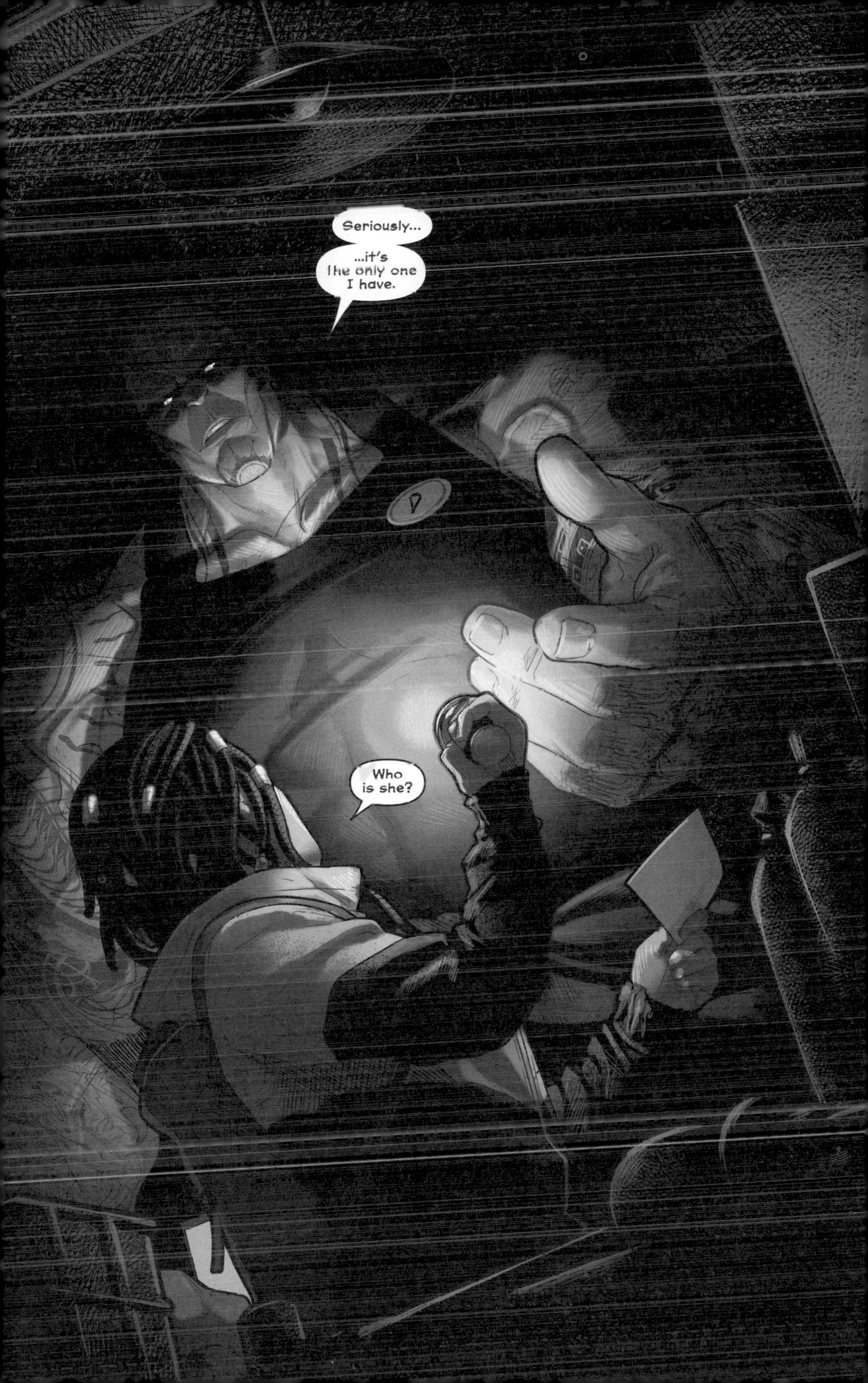
Seriously...
...it's the only one I have.
Who is she?

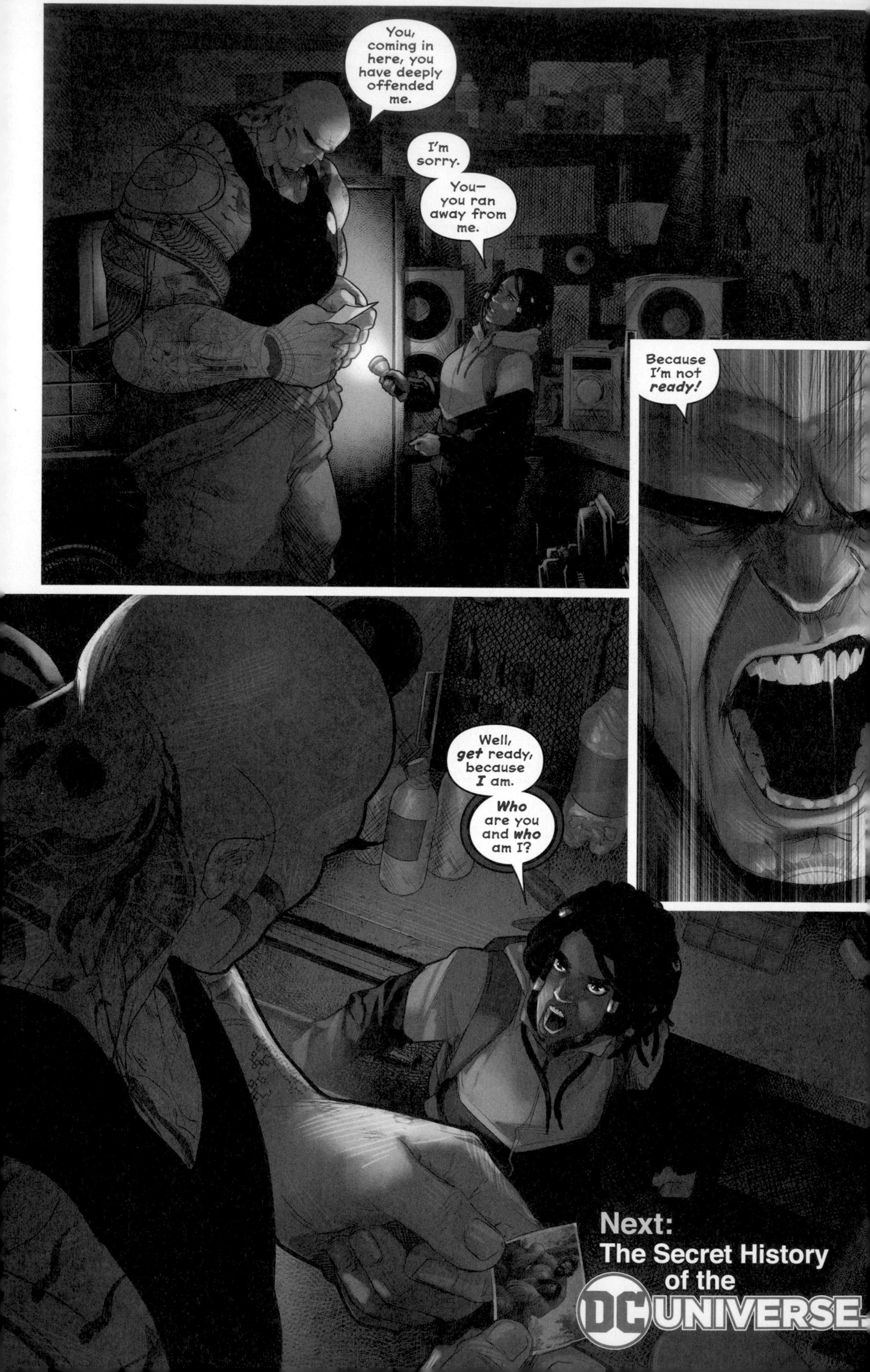

You, coming in here, you have deeply offended me.
I'm sorry.
You— you ran away from me.
Because I'm not ready!
Well, get ready, because I am.
Who are you and who am I?
Next: The Secret History of the DC UNIVERSE

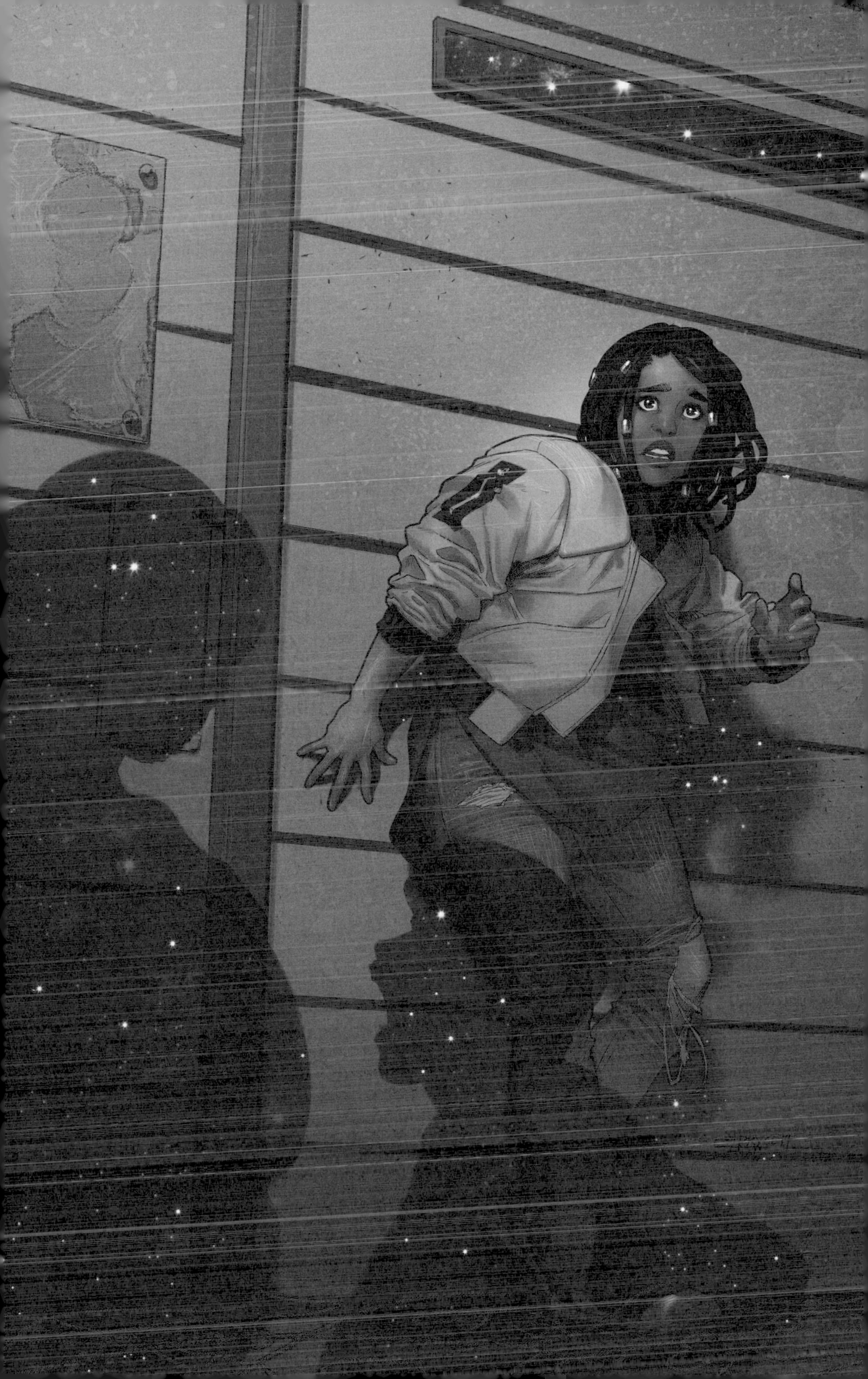

THREE

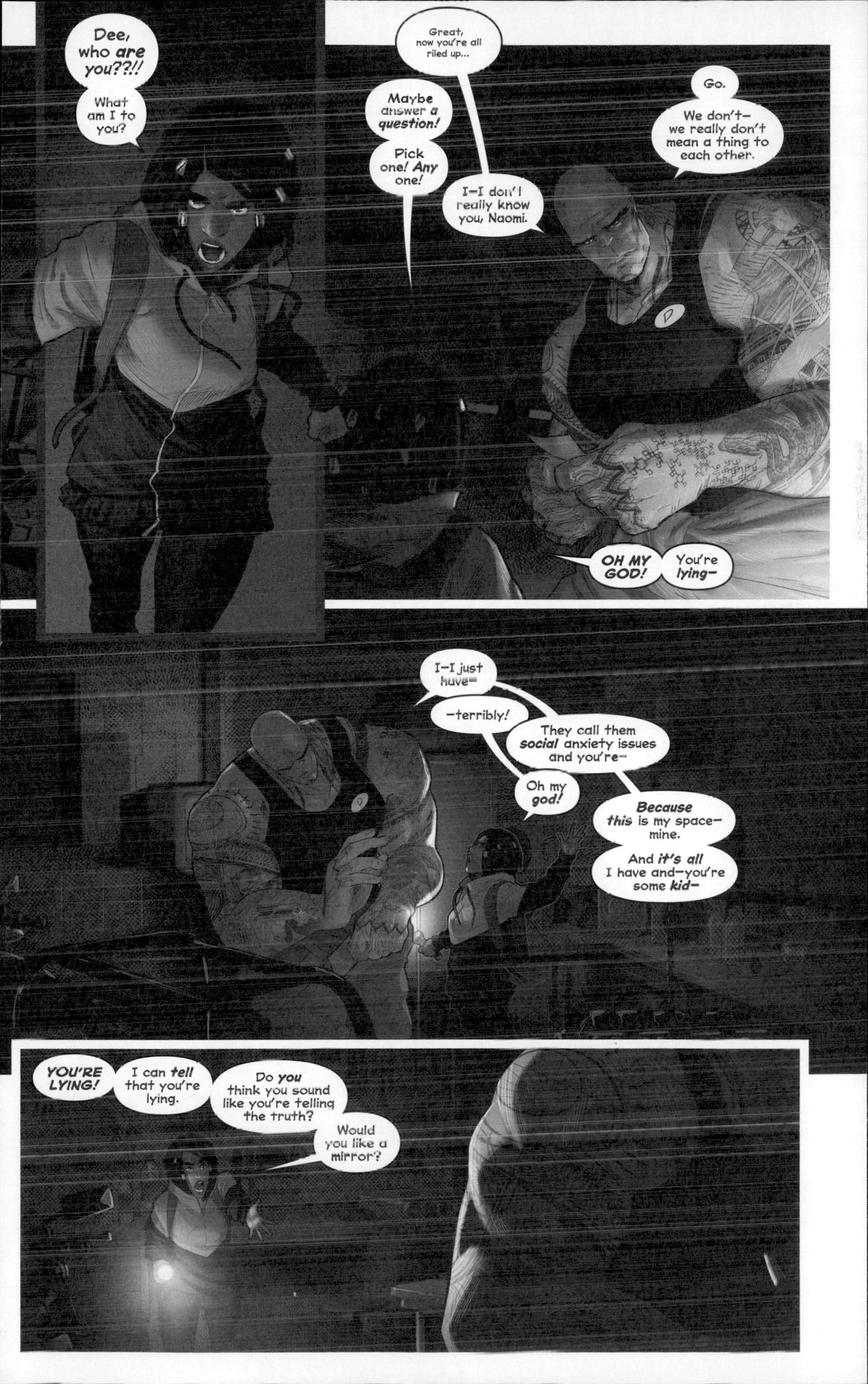

Dee, who are you??!!
What am I to you?
Great, now you're all riled up...
Maybe answer a question!
Pick one! Any one!
I—I don't really know you, Naomi.
Go.
We don't—we really don't mean a thing to each other.
OH MY GOD!
You're lying—
I—I just have—
—terribly!
They call them social anxiety issues and you're—
Oh my god!
Because this is my space—mine.
And it's all I have and—you're some kid—
YOU'RE LYING!
I can tell that you're lying.
Do you think you sound like you're telling the truth?
Would you like a mirror?

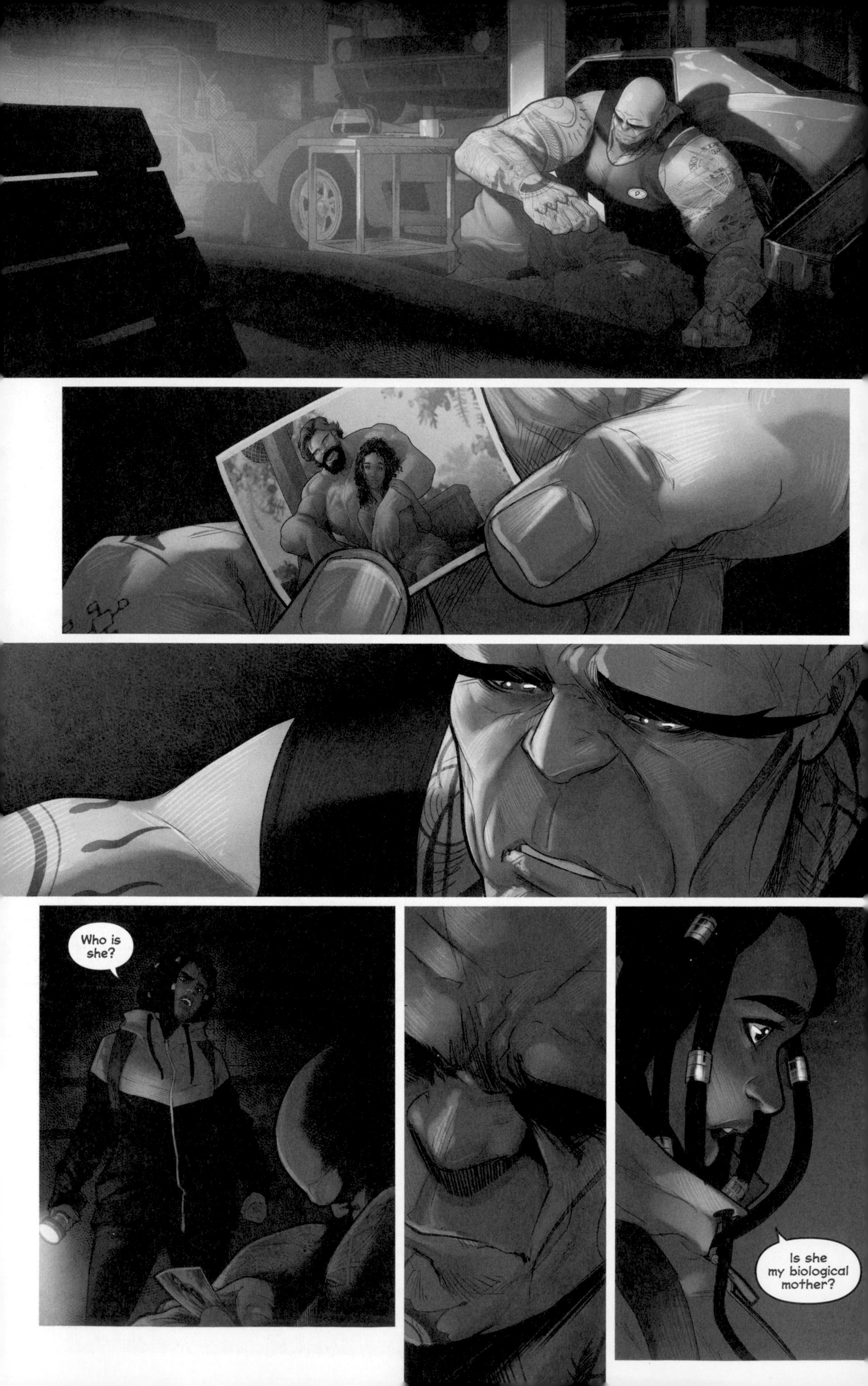
Who is she?
Is she my biological mother?

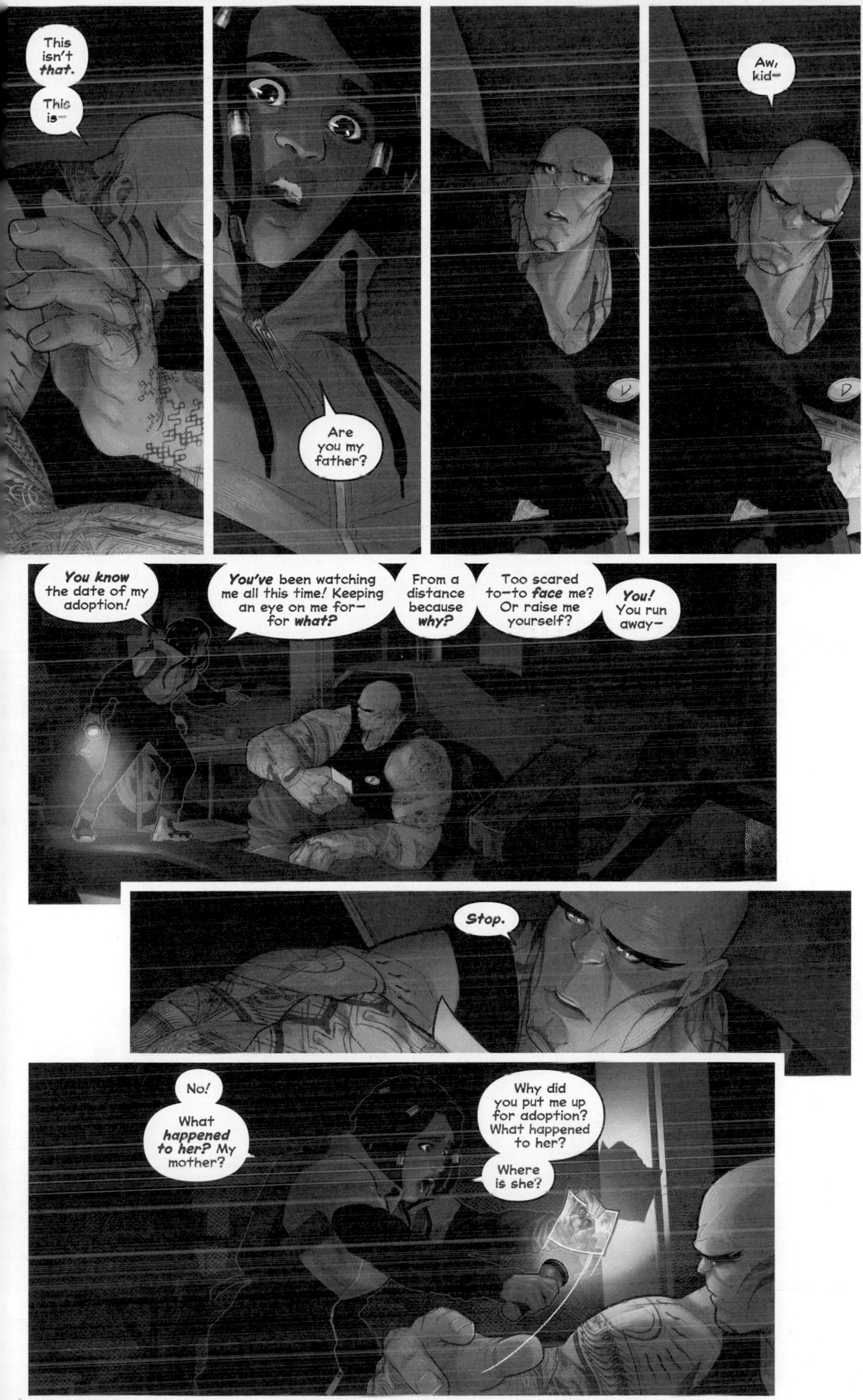
This isn't *that*.
This is—
Are you my father?
Aw, kid—
You know the date of my adoption!
You've been watching me all this time! Keeping an eye on me for— for *what?*
From a distance because *why?*
Too scared to—to *face* me? Or raise me yourself?
You! You run away—
Stop.
No!
What *happened to her?* My mother?
Why did you put me up for adoption? What happened to her?
Where is she?

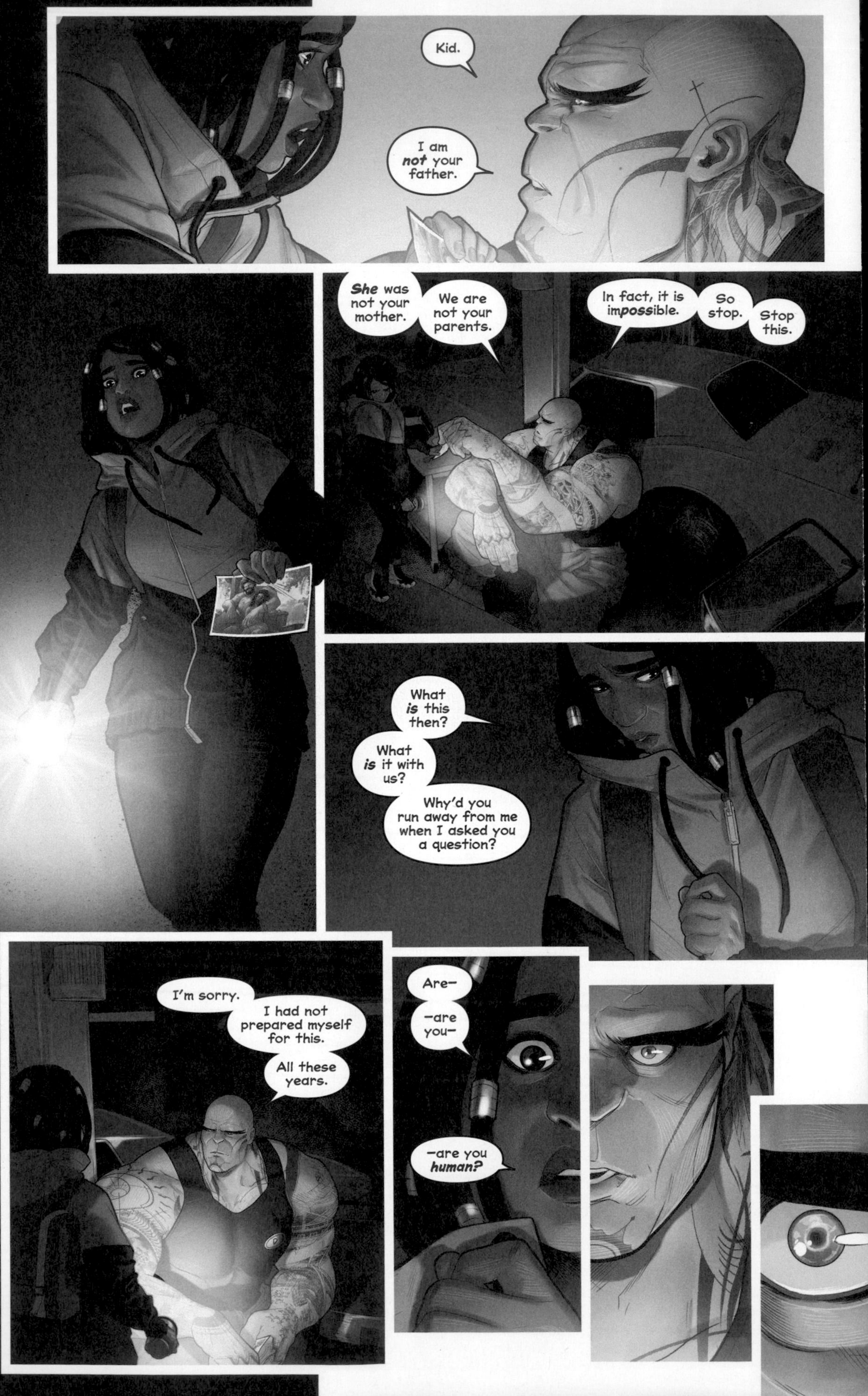
Kid.
I am *not* your father.
She was not your mother.
We are not your parents.
In fact, it is im*poss*ible.
So stop.
Stop this.
What *is* this then?
What *is* it with us?
Why'd you run away from me when I asked you a question?
I'm sorry.
I had not prepared myself for this.
All these years.
Are–
–are you–
–are you *human?*

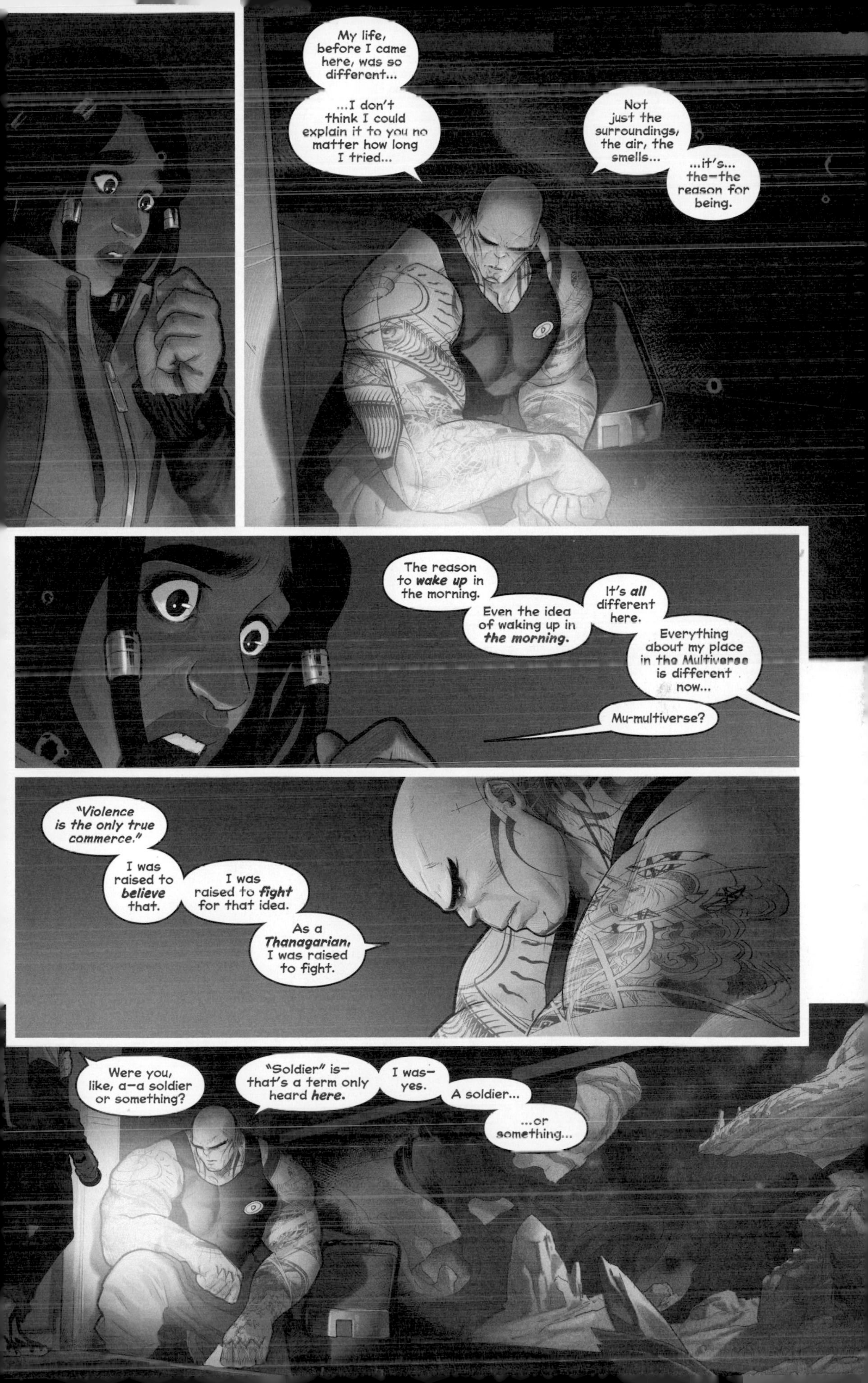
My life, before I came here, was so different...
...I don't think I could explain it to you no matter how long I tried...
Not just the surroundings, the air, the smells...
...it's... the—the reason for being.
The reason to *wake up* in the morning.
Even the idea of waking up in *the morning.*
It's *all* different here.
Everything about my place in the Multiverse is different now...
Mu-multiverse?
"Violence is the only true commerce."
I was raised to *believe* that.
I was raised to *fight* for that idea.
As a *Thanagarian,* I was raised to fight.
Were you, like, a—a soldier or something?
"Soldier" is—that's a term only heard *here.*
I was—yes.
A soldier...
...or something...

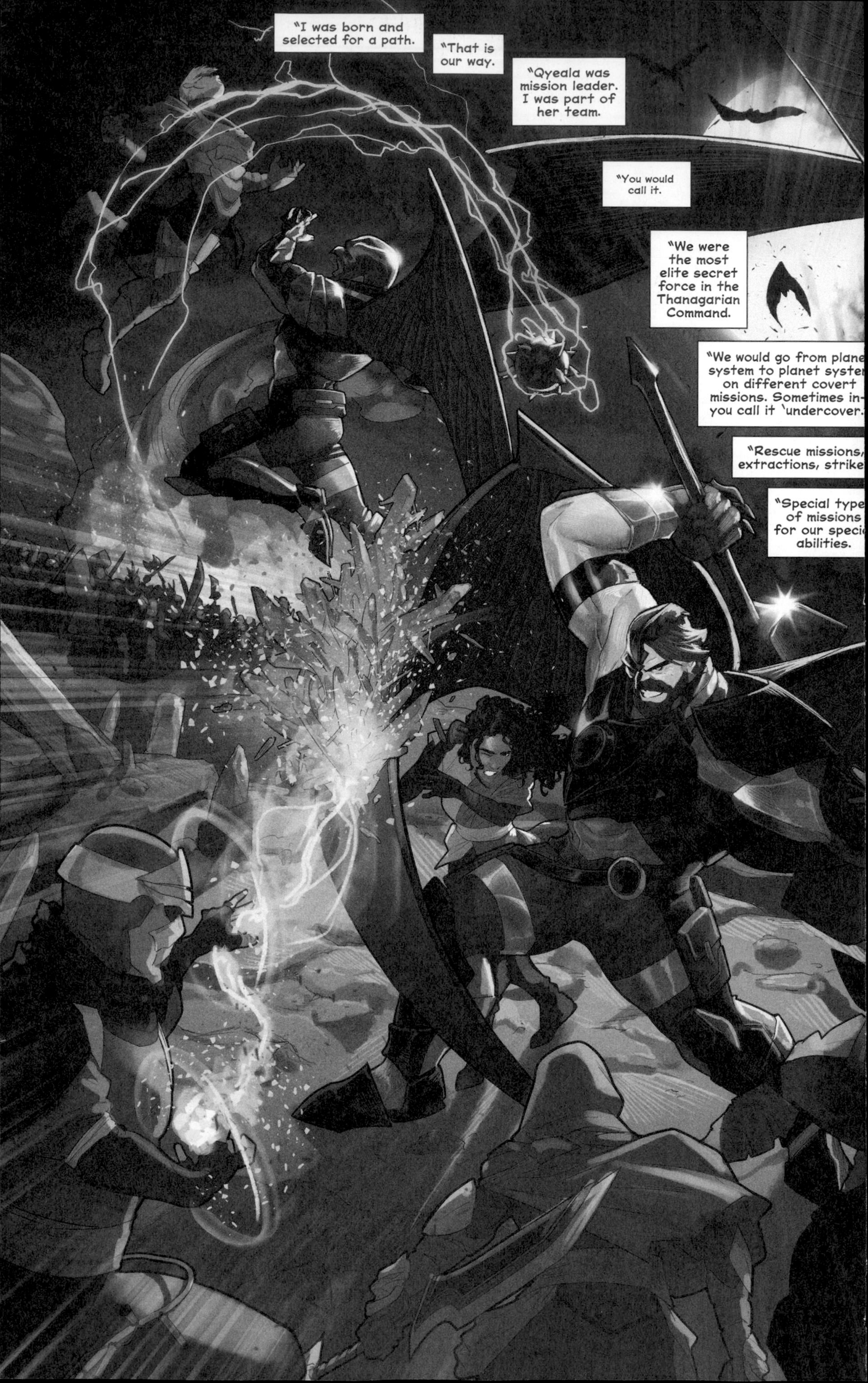
"I was born and selected for a path.
"That is our way.
"Qyeala was mission leader. I was part of her team.
"You would call it.
"We were the most elite secret force in the Thanagarian Command.
"We would go from plane system to planet syster on different covert missions. Sometimes in- you call it 'undercover.
"Rescue missions, extractions, strike
"Special type of missions for our speci abilities.

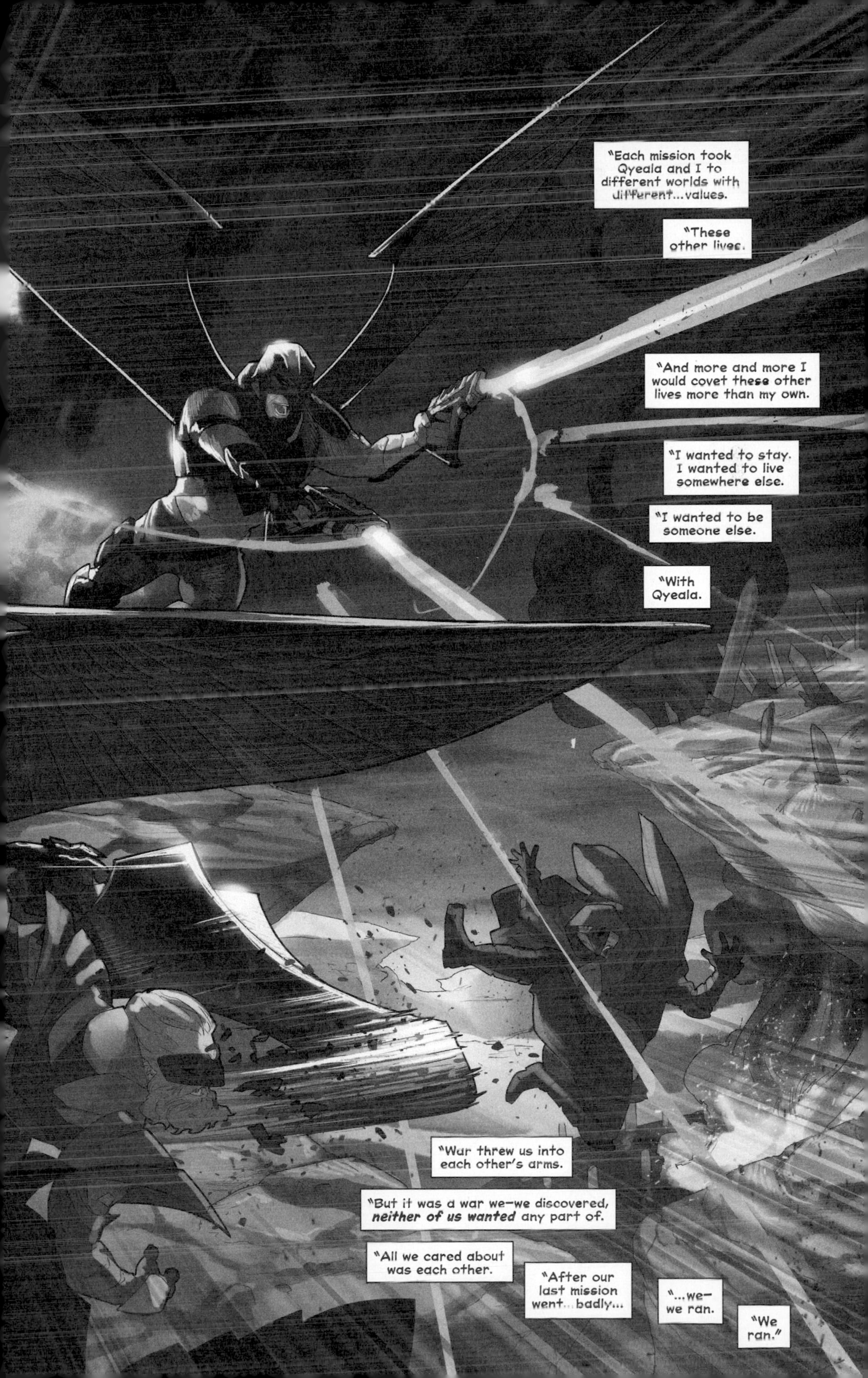
"Each mission took Qyeala and I to different worlds with different...values.
"These other lives.
"And more and more I would covet these other lives more than my own.
"I wanted to stay. I wanted to live somewhere else.
"I wanted to be someone else.
"With Qyeala.
"War threw us into each other's arms.
"But it was a war we—we discovered, ***neither of us wanted*** any part of.
"All we cared about was each other.
"After our last mission went...badly...
"...we—we ran.
"We ran."

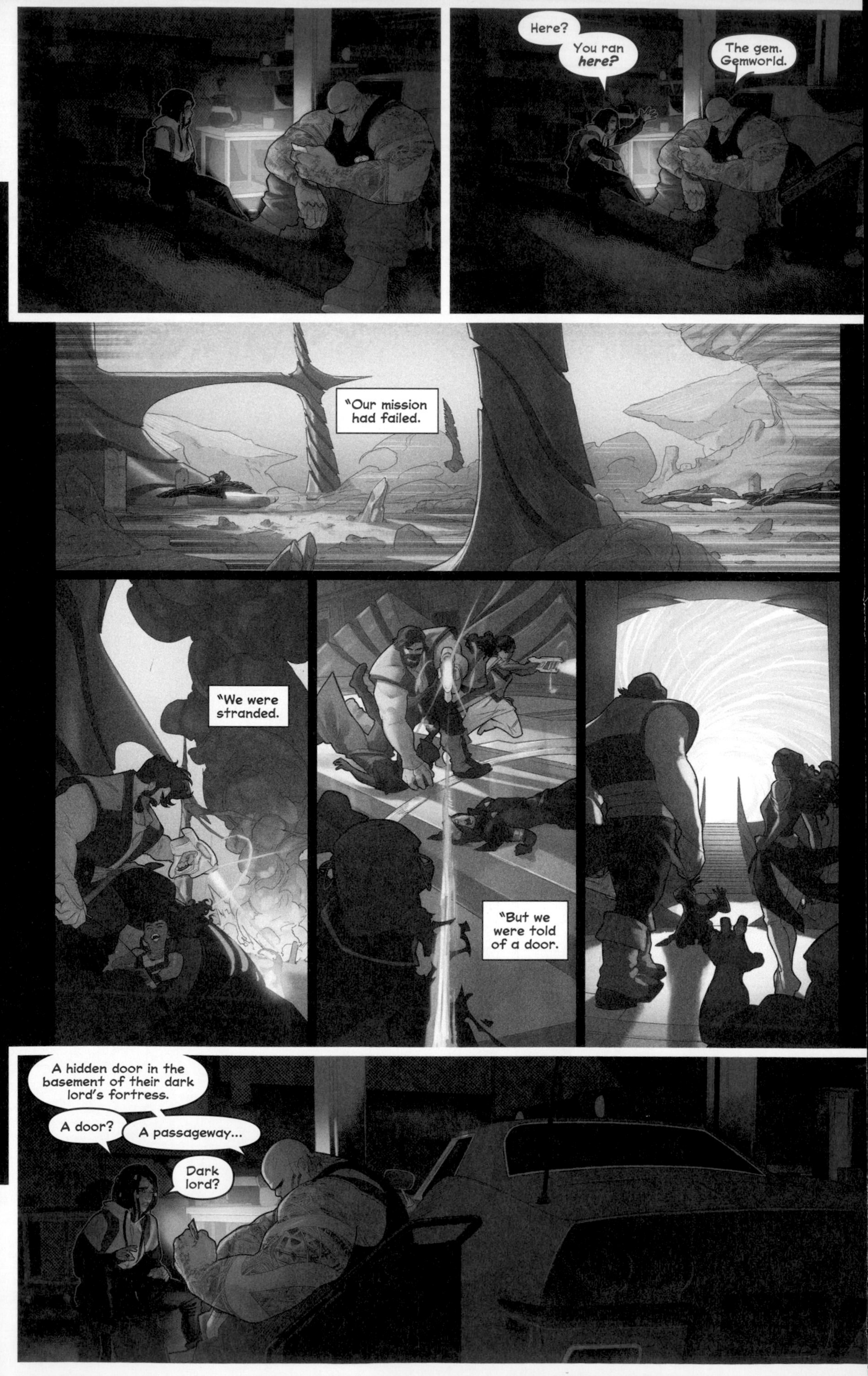
Here?
You ran here?
The gem. Gemworld.
"Our mission had failed.
"We were stranded.
"But we were told of a door.
A hidden door in the basement of their dark lord's fortress.
A door?
A passageway...
Dark lord?

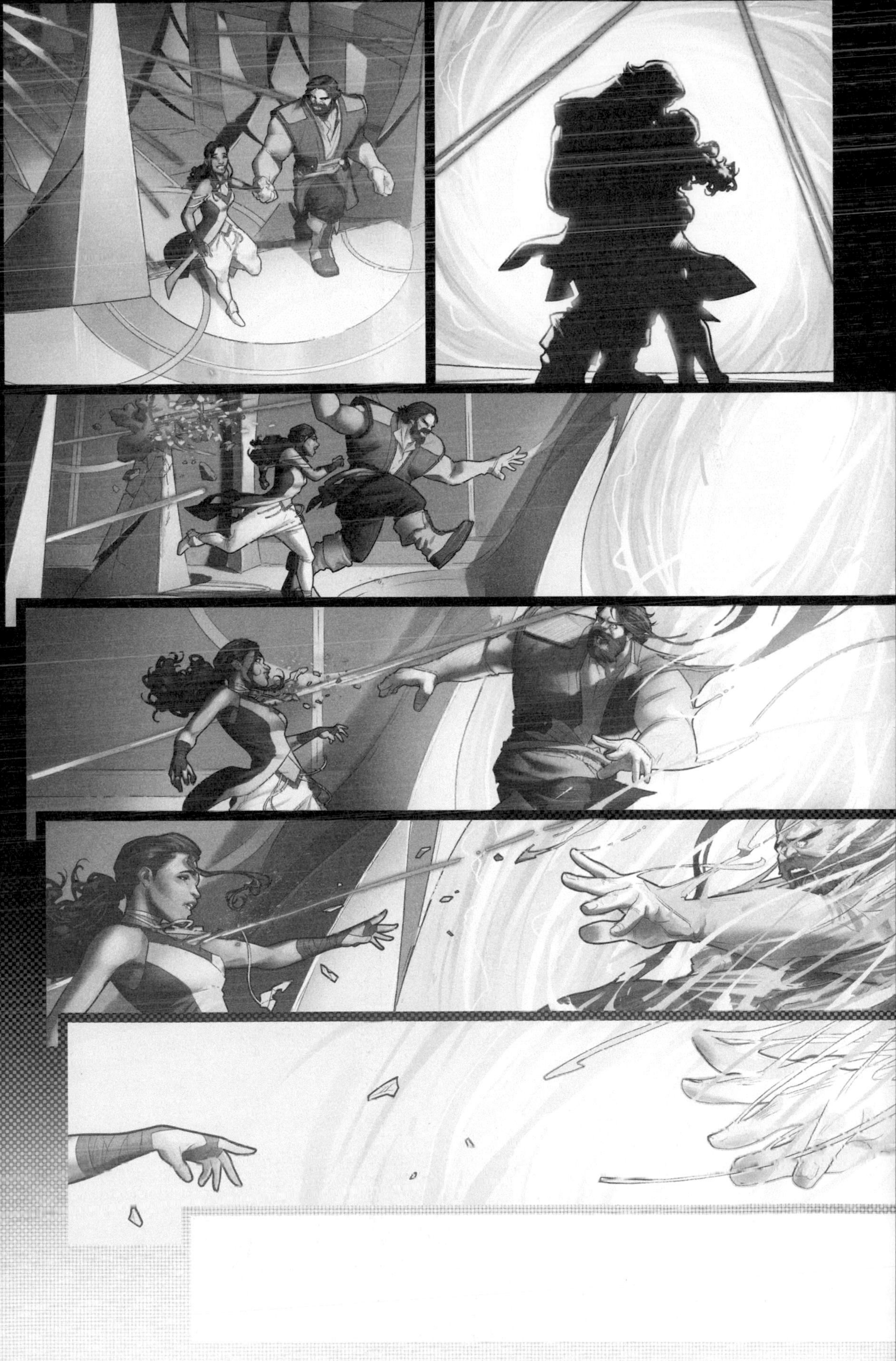

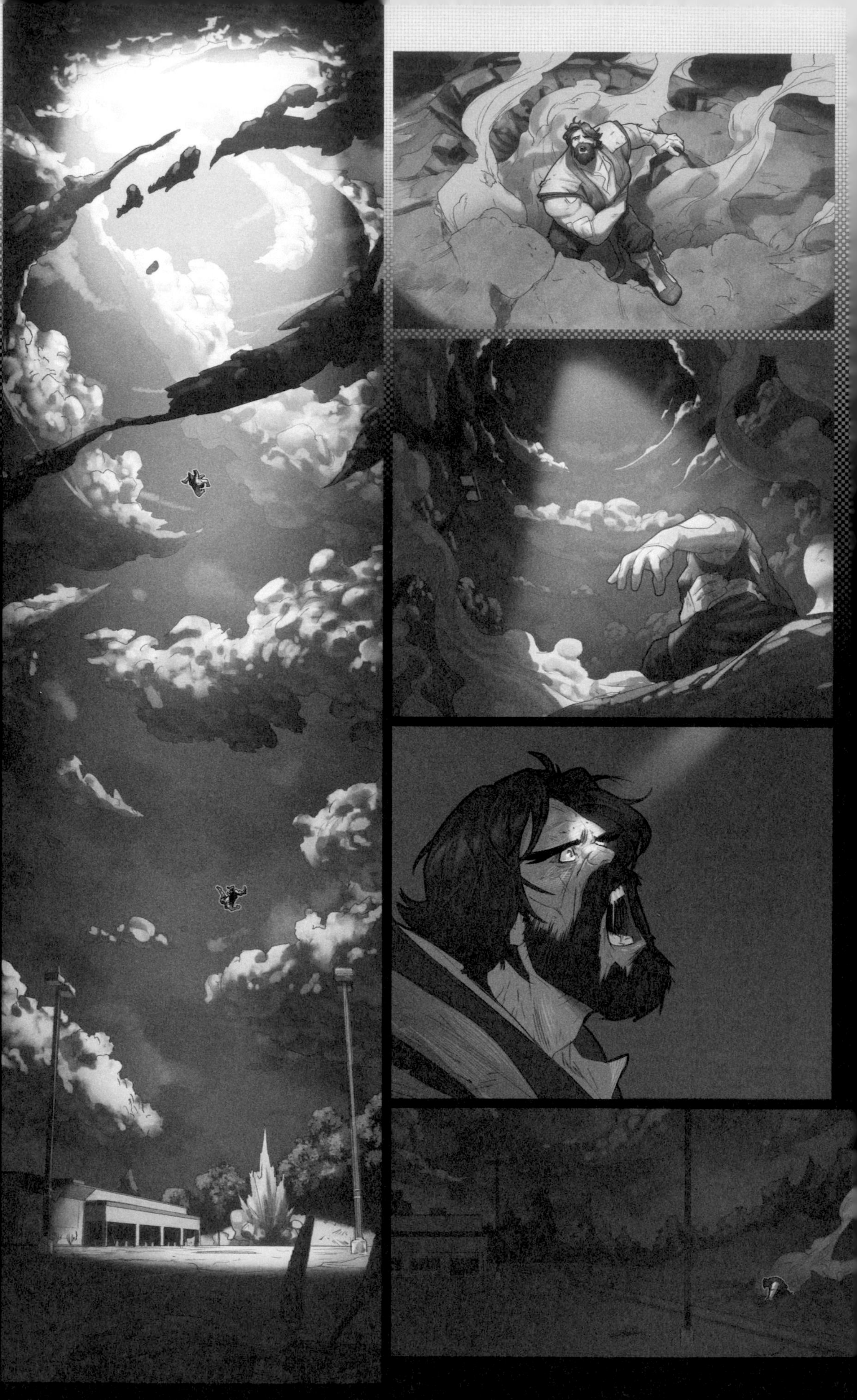

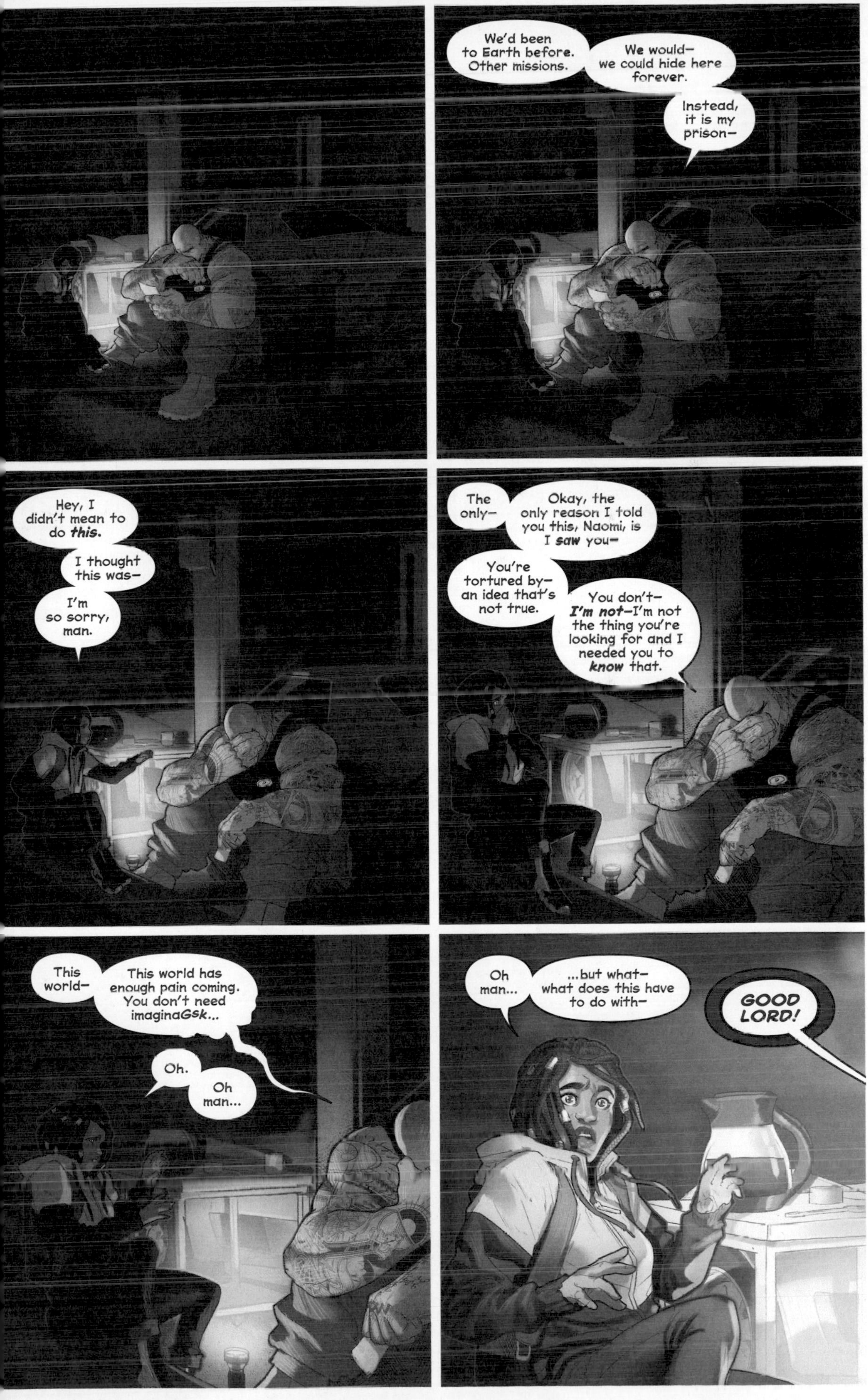
We'd been to Earth before. Other missions.
We would— we could hide here forever.
Instead, it is my prison—
Hey, I didn't mean to do **this.**
I thought this was—
I'm so sorry, man.
The only—
Okay, the only reason I told you this, Naomi, is I **saw** you—
You're tortured by— an idea that's not true.
You don't— ***I'm not***—I'm not the thing you're looking for and I needed you to **know** that.
This world—
This world has enough pain coming. You don't need imagina**Gsk...**
Oh.
Oh man...
Oh man...
...but what— what does this have to do with—
GOOD LORD!

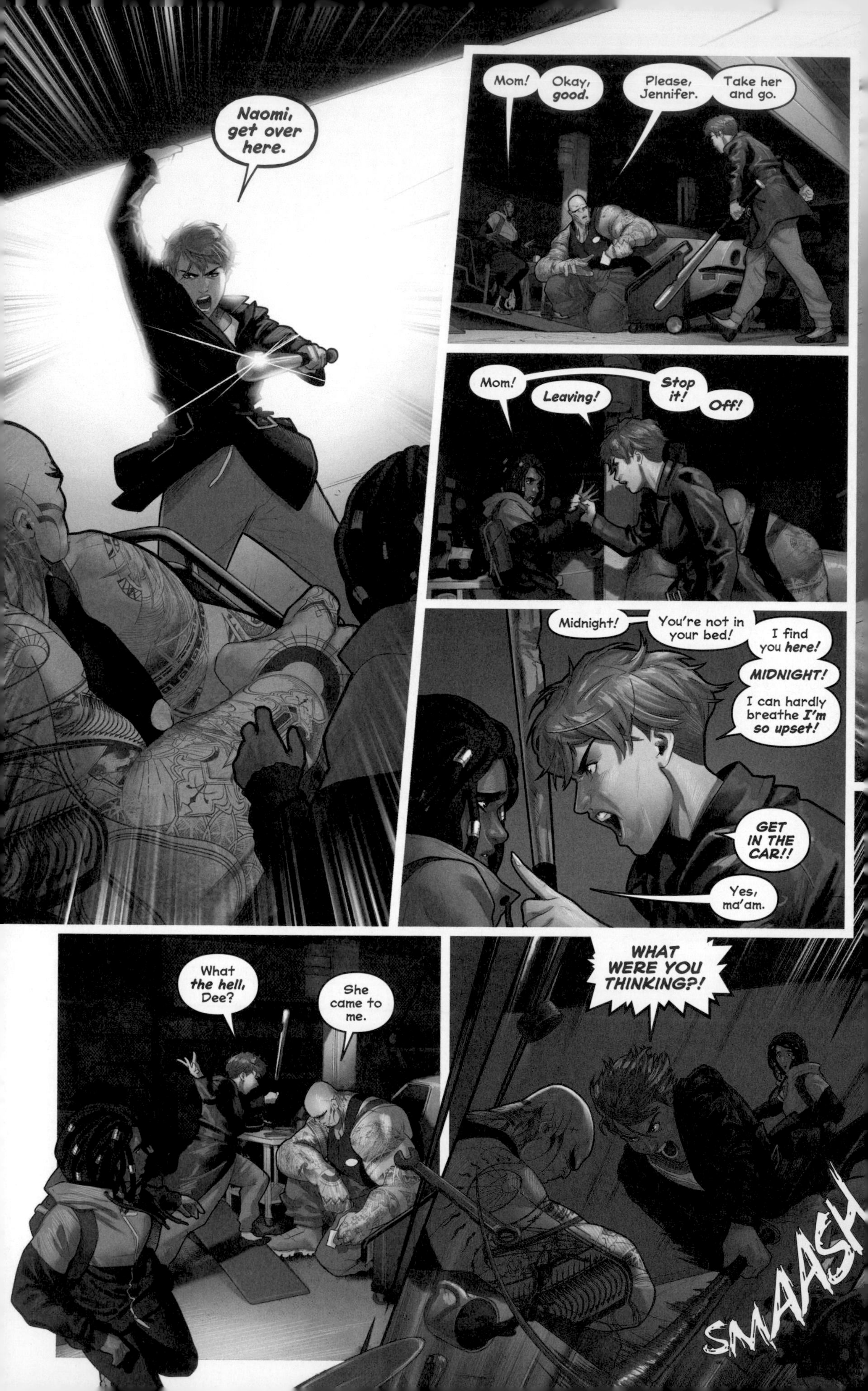

Naomi, get over here.
Mom!
Okay, good.
Please, Jennifer.
Take her and go.
Mom!
Leaving!
Stop it!
Off!
Midnight!
You're not in your bed!
I find you here!
MIDNIGHT!
I can hardly breathe I'm so upset!
GET IN THE CAR!!
Yes, ma'am.
What the hell, Dee?
She came to me.
WHAT WERE YOU THINKING?!
SMAASH

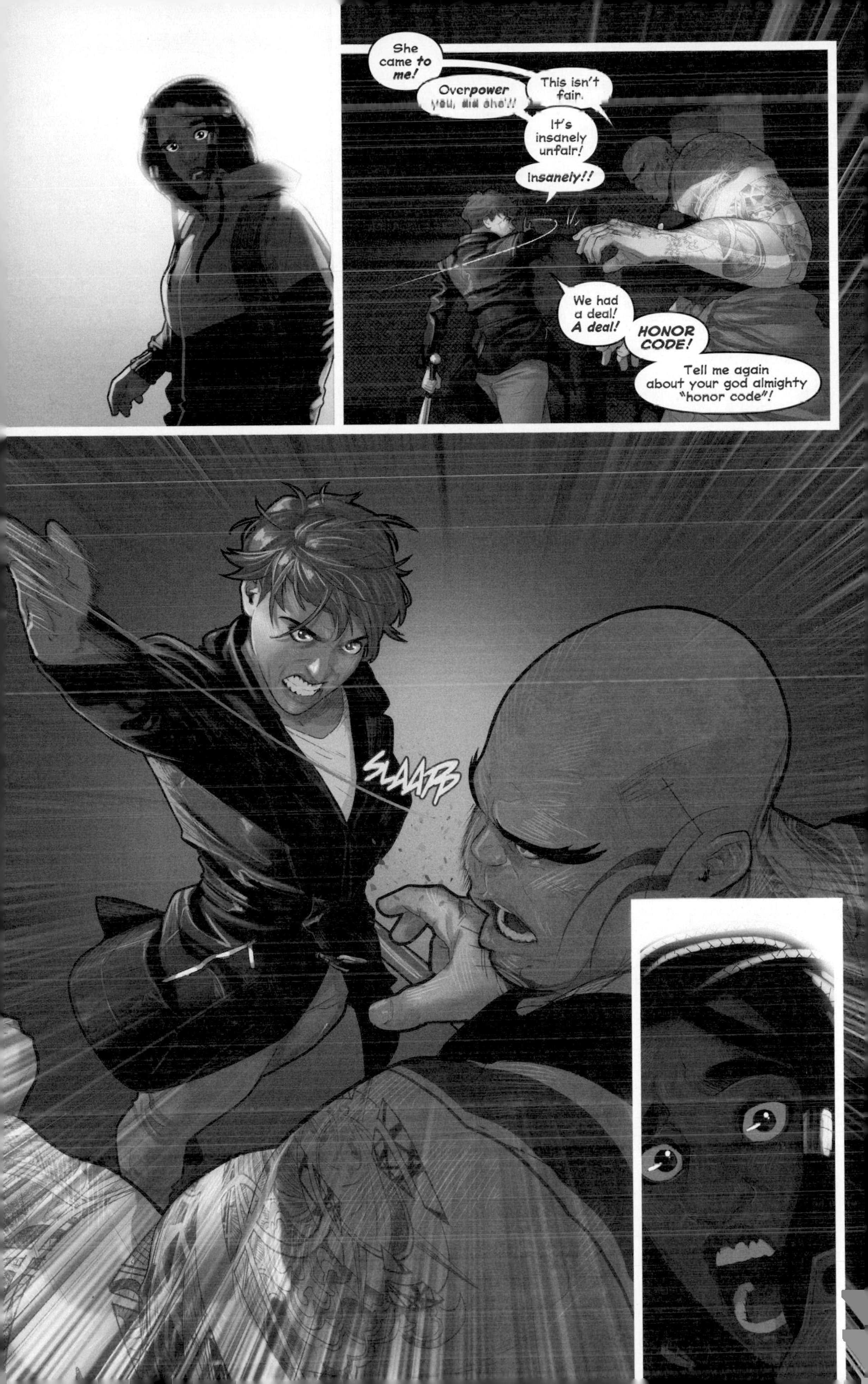
She came to me!
This isn't fair.
Overpower you, did she?!
It's insanely unfair!
Insanely!!
We had a deal! A deal!
HONOR CODE!
Tell me again about your god almighty "honor code"!
SLAAAP

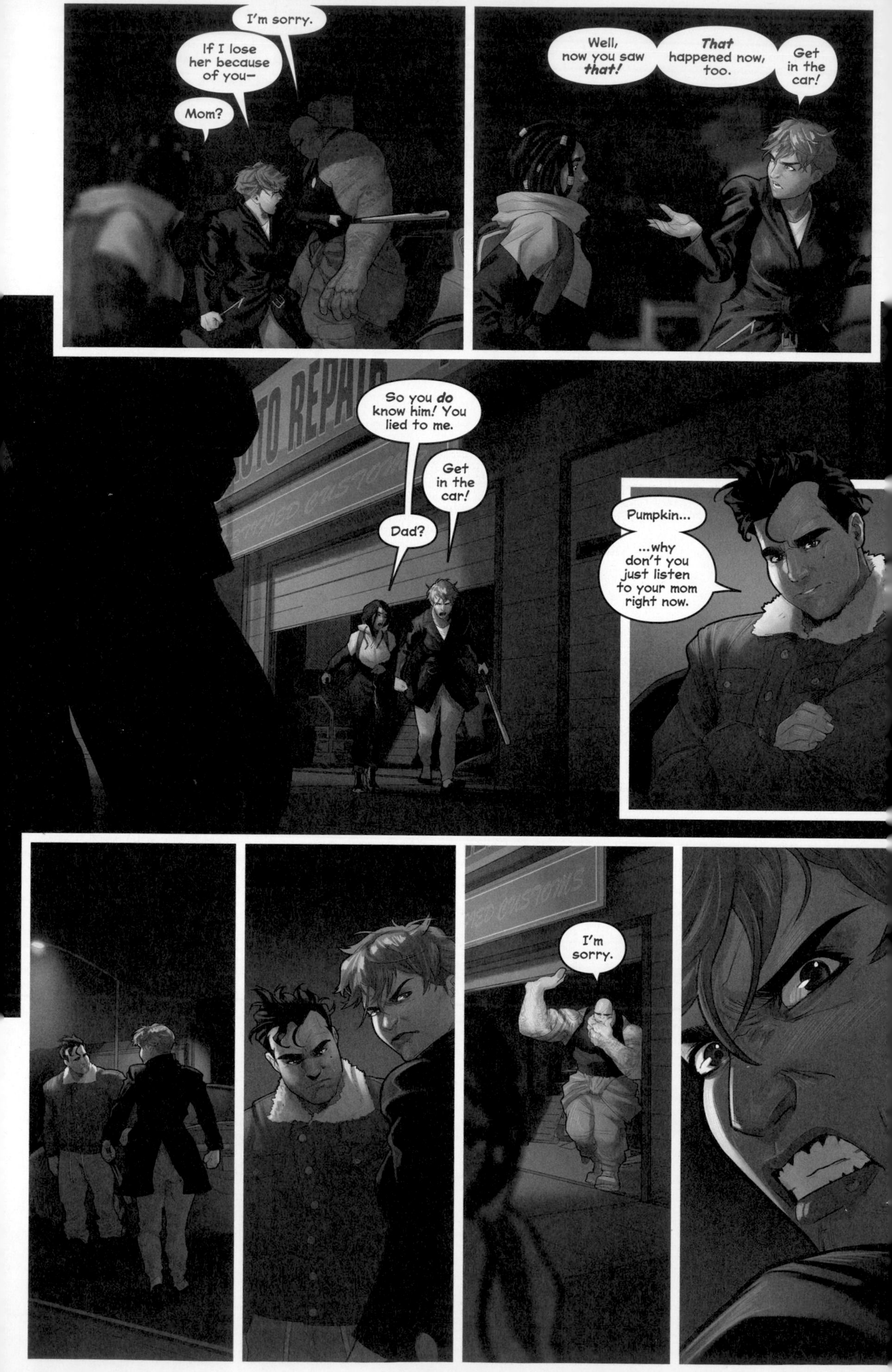
If I lose her because of you—
I'm sorry.
Mom?
Well, now you saw *that!*
That happened now, too.
Get in the car!
So you *do* know him! You lied to me.
Get in the car!
Dad?
Pumpkin...
...why don't you just listen to your mom right now.
I'm sorry.

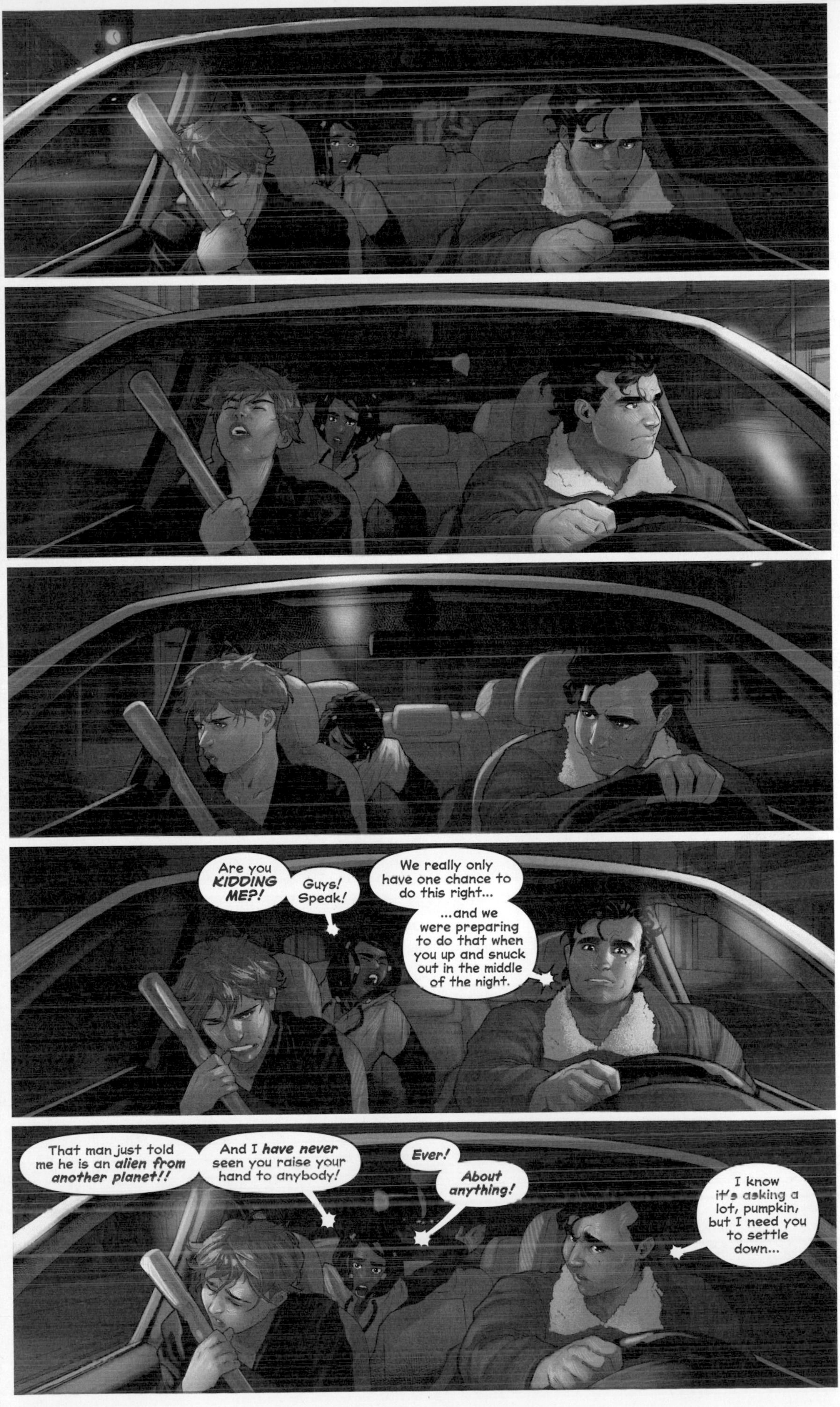
Are you KIDDING ME?!
Guys! Speak!
We really only have one chance to do this right...
...and we were preparing to do that when you up and snuck out in the middle of the night.
That man just told me he is an alien from another planet!!
And I have never seen you raise your hand to anybody!
Ever!
About anything!
I know it's asking a lot, pumpkin, but I need you to settle down...

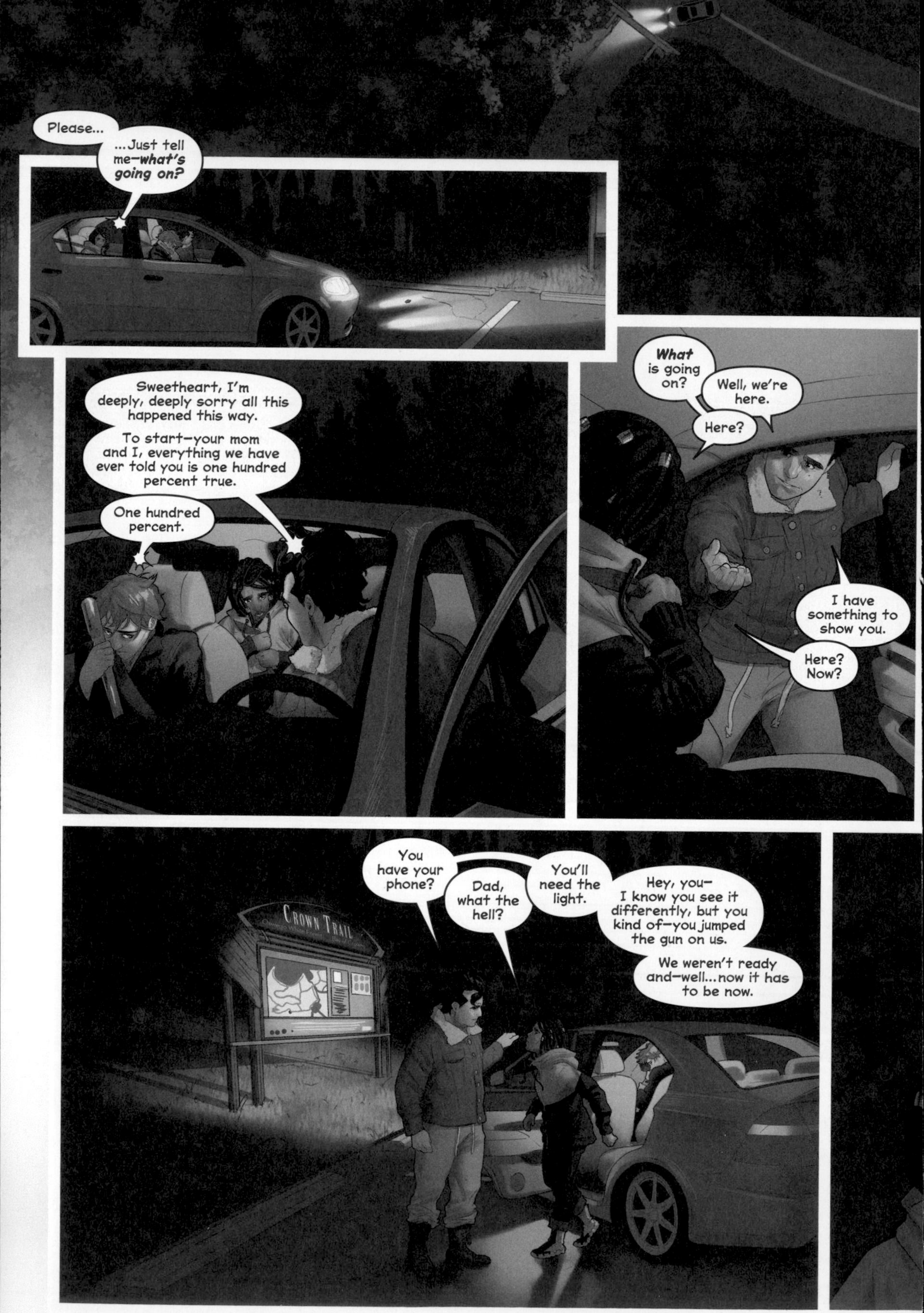
Please...
...Just tell me—*what's going on?*
Sweetheart, I'm deeply, deeply sorry all this happened this way.
To start—your mom and I, everything we have ever told you is one hundred percent true.
One hundred percent.
What is going on?
Well, we're here.
Here?
I have something to show you.
Here? Now?
CROWN TRAIL
You have your phone?
Dad, what the hell?
You'll need the light.
Hey, you—I know you see it differently, but you kind of—you jumped the gun on us.
We weren't ready and—well...now it has to be now.

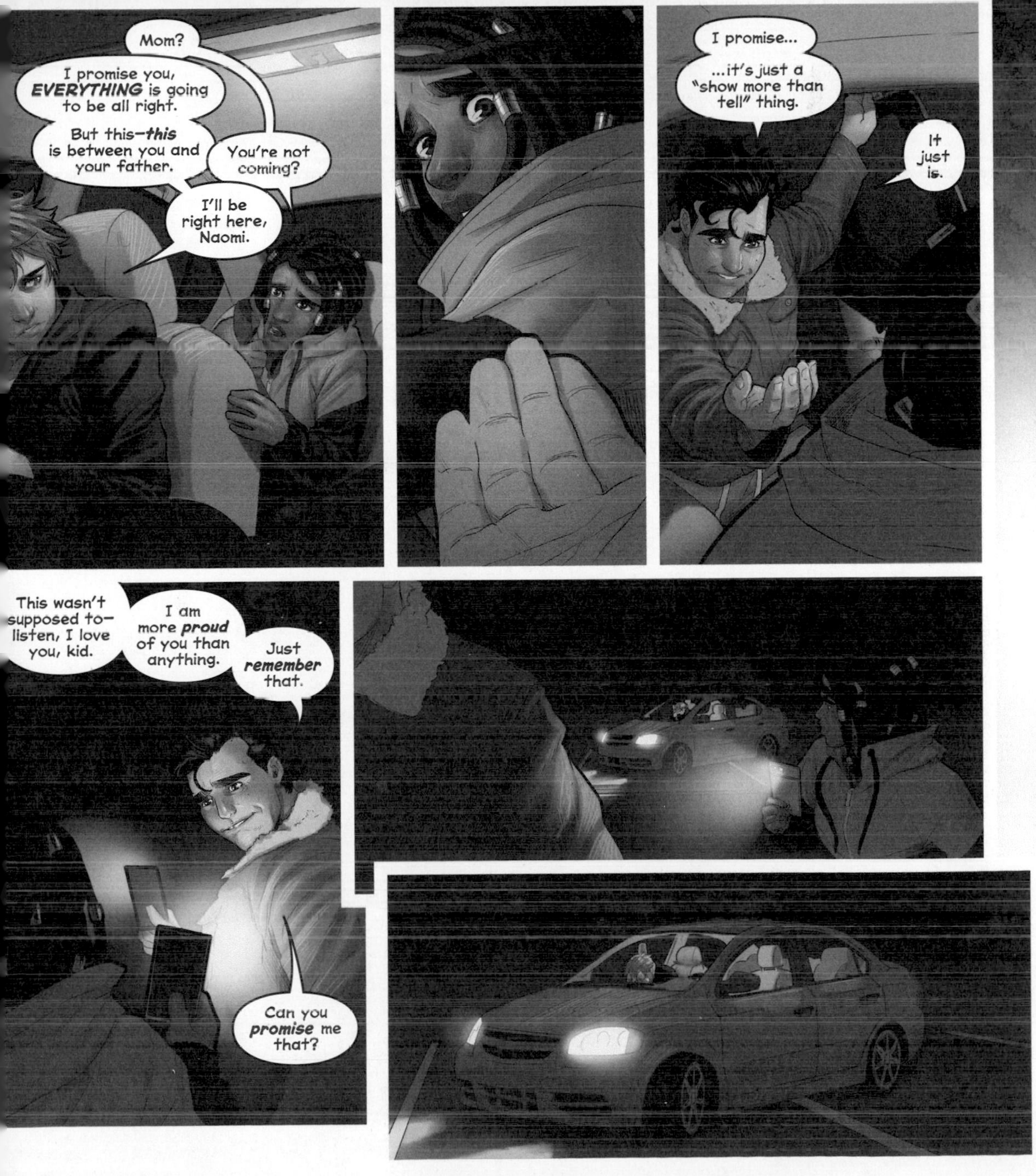
Mom?
I promise you, EVERYTHING is going to be all right.
But this—this is between you and your father.
You're not coming?
I'll be right here, Naomi.
I promise...
...it's just a "show more than tell" thing.
It just is.
This wasn't supposed to—listen, I love you, kid.
I am more proud of you than anything.
Just remember that.
Can you promise me that?

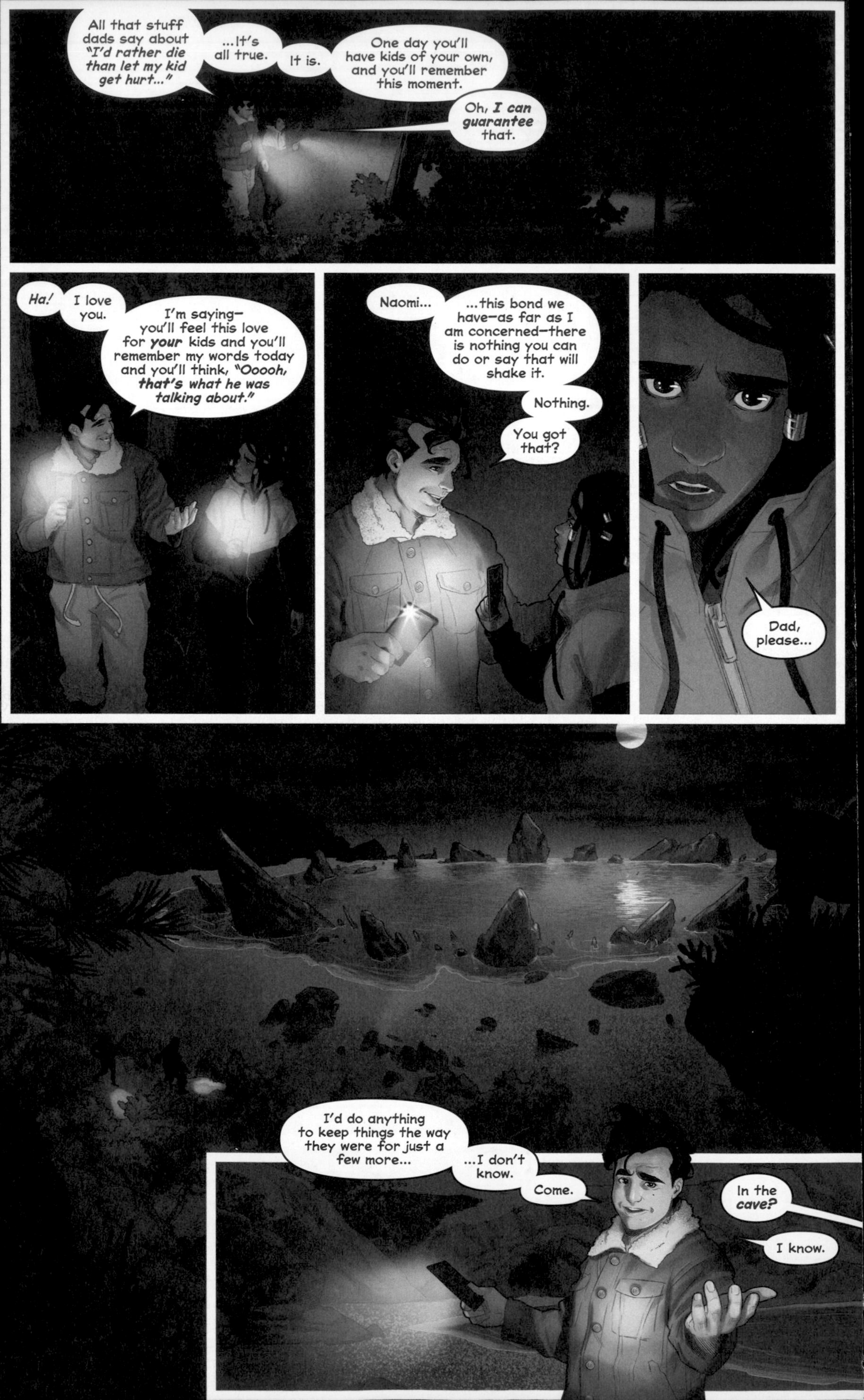
All that stuff dads say about "I'd rather die than let my kid get hurt..."
...It's all true.
It is.
One day you'll have kids of your own, and you'll remember this moment.
Oh, I can guarantee that.
Ha!
I love you.
I'm saying— you'll feel this love for your kids and you'll remember my words today and you'll think, "Ooooh, that's what he was talking about."
Naomi...
...this bond we have—as far as I am concerned—there is nothing you can do or say that will shake it.
Nothing.
You got that?
Dad, please...
I'd do anything to keep things the way they were for just a few more...
...I don't know.
Come.
In the cave?
I know.

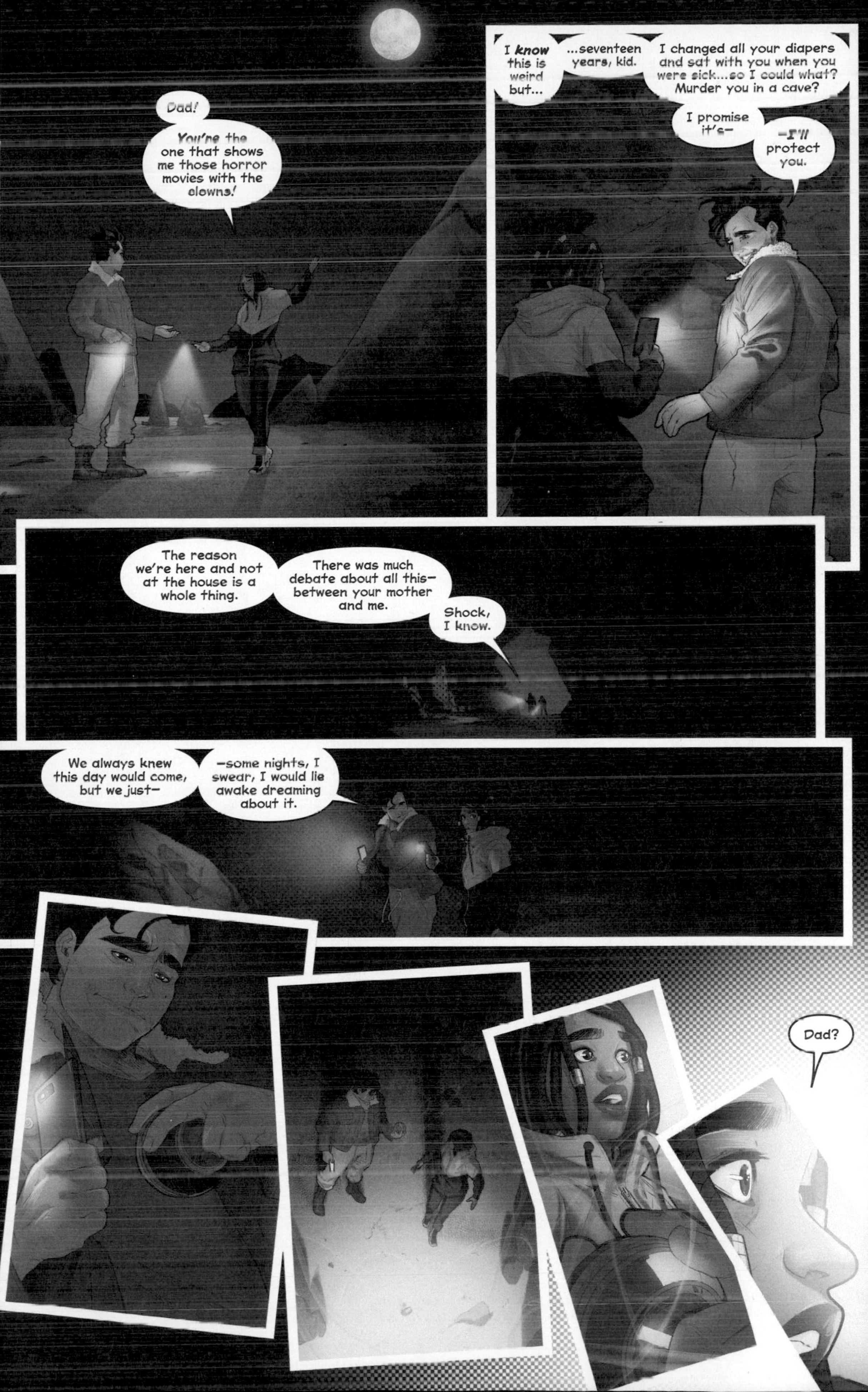
Dad!
You're the one that shows me those horror movies with the clowns!
I know this is weird but...
...seventeen years, kid.
I changed all your diapers and sat with you when you were sick...so I could what? Murder you in a cave?
I promise it's—
—I'll protect you.
The reason we're here and not at the house is a whole thing.
There was much debate about all this—between your mother and me.
Shock, I know.
We always knew this day would come, but we just—
—some nights, I swear, I would lie awake dreaming about it.
Dad?

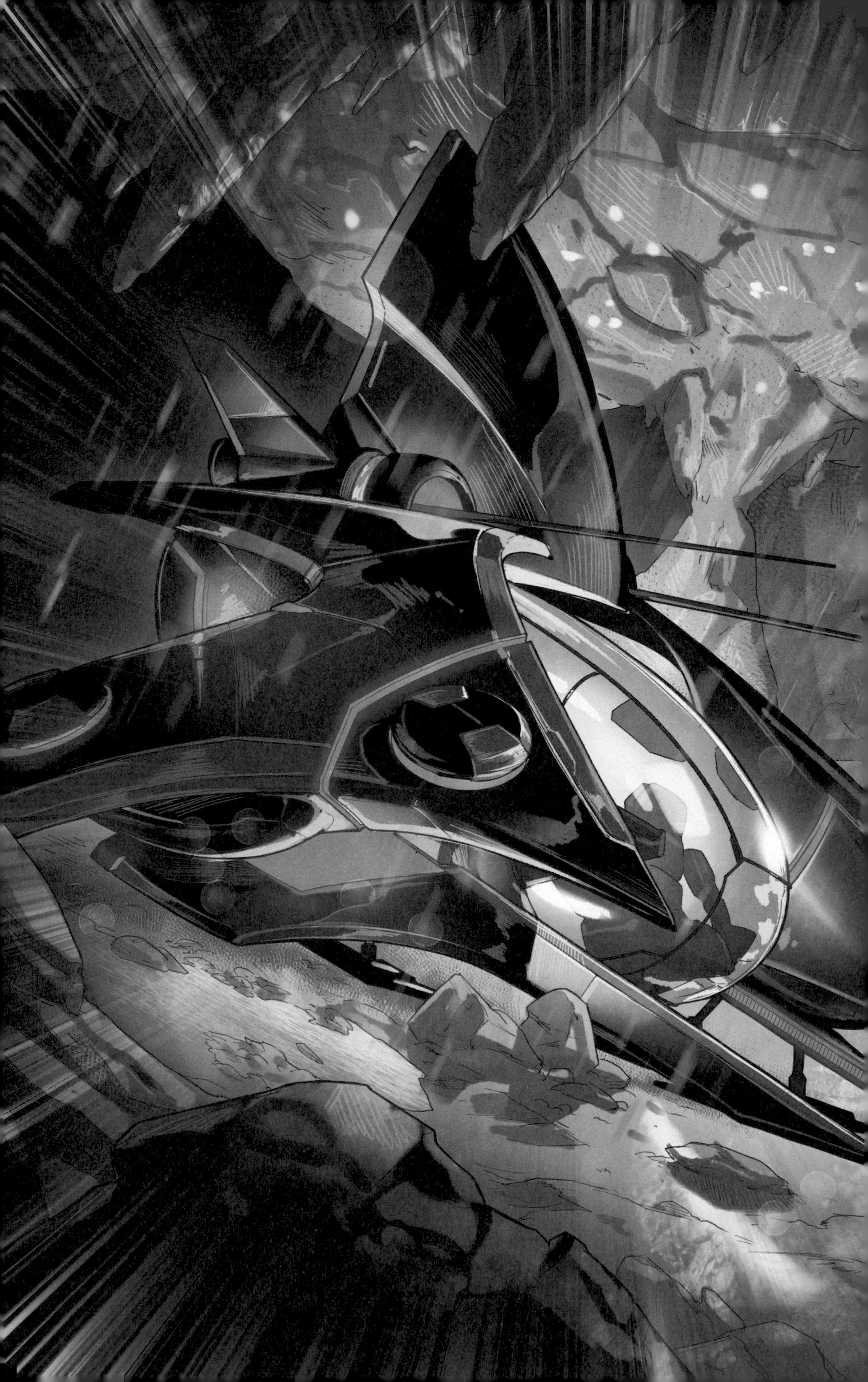

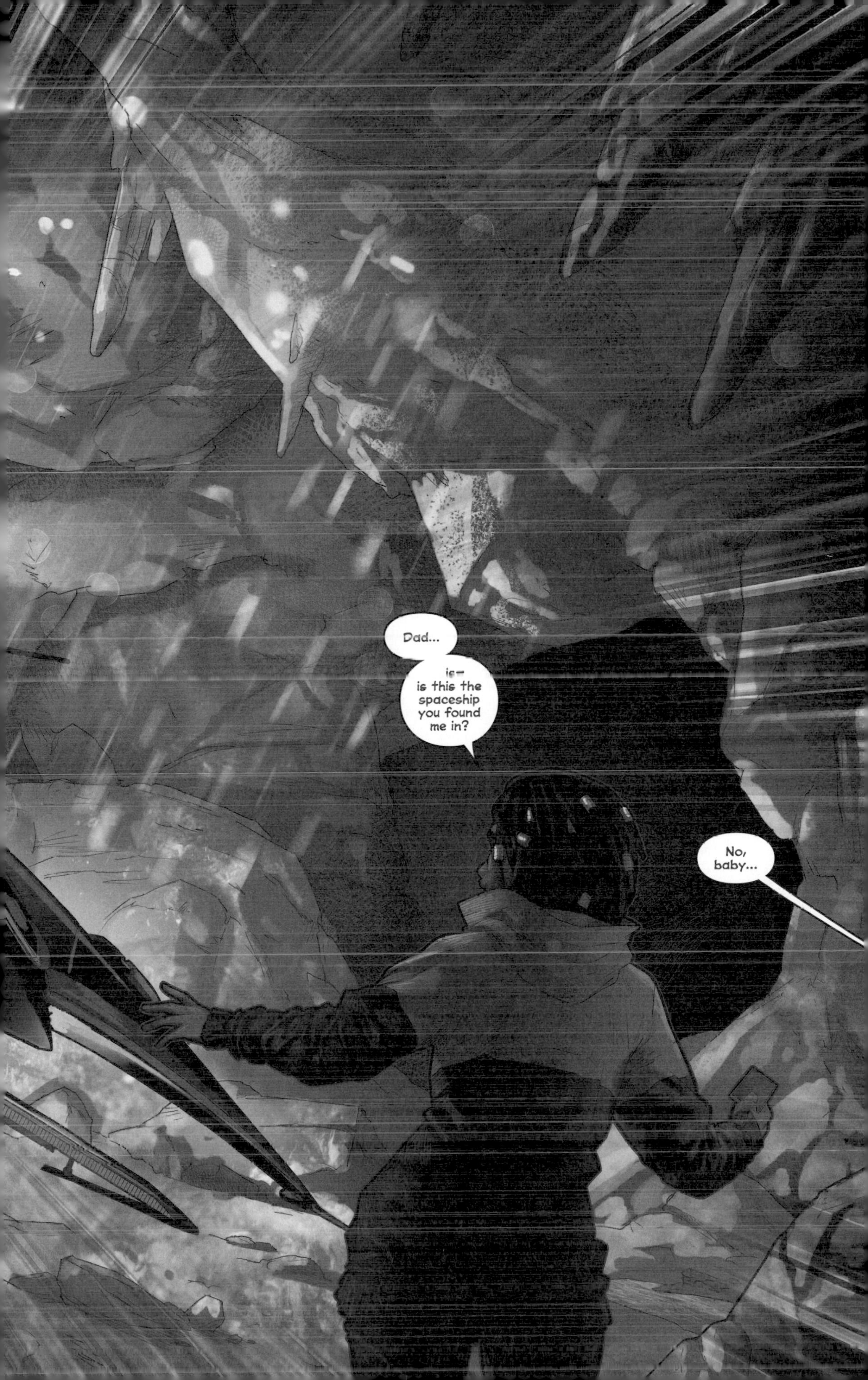
Dad...
is–
is this the spaceship you found me in?
No, baby...

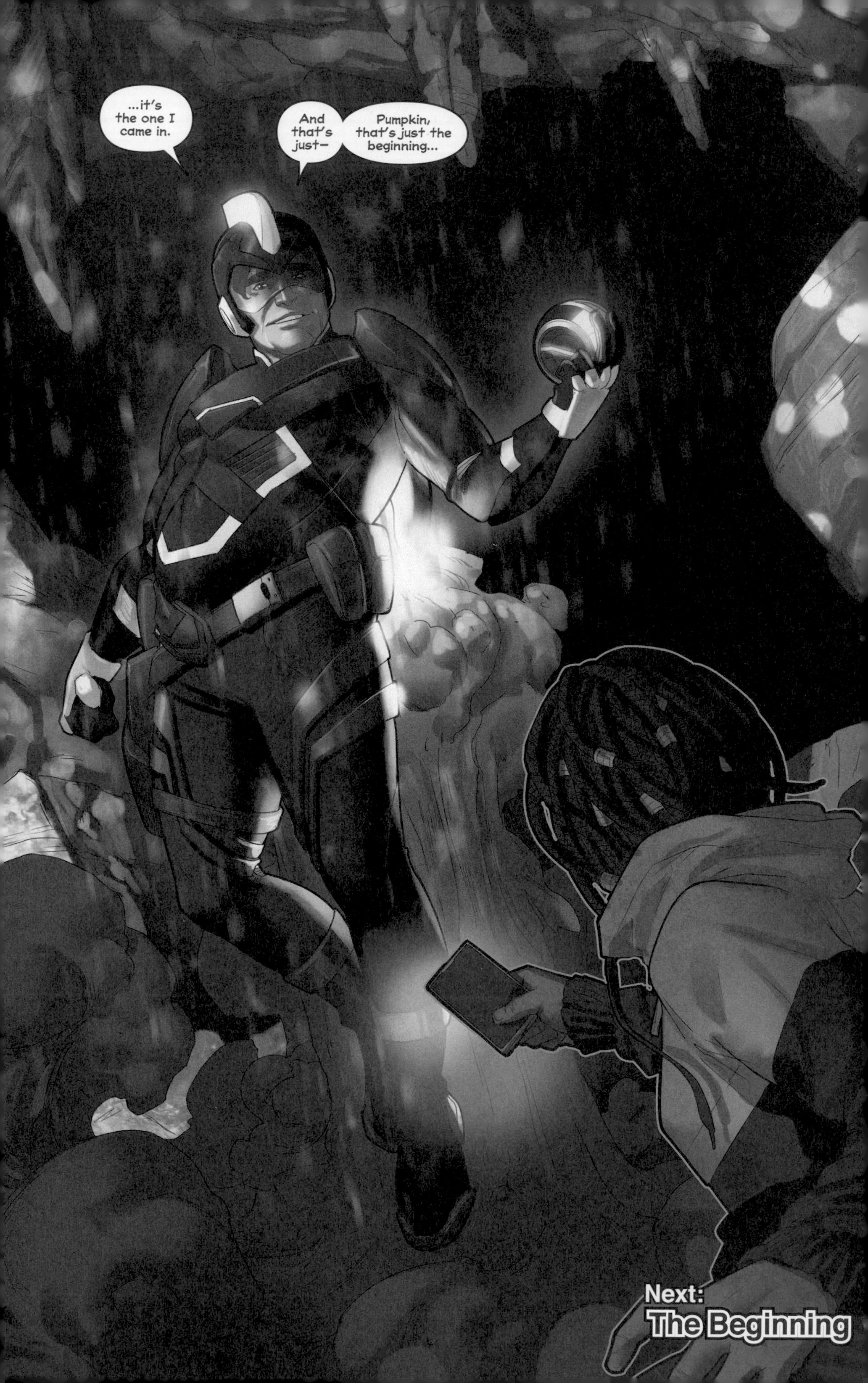
...it's the one I came in.
And that's just—
Pumpkin, that's just the beginning...
Next:
The Beginning

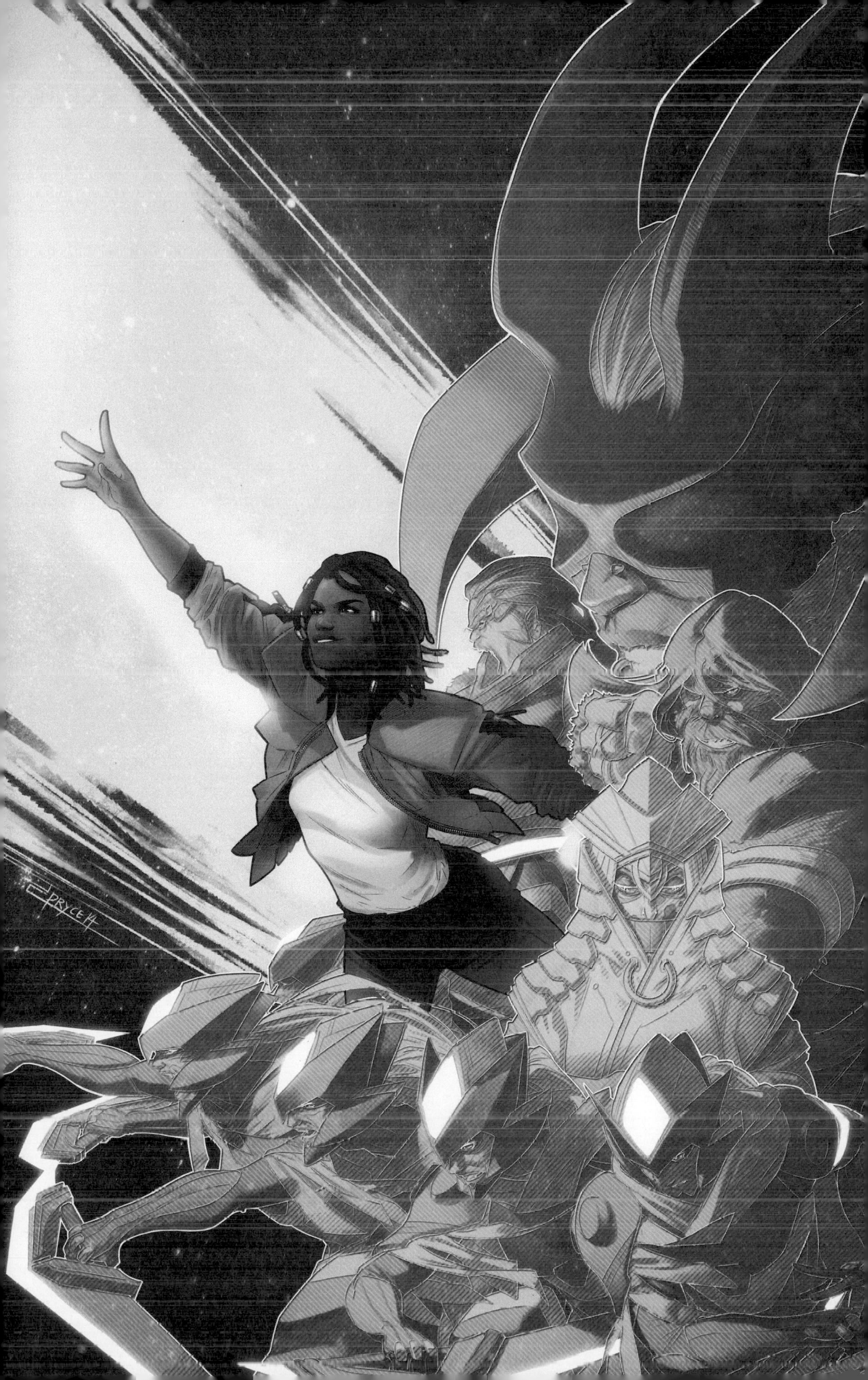

FOUR

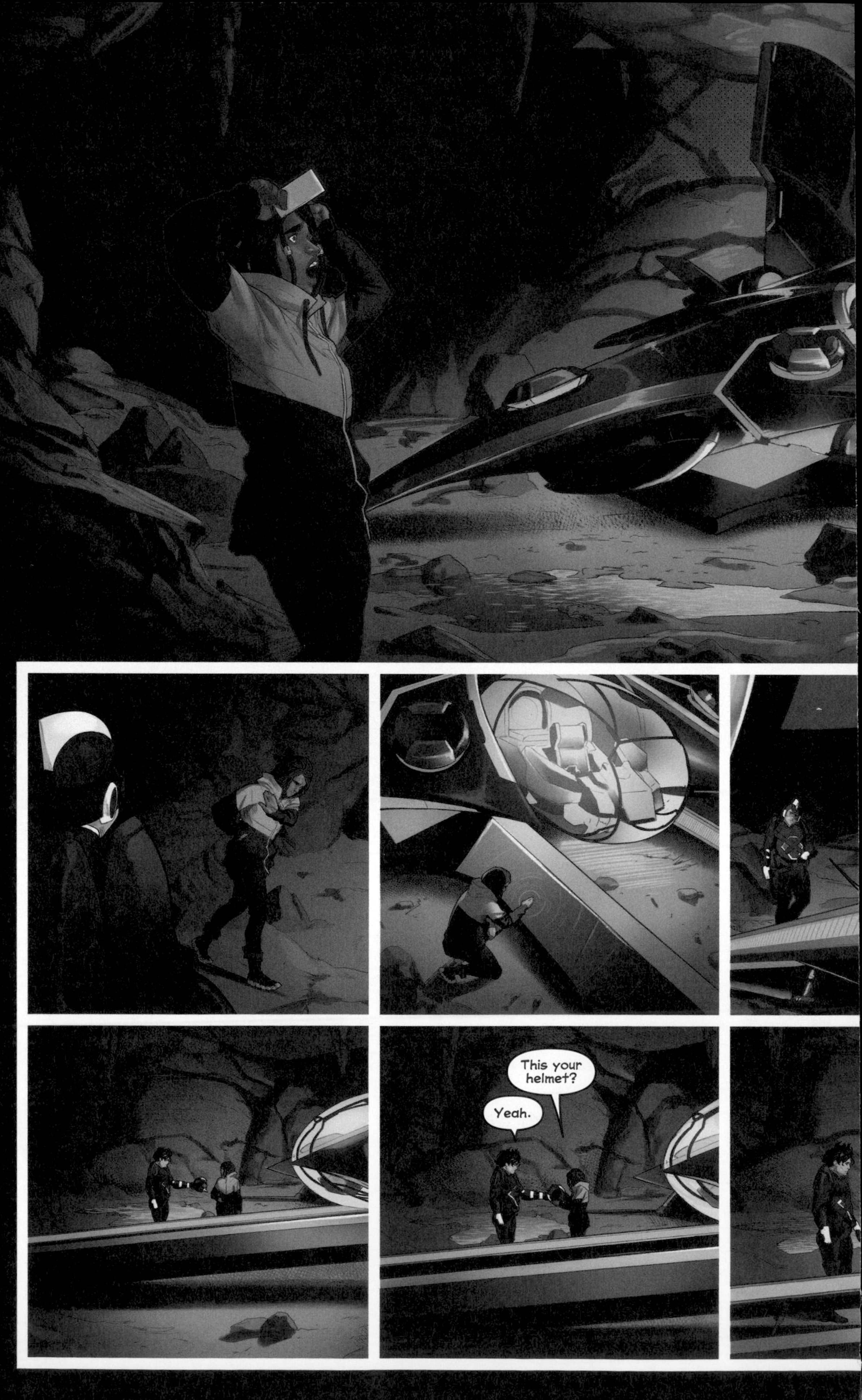
This your helmet?
Yeah.

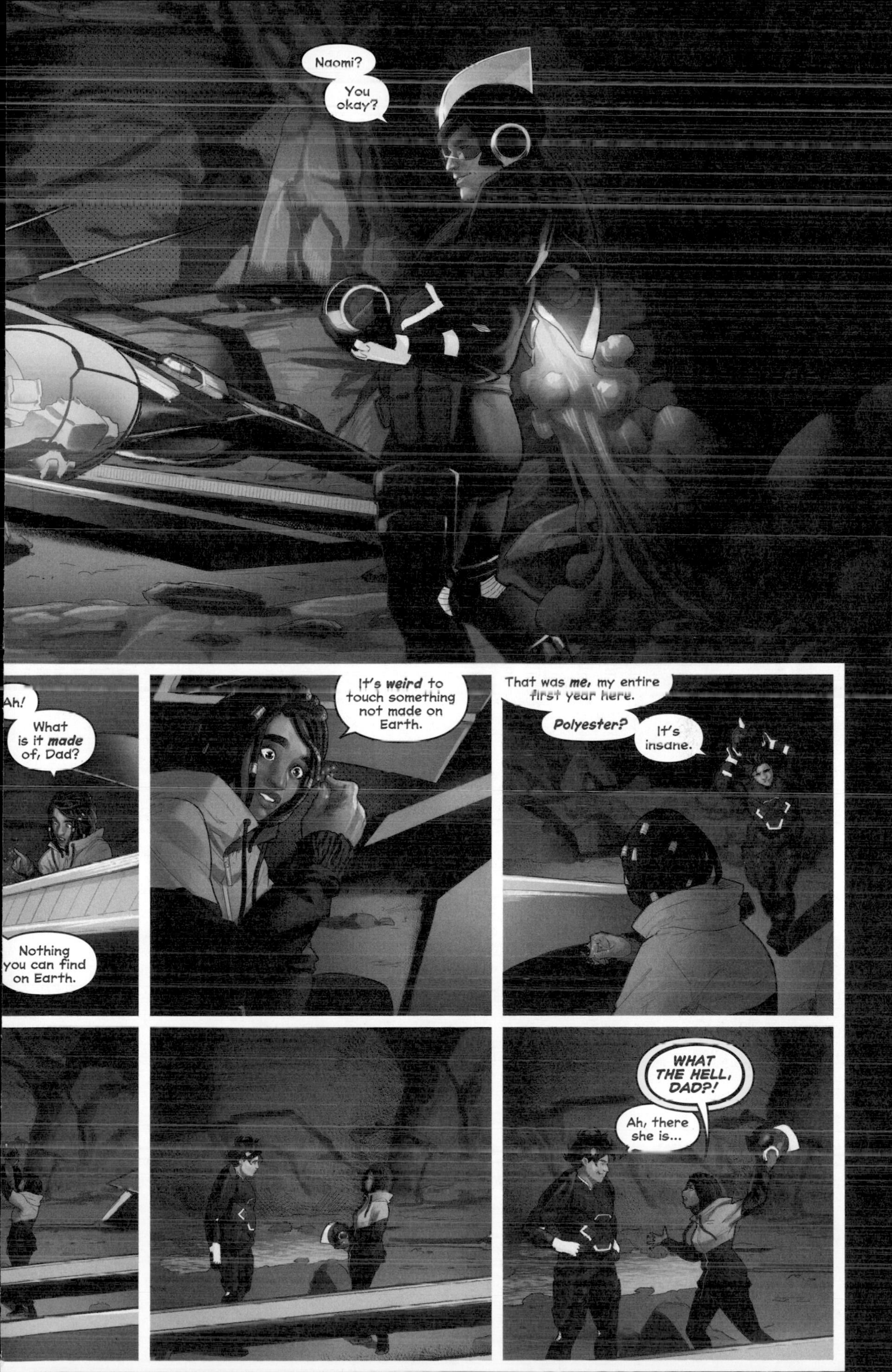
Naomi?
You okay?
Ah!
What is it *made* of, Dad?
Nothing you can find on Earth.
It's *weird* to touch something not made on Earth.
That was *me*, my entire first year here.
Polyester?
It's insane.
WHAT THE HELL, DAD?!
Ah, there she is...

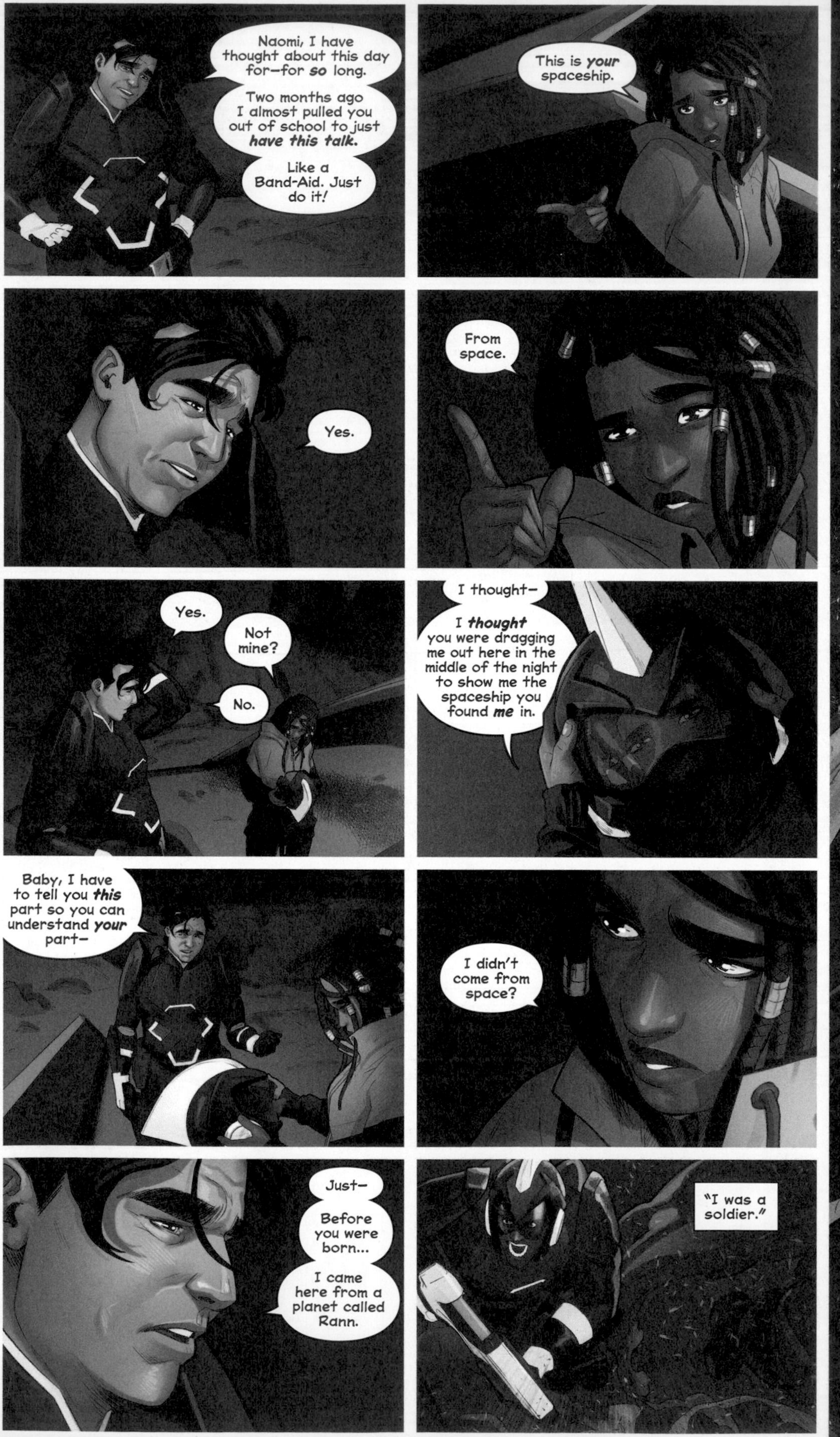
Naomi, I have thought about this day for—for **so** long.
Two months ago I almost pulled you out of school to just ***have this talk.***
Like a Band-Aid. Just do it!
This is ***your*** spaceship.
Yes.
From space.
Yes.
Not mine?
No.
I thought—
I ***thought*** you were dragging me out here in the middle of the night to show me the spaceship you found ***me*** in.
Baby, I have to tell you ***this*** part so you can understand ***your*** part—
I didn't come from space?
Just—
Before you were born...
I came here from a planet called Rann.
"I was a soldier."

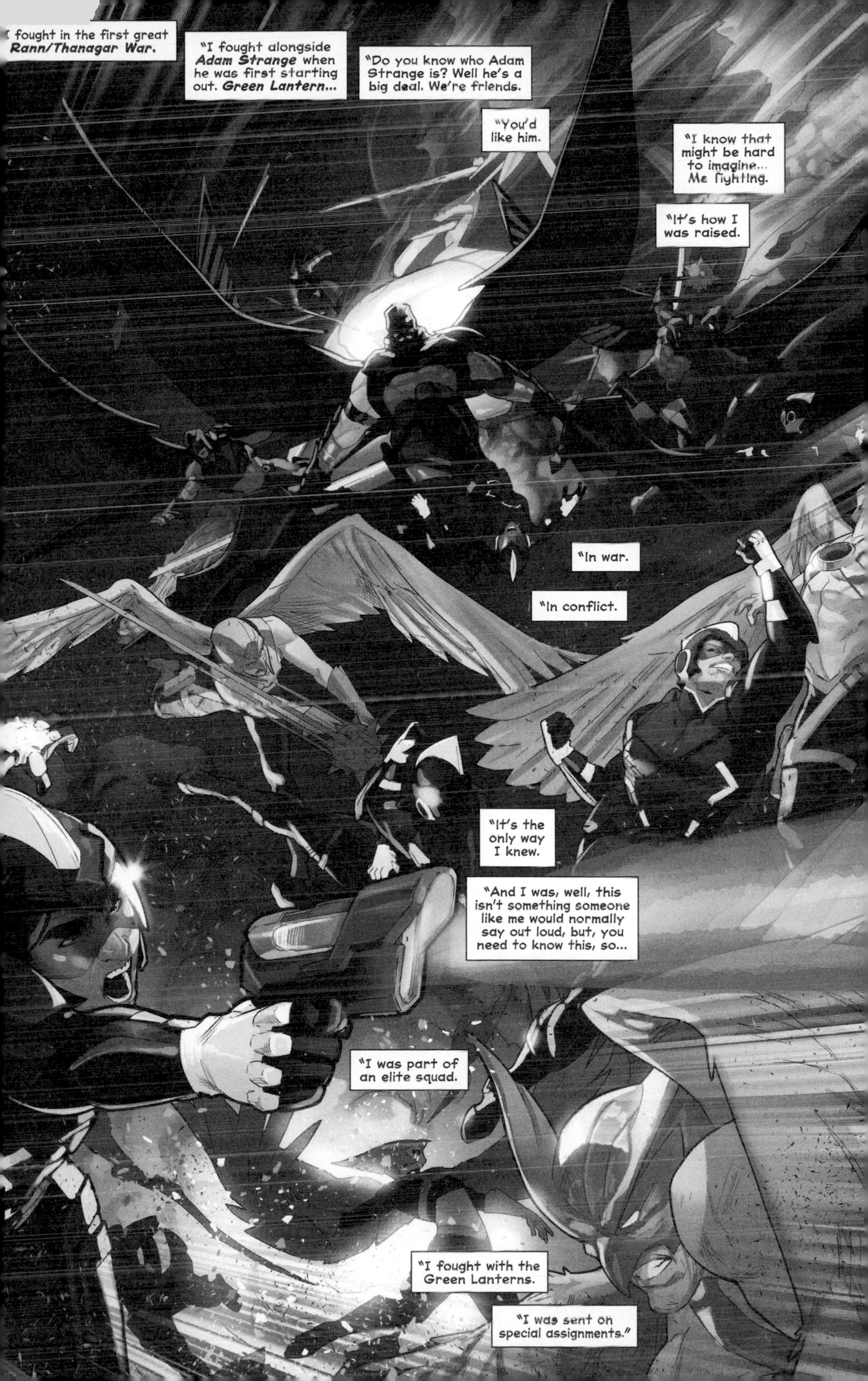

I fought in the first great Rann/Thanagar War.
"I fought alongside Adam Strange when he was first starting out. Green Lantern...
"Do you know who Adam Strange is? Well he's a big deal. We're friends.
"You'd like him.
"I know that might be hard to imagine... Me fighting.
"It's how I was raised.
"In war.
"In conflict.
"It's the only way I knew.
"And I was, well, this isn't something someone like me would normally say out loud, but, you need to know this, so...
"I was part of an elite squad.
"I fought with the Green Lanterns.
"I was sent on special assignments."

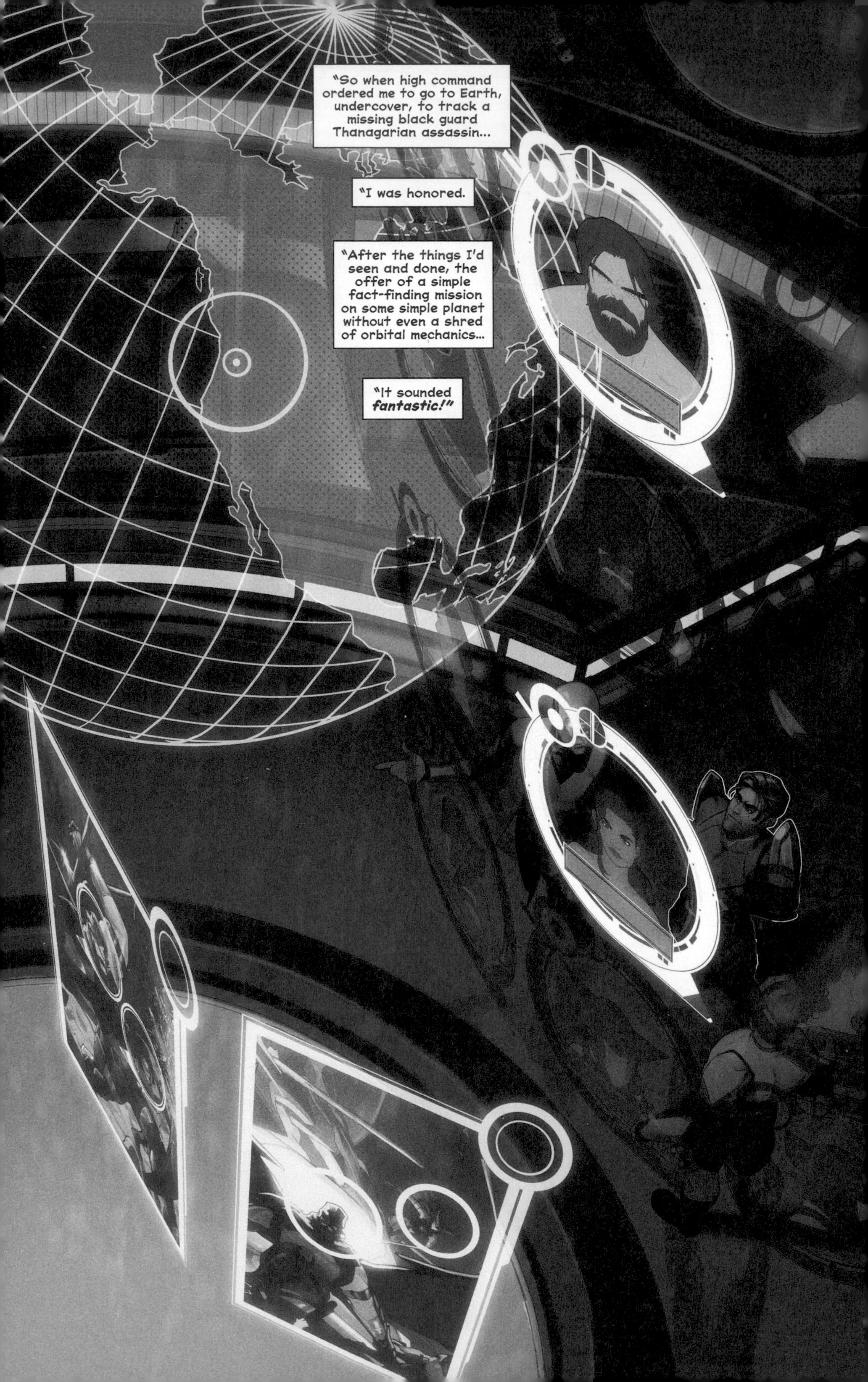
"So when high command ordered me to go to Earth, undercover, to track a missing black guard Thanagarian assassin...
"I was honored.
"After the things I'd seen and done, the offer of a simple fact-finding mission on some simple planet without even a shred of orbital mechanics...
"It sounded *fantastic!"*

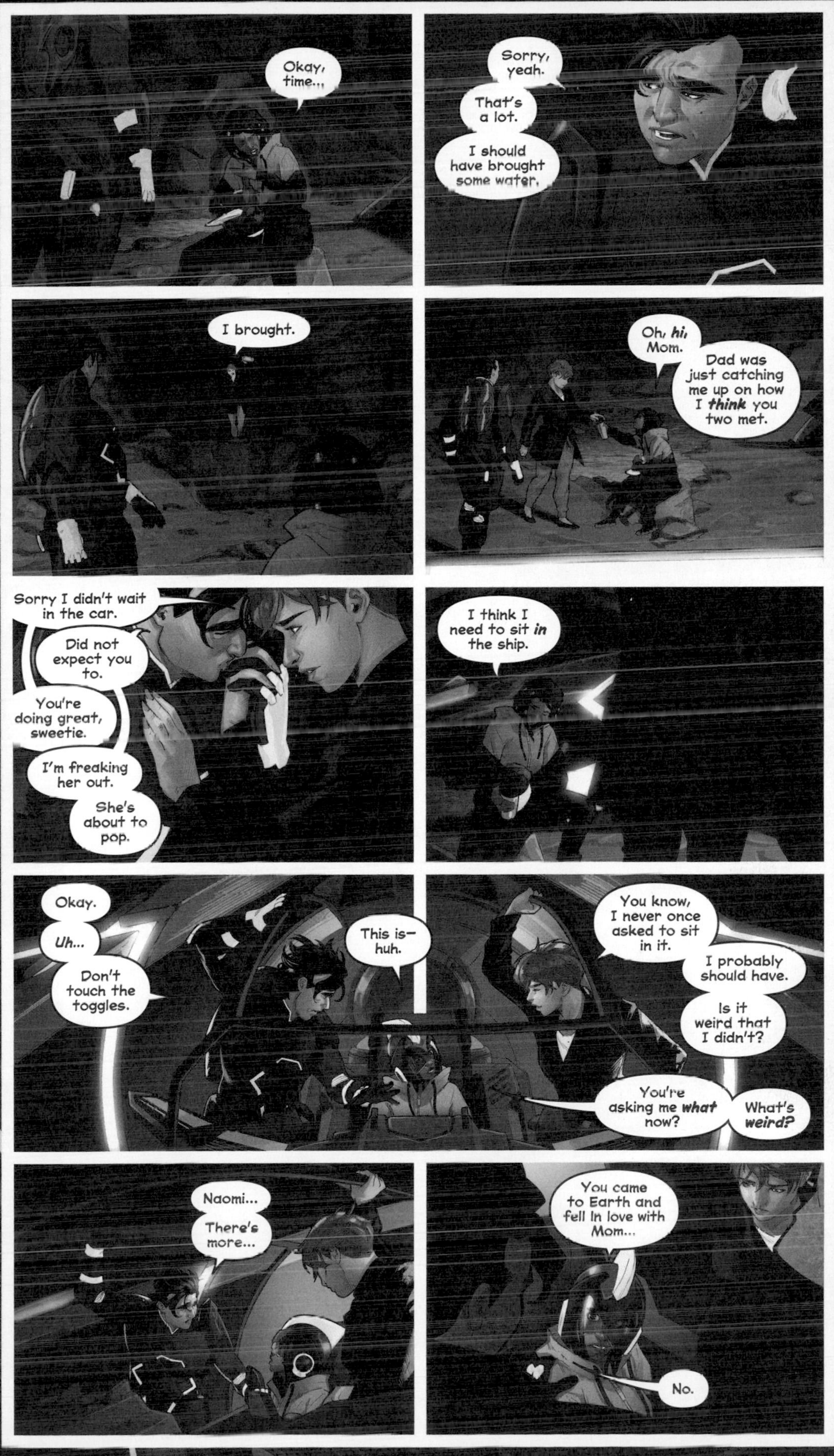
Okay, time...
Sorry, yeah.
That's a lot.
I should have brought some water.
I brought.
Oh, *hi*, Mom.
Dad was just catching me up on how I *think* you two met.
Sorry I didn't wait in the car.
Did not expect you to.
You're doing great, sweetie.
I'm freaking her out.
She's about to pop.
I think I need to sit *in* the ship.
Okay.
Uh...
Don't touch the toggles.
This is— huh.
You know, I never once asked to sit in it.
I probably should have.
Is it weird that I didn't?
You're asking me *what* now?
What's *weird?*
Naomi...
There's more...
You came to Earth and fell In love with Mom...
No.

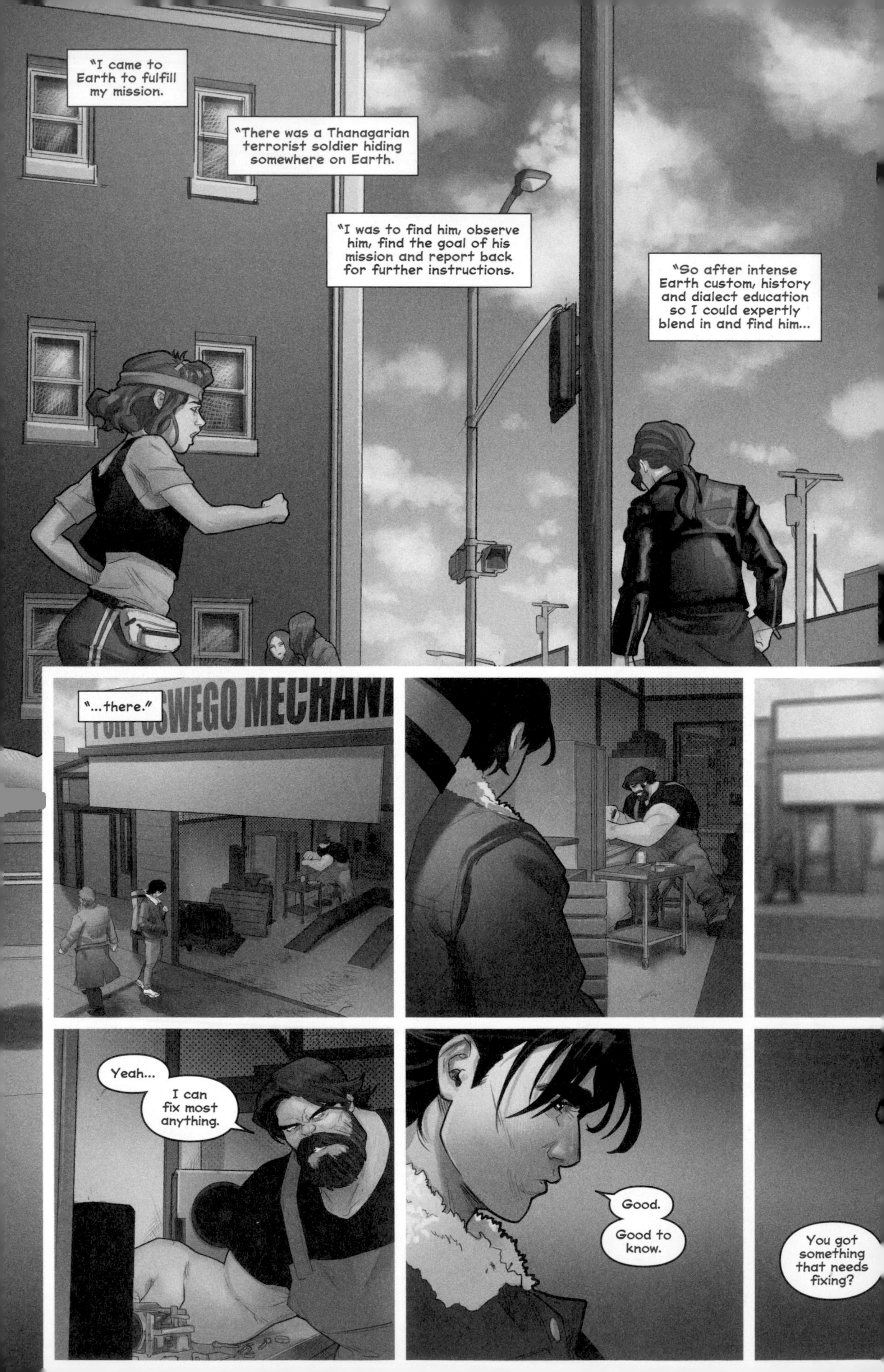
"I came to Earth to fulfill my mission.
"There was a Thanagarian terrorist soldier hiding somewhere on Earth.
"I was to find him, observe him, find the goal of his mission and report back for further instructions.
"So after intense Earth custom, history and dialect education so I could expertly blend in and find him...
"...there."
PORT OSWEGO MECHAN
Yeah...
I can fix most anything.
Good.
Good to know.
You got something that needs fixing?

You'd imagine my, well, deep annoyance, when I found him just...

Can I help you?

You're the mechanic in town?

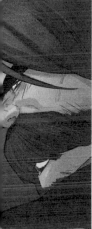

Um...

How long has that shop been for rent?

Couldn't say.

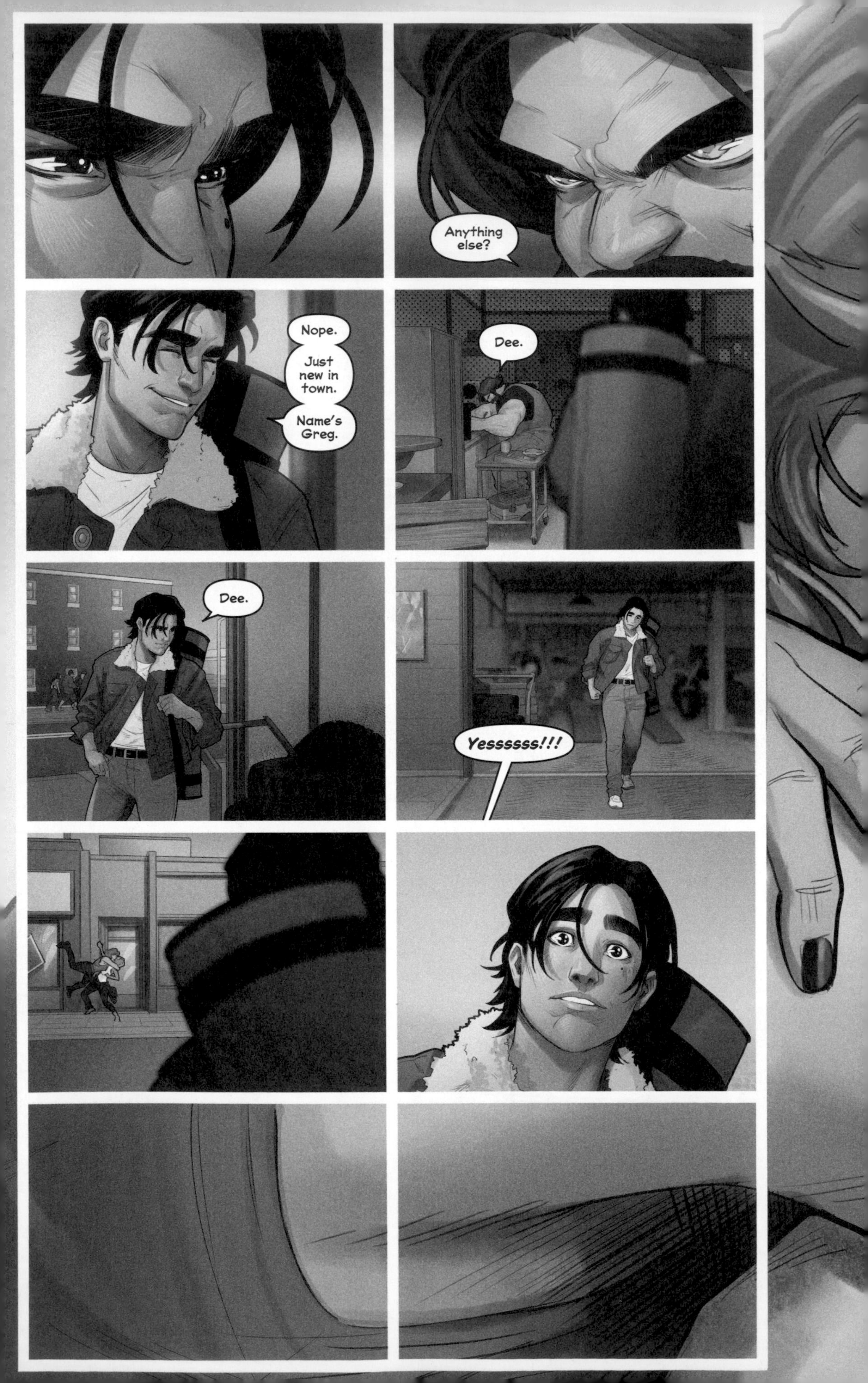

Anything else?
Nope.
Just new in town.
Name's Greg.
Dee.
Dee.
Yessssss!!!

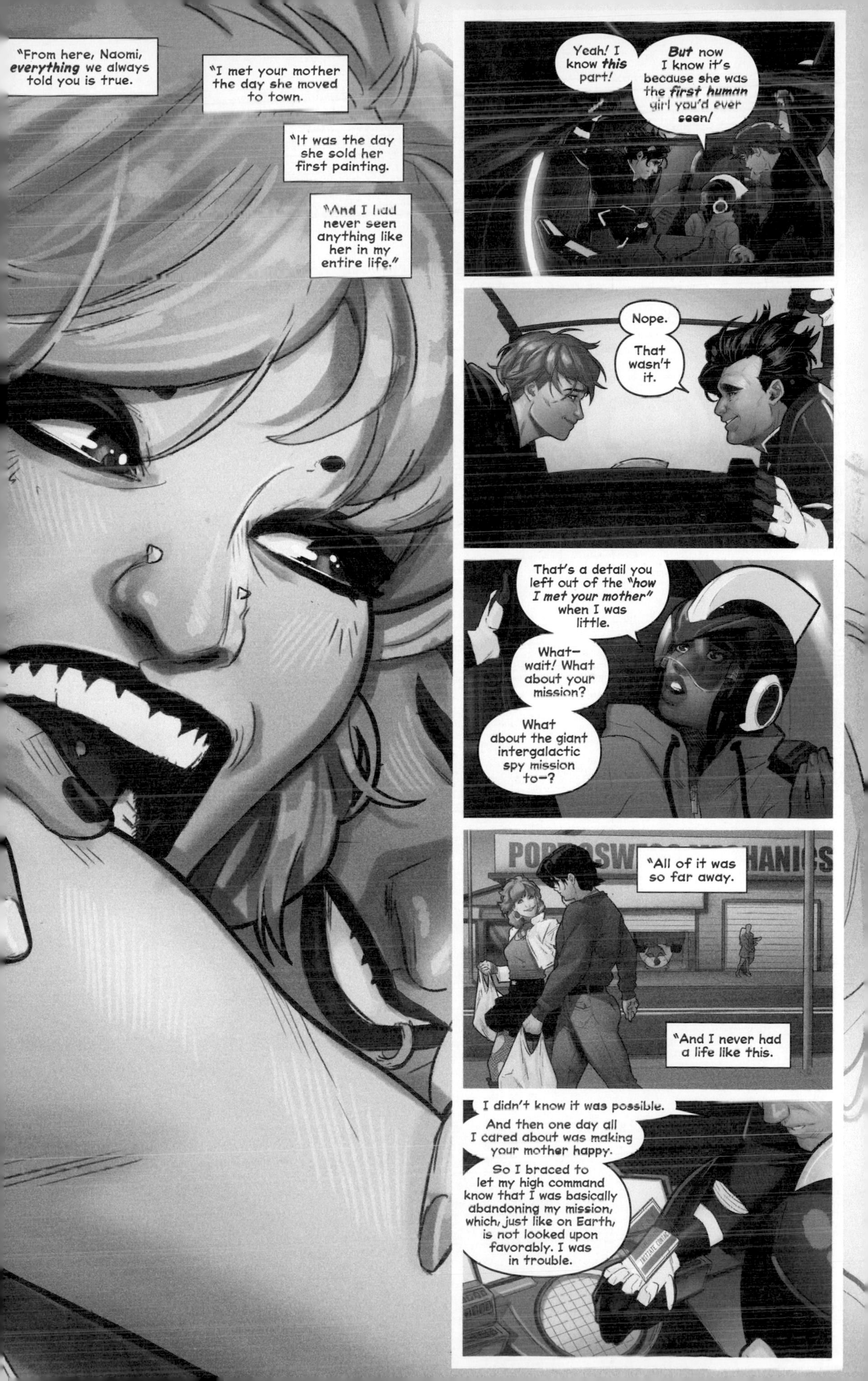
"From here, Naomi, ***everything*** we always told you is true.
"I met your mother the day she moved to town.
"It was the day she sold her first painting.
"And I had never seen anything like her in my entire life."
Yeah! I know ***this*** part!
But now I know it's because she was the ***first human*** girl you'd ever seen!
Nope.
That wasn't it.
That's a detail you left out of the *"how I met your mother"* when I was little.
What— wait! What about your mission?
What about the giant intergalactic spy mission to—?
PORDOSWE... HANICS
"All of it was so far away.
"And I never had a life like this.
I didn't know it was possible.
And then one day all I cared about was making your mother happy.
So I braced to let my high command know that I was basically abandoning my mission, which, just like on Earth, is not looked upon favorably. I was in trouble.

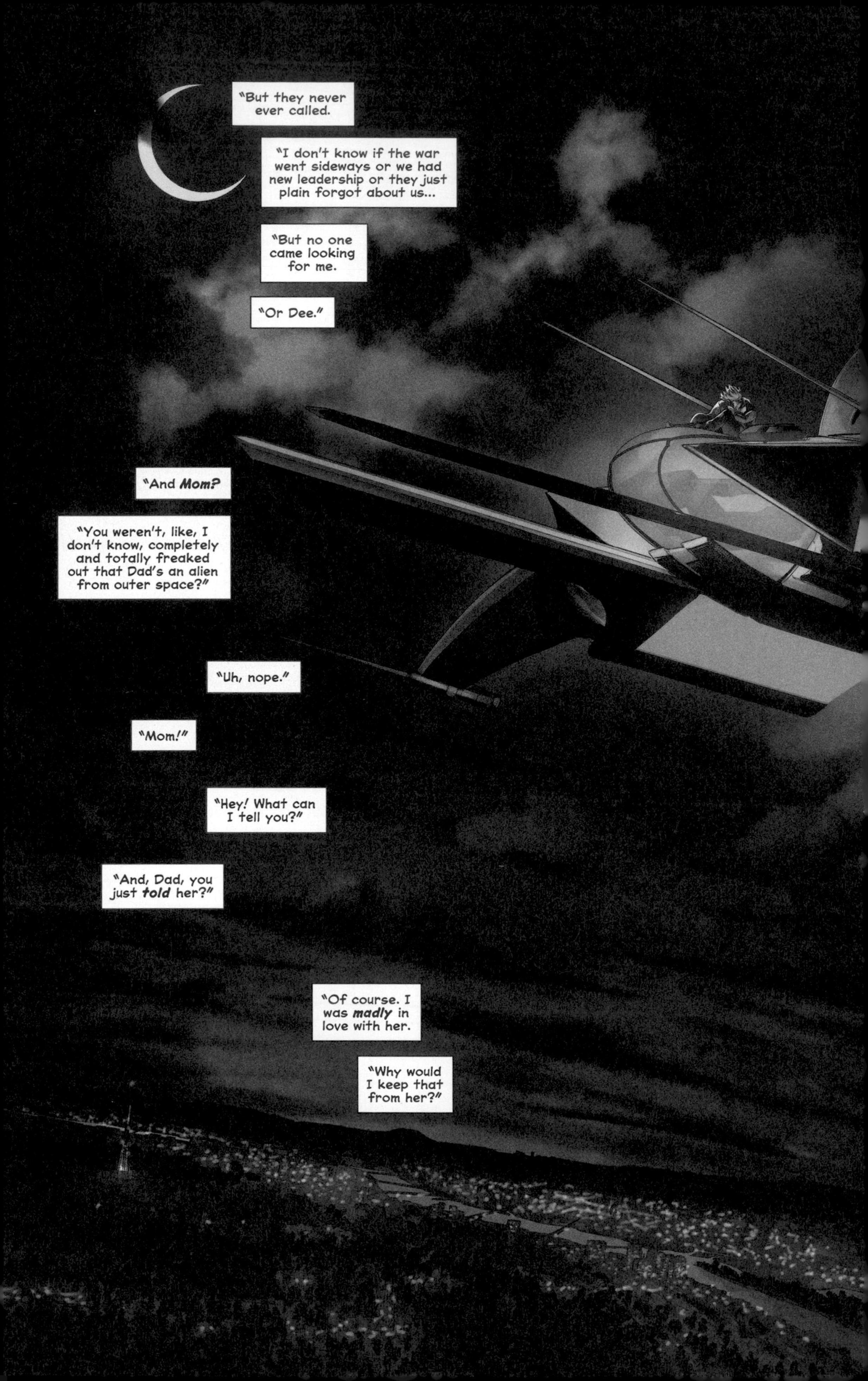
"But they never ever called.
"I don't know if the war went sideways or we had new leadership or they just plain forgot about us...
"But no one came looking for me.
"Or Dee."
"And *Mom?*
"You weren't, like, I don't know, completely and totally freaked out that Dad's an alien from outer space?"
"Uh, nope."
"Mom!"
"Hey! What can I tell you?"
"And, Dad, you just *told* her?"
"Of course. I was *madly* in love with her.
"Why would I keep that from her?"

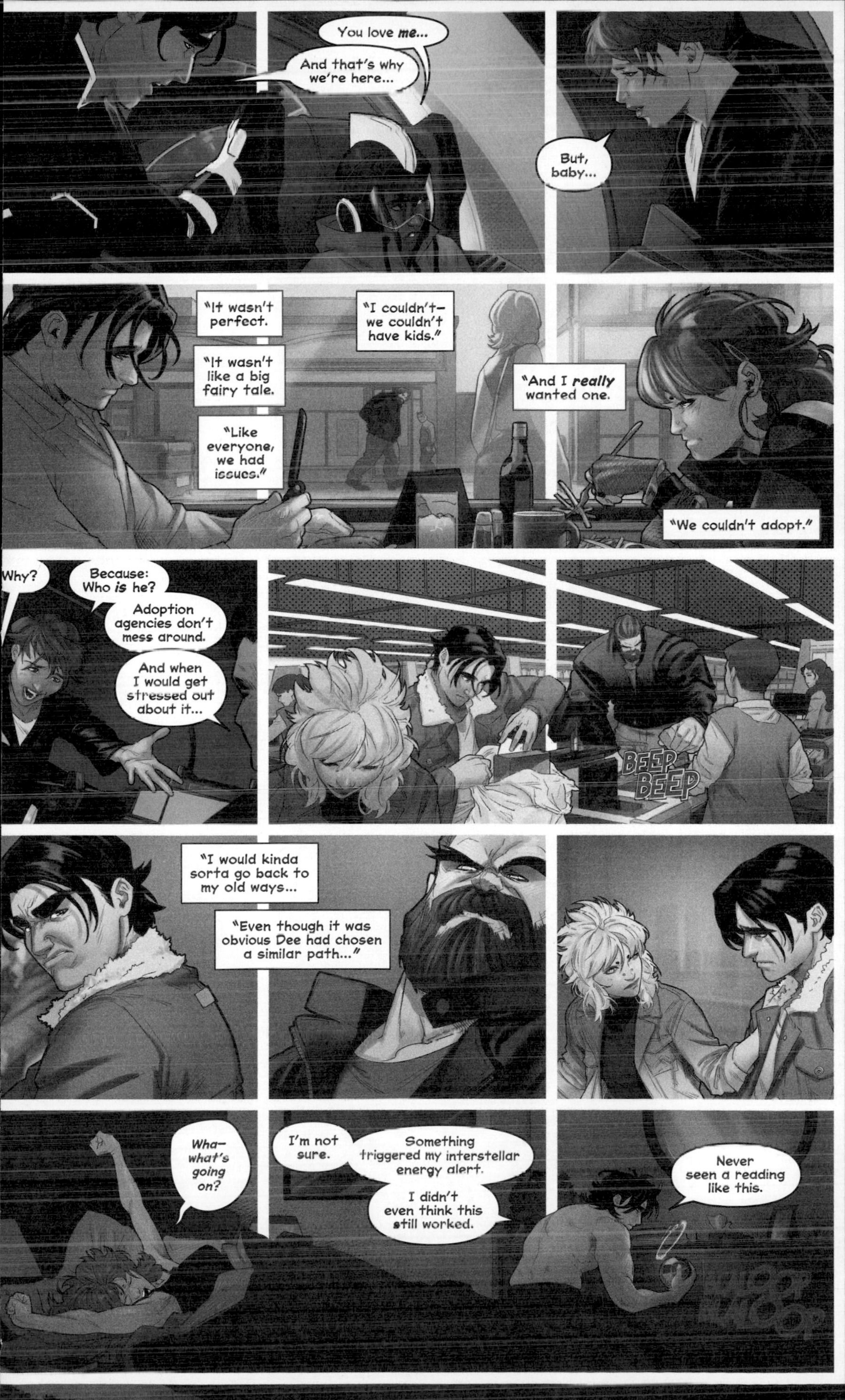
You love me...
And that's why we're here...
But, baby...
"It wasn't perfect.
"It wasn't like a big fairy tale.
"Like everyone, we had issues."
"I couldn't— we couldn't have kids."
"And I really wanted one.
"We couldn't adopt."
Why?
Because: Who is he?
Adoption agencies don't mess around.
And when I would get stressed out about it...
BEEP BEEP
"I would kinda sorta go back to my old ways...
"Even though it was obvious Dee had chosen a similar path..."
Wha— what's going on?
I'm not sure.
Something triggered my interstellar energy alert.
I didn't even think this still worked.
Never seen a reading like this.

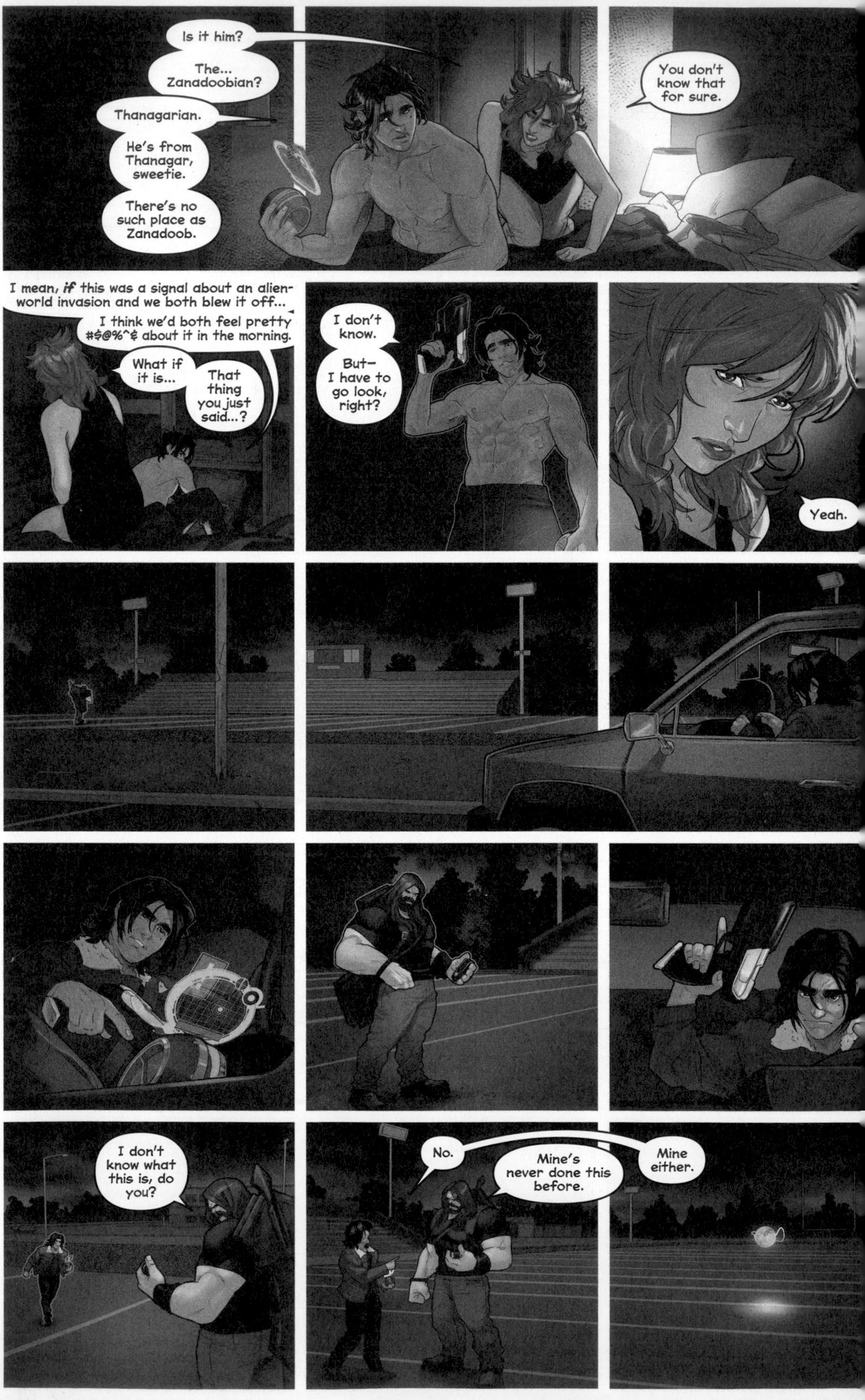
Is it him?
The... Zanadoobian?
Thanagarian.
He's from Thanagar, sweetie.
There's no such place as Zanadoob.
You don't know that for sure.
I mean, if this was a signal about an alien-world invasion and we both blew it off...
I think we'd both feel pretty #$@%^& about it in the morning.
What if it is...
That thing you just said...?
I don't know.
But— I have to go look, right?
Yeah.
I don't know what this is, do you?
No.
Mine's never done this before.
Mine either.

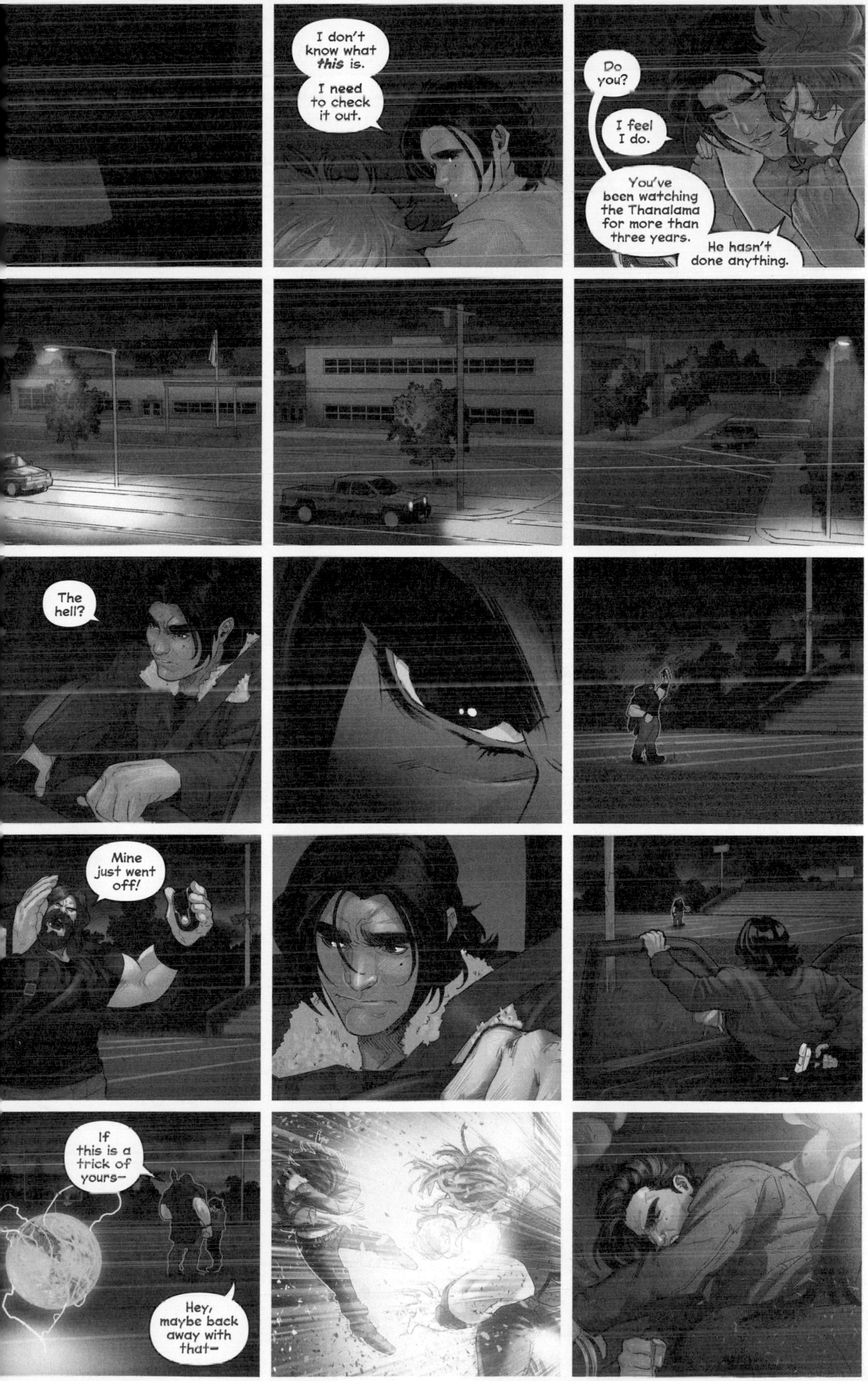

I don't know what *this* is.
I need to check it out.
Do you?
I feel I do.
You've been watching the Thanalama for more than three years.
He hasn't done anything.
The hell?
Mine just went off!
If this is a trick of yours—
Hey, maybe back away with that—

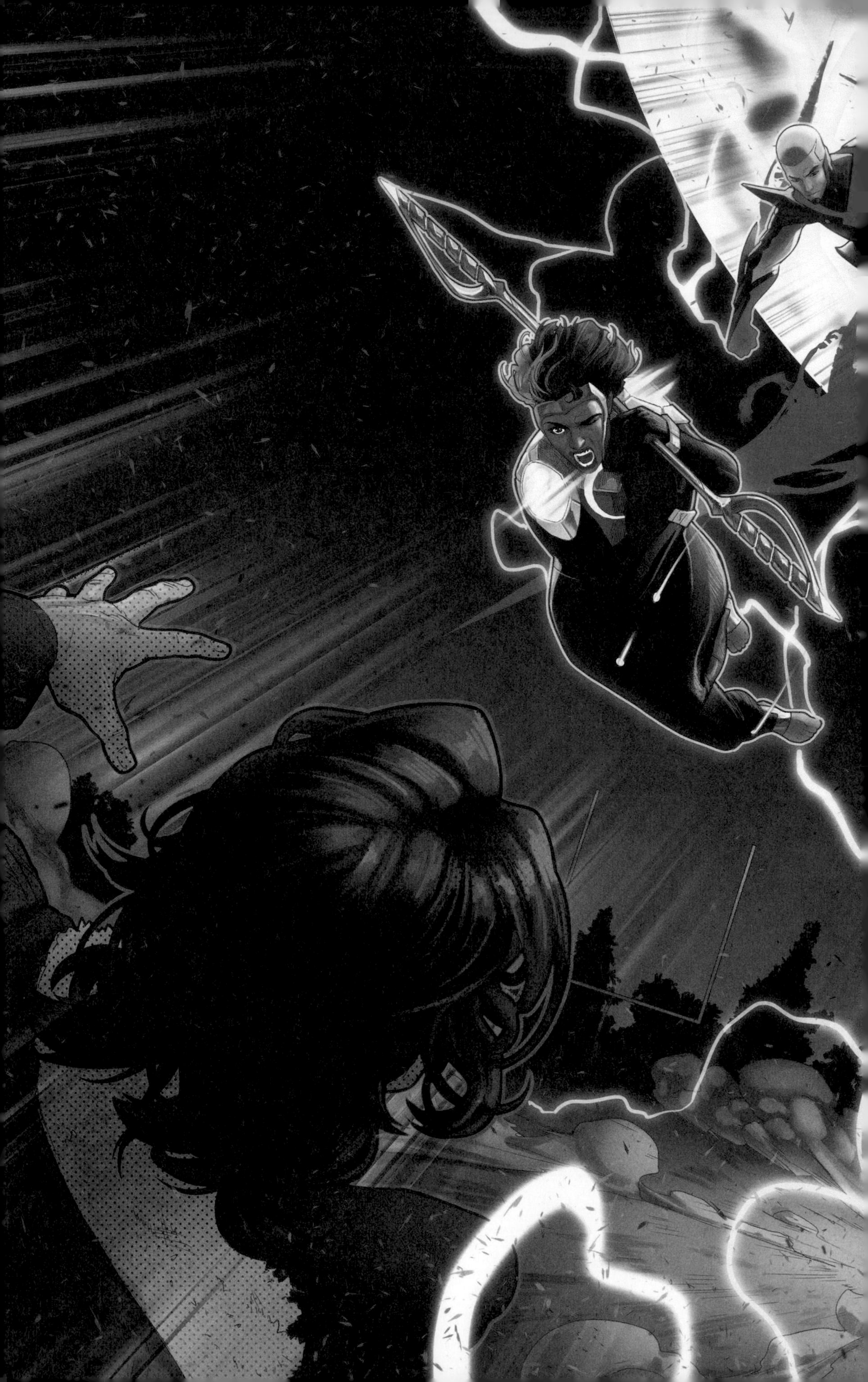

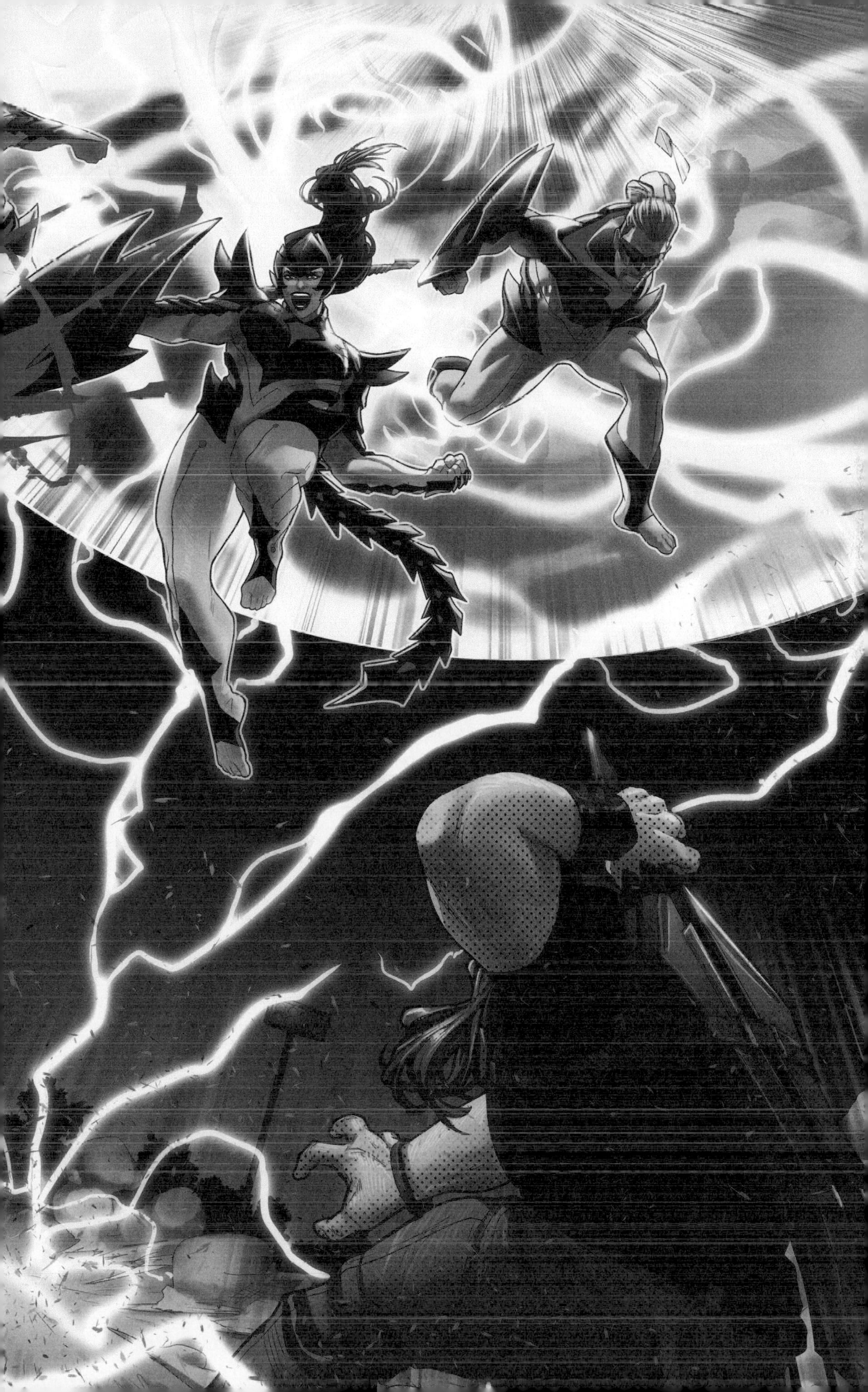

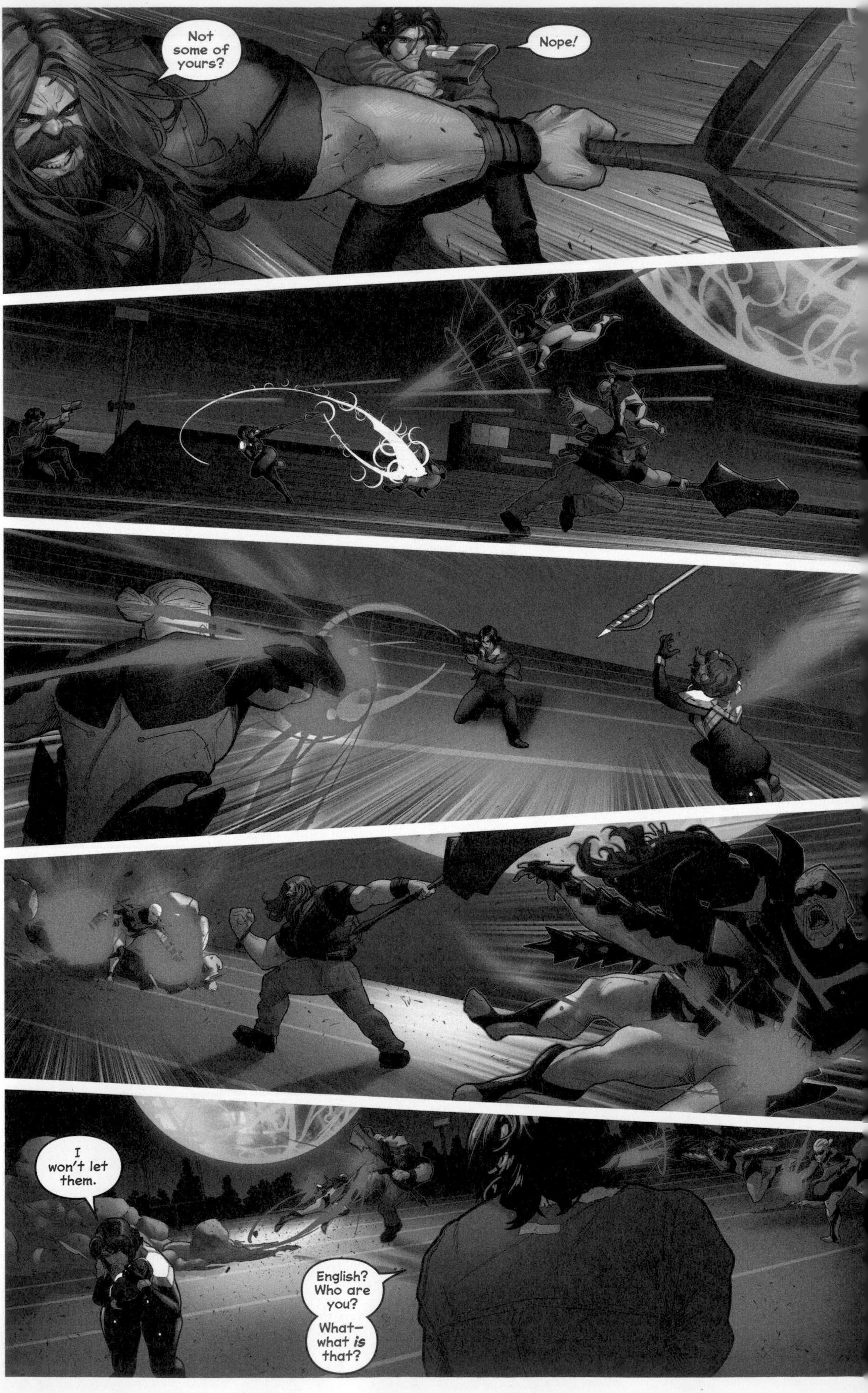
Not some of yours?
Nope!
I won't let them.
English? Who are you?
What— what *is* that?

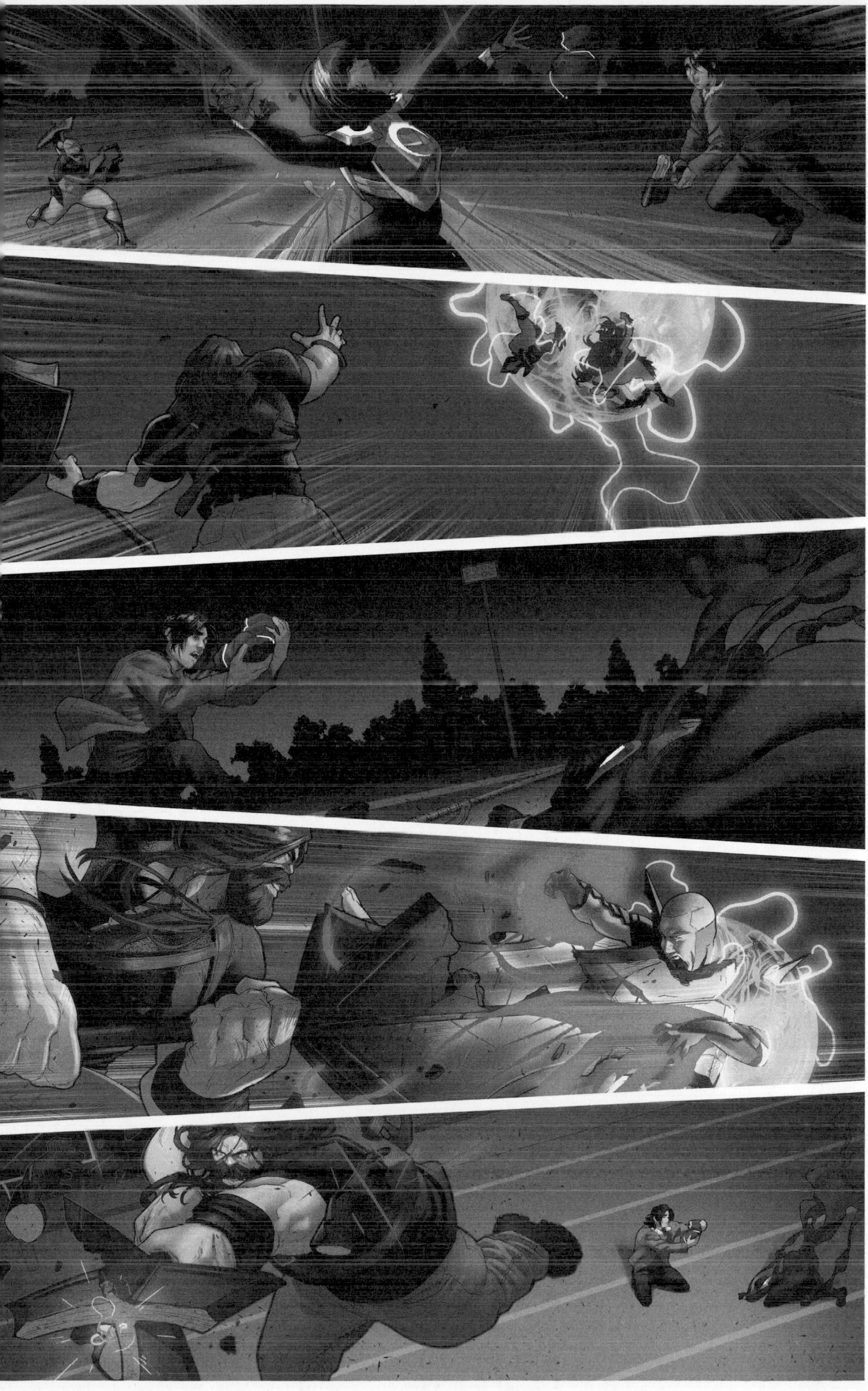

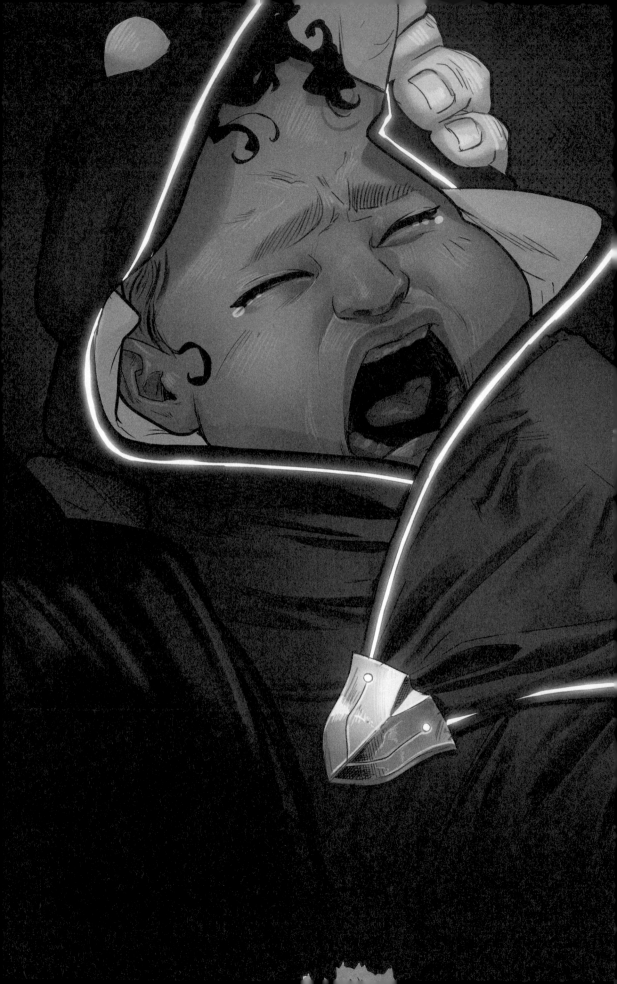

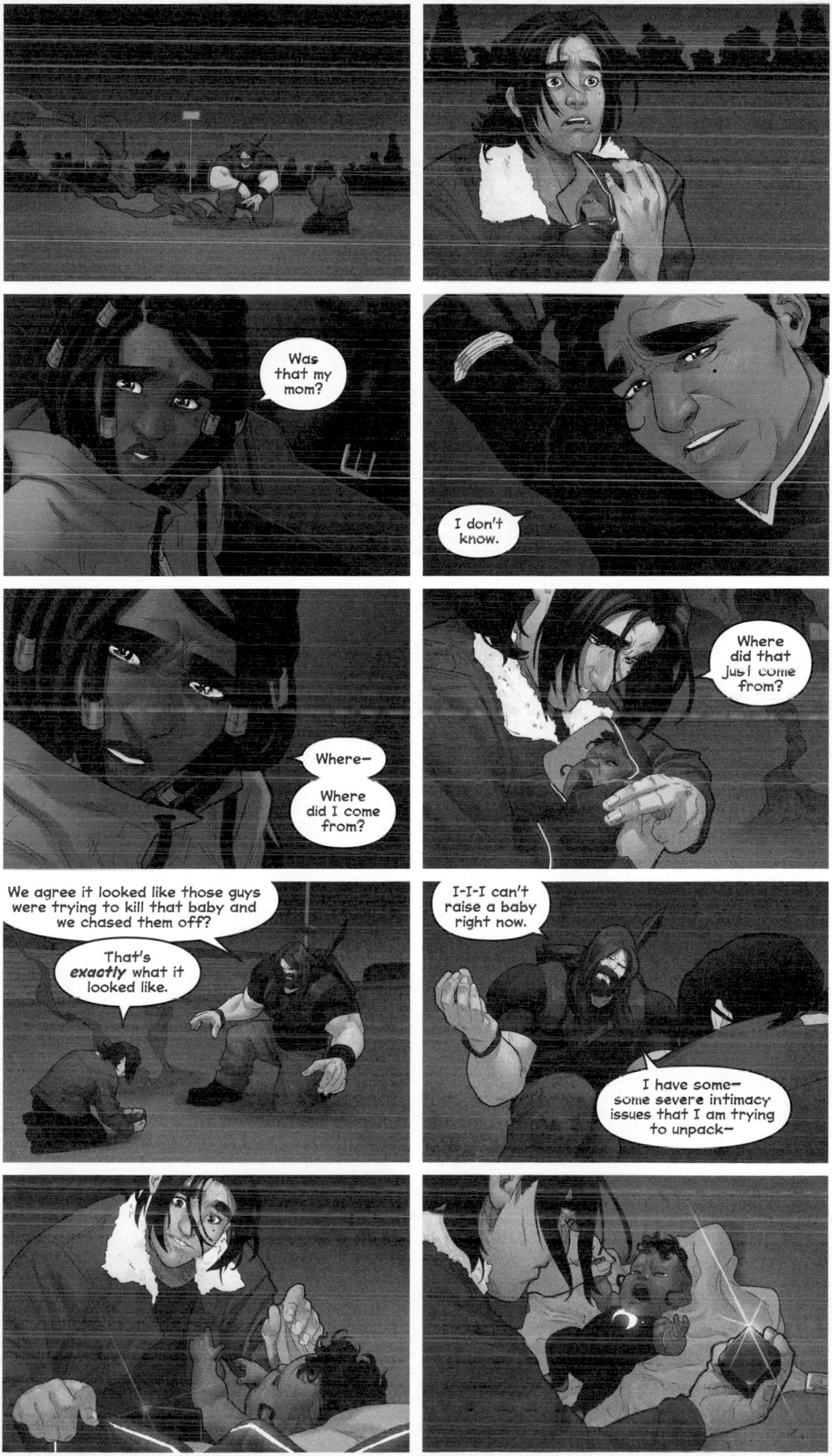
Was that my mom?
I don't know.
Where-
Where did I come from?
Where did that just come from?
We agree it looked like those guys were trying to kill that baby and we chased them off?
That's *exactly* what it looked like.
I-I-I can't raise a baby right now.
I have some- some severe intimacy issues that I am trying to unpack-

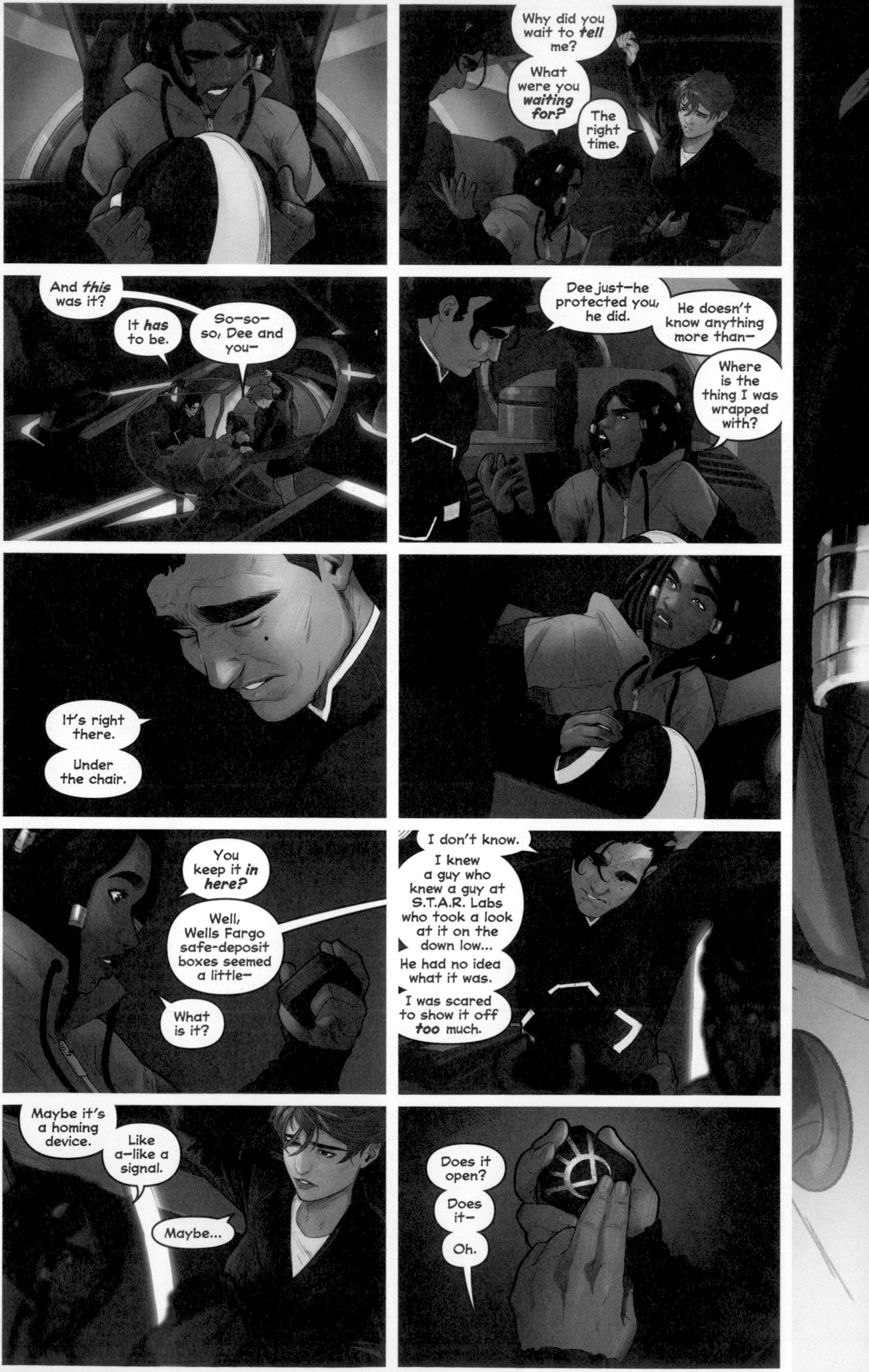
Why did you wait to *tell* me?
What were you *waiting for?*
The right time.
And *this* was it?
It *has* to be.
So-so-so, Dee and you—
Dee just—he protected you, he did.
He doesn't know anything more than—
Where is the thing I was wrapped with?
It's right there.
Under the chair.
You keep it *in here?*
Well, Wells Fargo safe-deposit boxes seemed a little—
What is it?
I don't know.
I knew a guy who knew a guy at S.T.A.R. Labs who took a look at it on the down low...
He had no idea what it was.
I was scared to show it off *too* much.
Maybe it's a homing device.
Like a—like a signal.
Maybe...
Does it open?
Does it—
Oh.

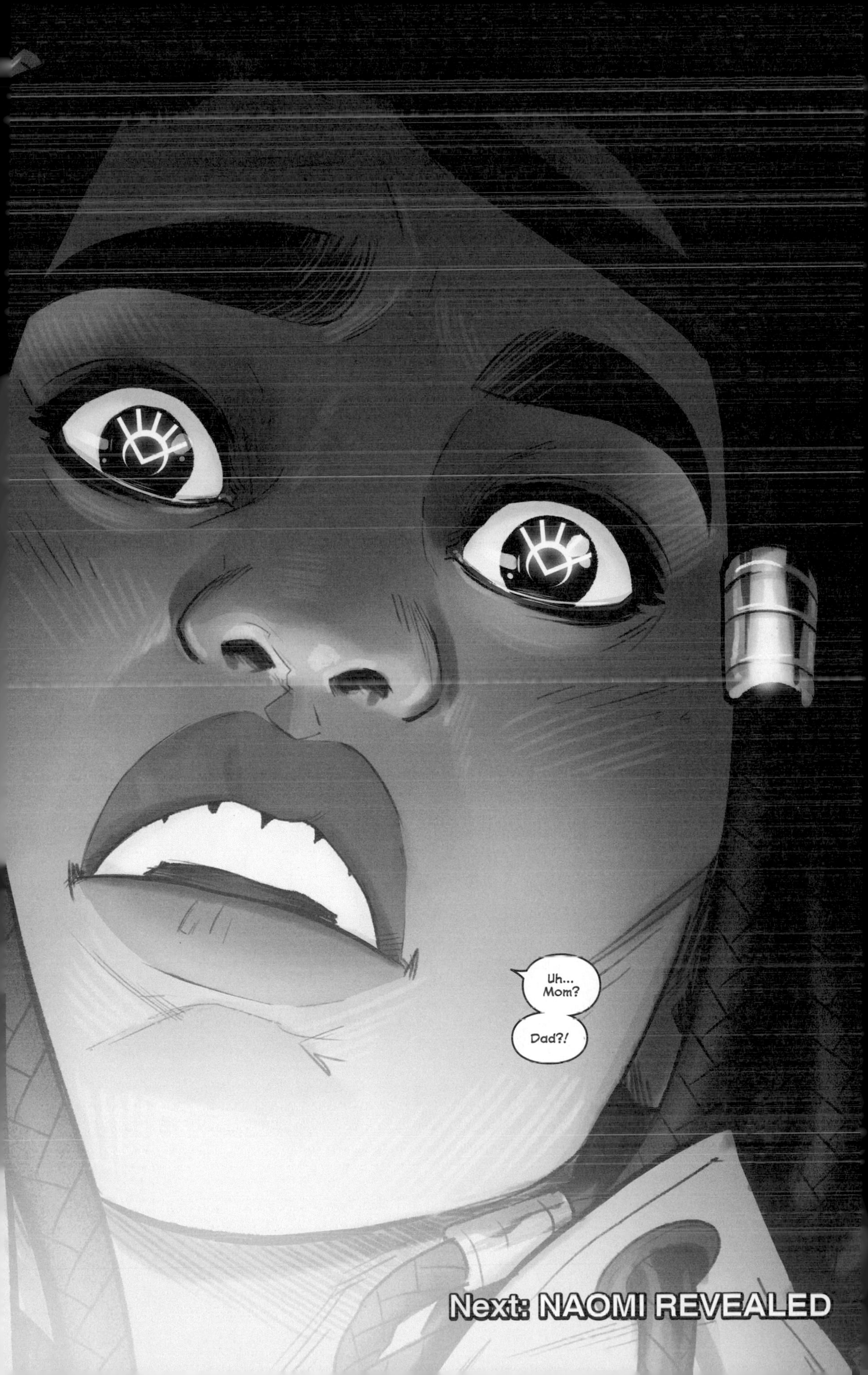
Uh... Mom?
Dad?!
Next: NAOMI REVEALED

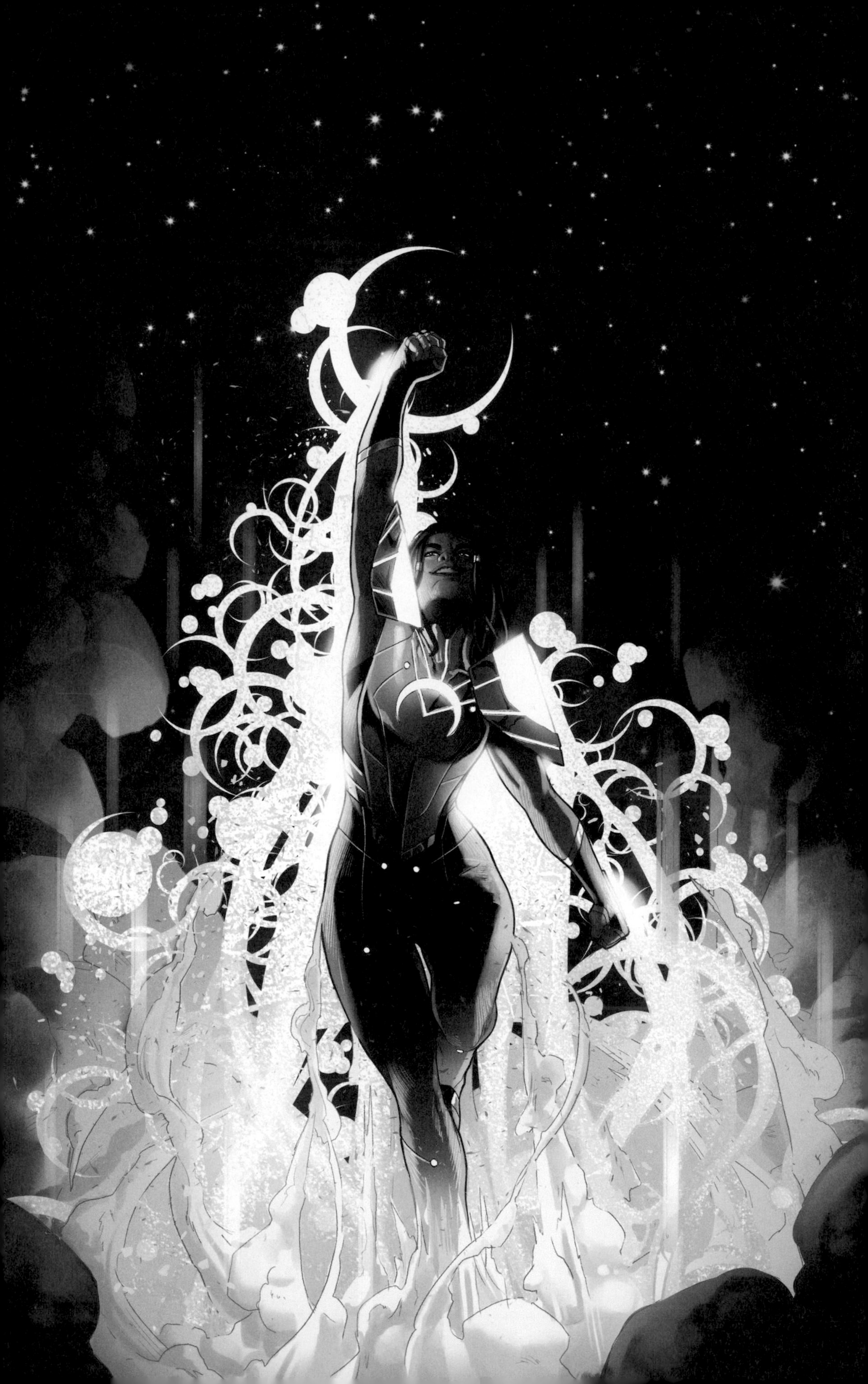

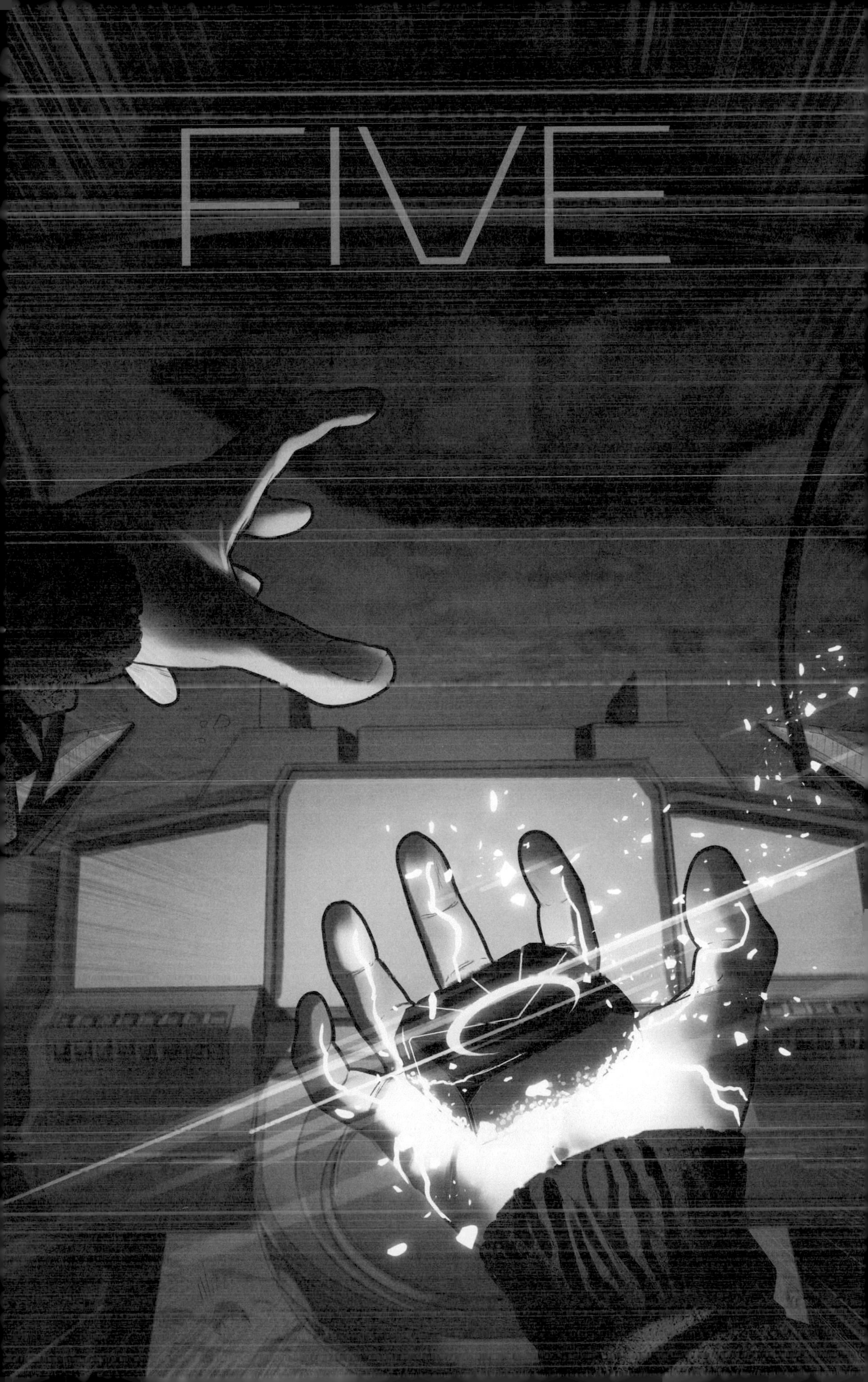
FIVE

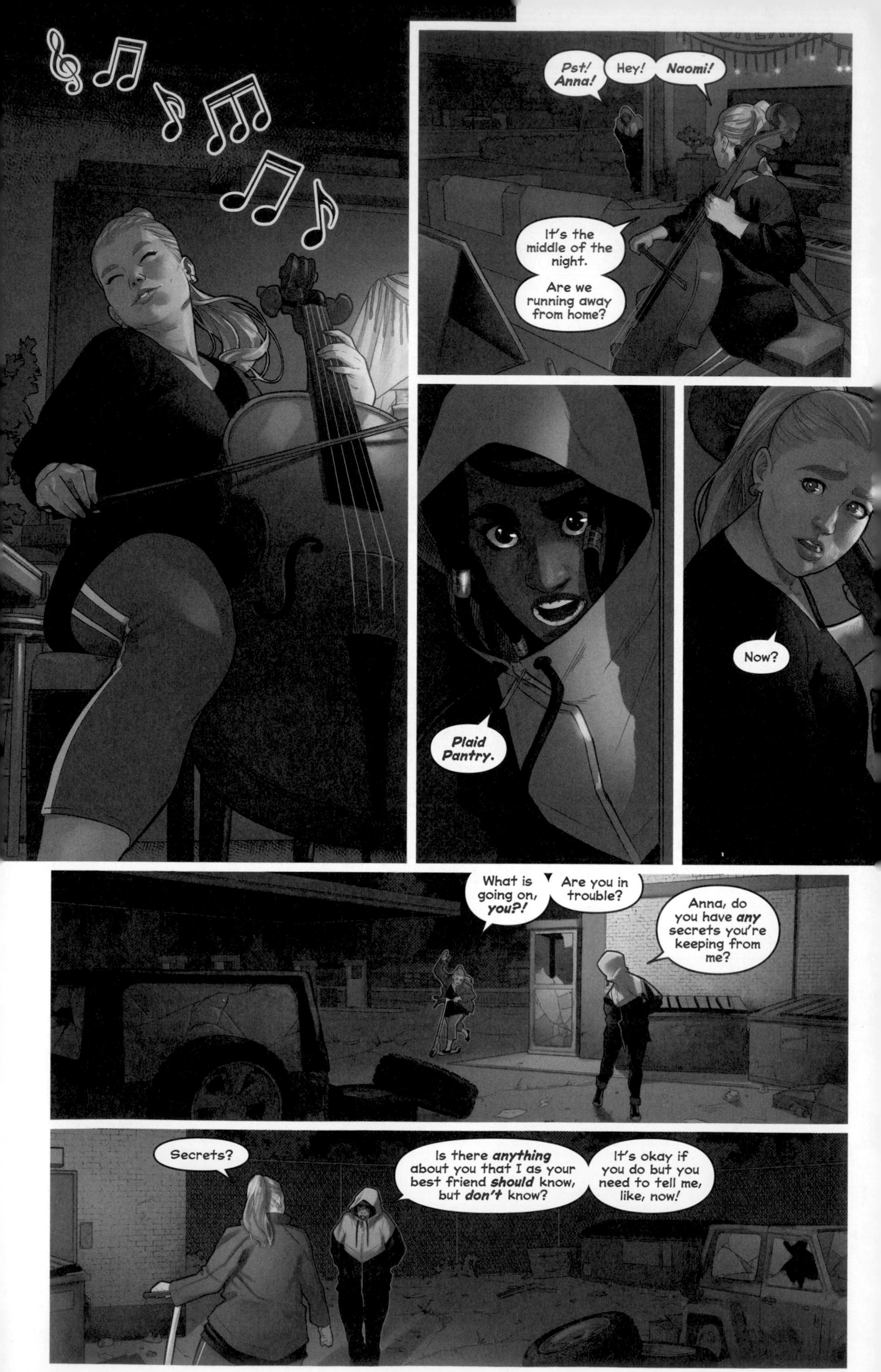
Pst! Anna!
Hey!
Naomi!
It's the middle of the night.
Are we running away from home?
Plaid Pantry.
Now?
What is going on, you?!
Are you in trouble?
Anna, do you have any secrets you're keeping from me?
Secrets?
Is there anything about you that I as your best friend should know, but don't know?
It's okay if you do but you need to tell me, like, now!

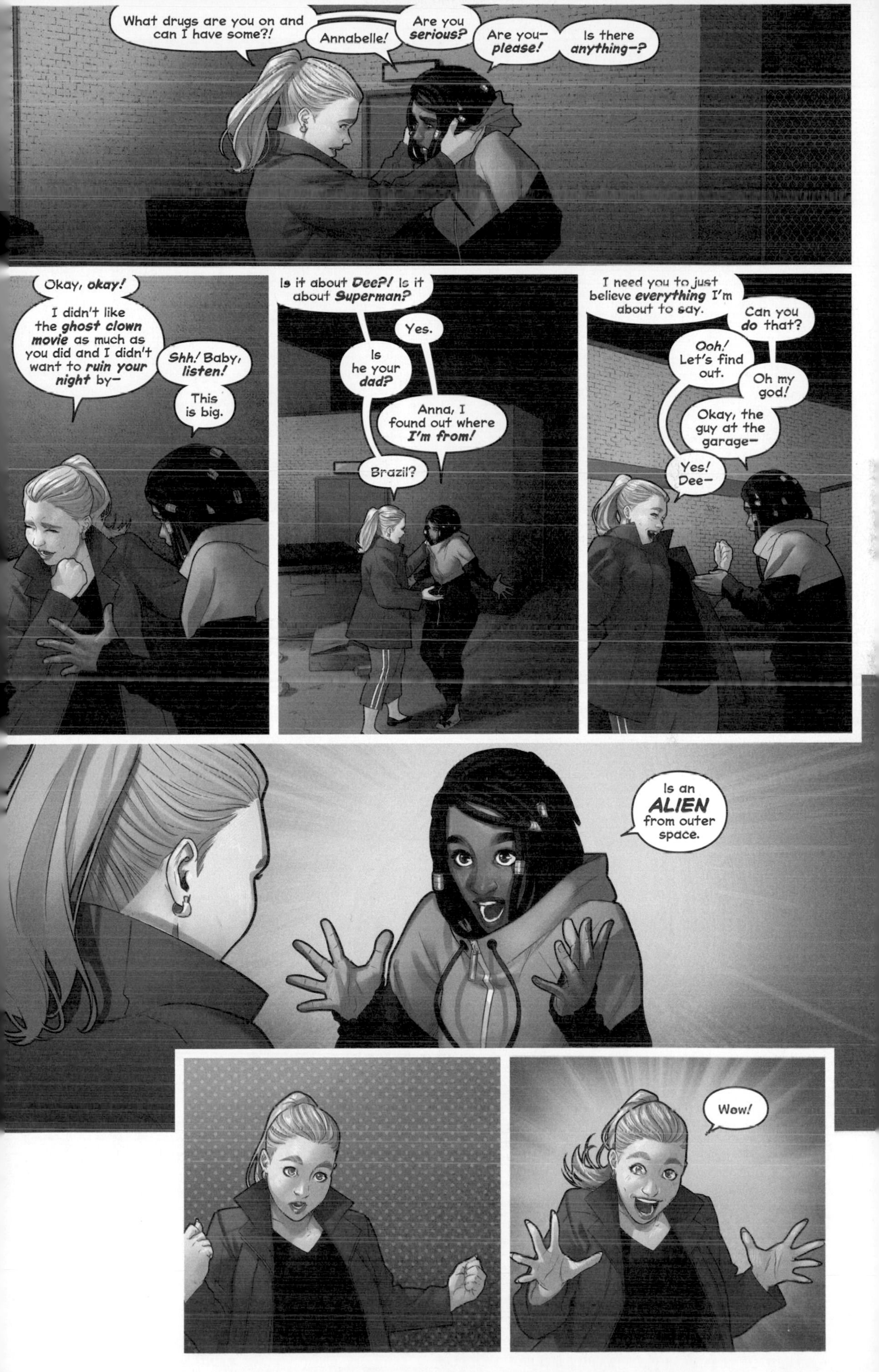
What drugs are you on and can I have some?!
Annabelle!
Are you *serious?*
Are you— *please!*
Is there *anything—?*
Okay, *okay!*
I didn't like the *ghost clown movie* as much as you did and I didn't want to *ruin your night* by—
Shh! Baby, *listen!*
This is big.
Is it about *Dee?!* Is it about *Superman?*
Yes.
Is he your *dad?*
Anna, I found out where *I'm from!*
Brazil?
I need you to just believe *everything* I'm about to say.
Can you *do* that?
Ooh! Let's find out.
Oh my god!
Okay, the guy at the garage—
Yes! Dee—
Is an *ALIEN* from outer space.
Wow!

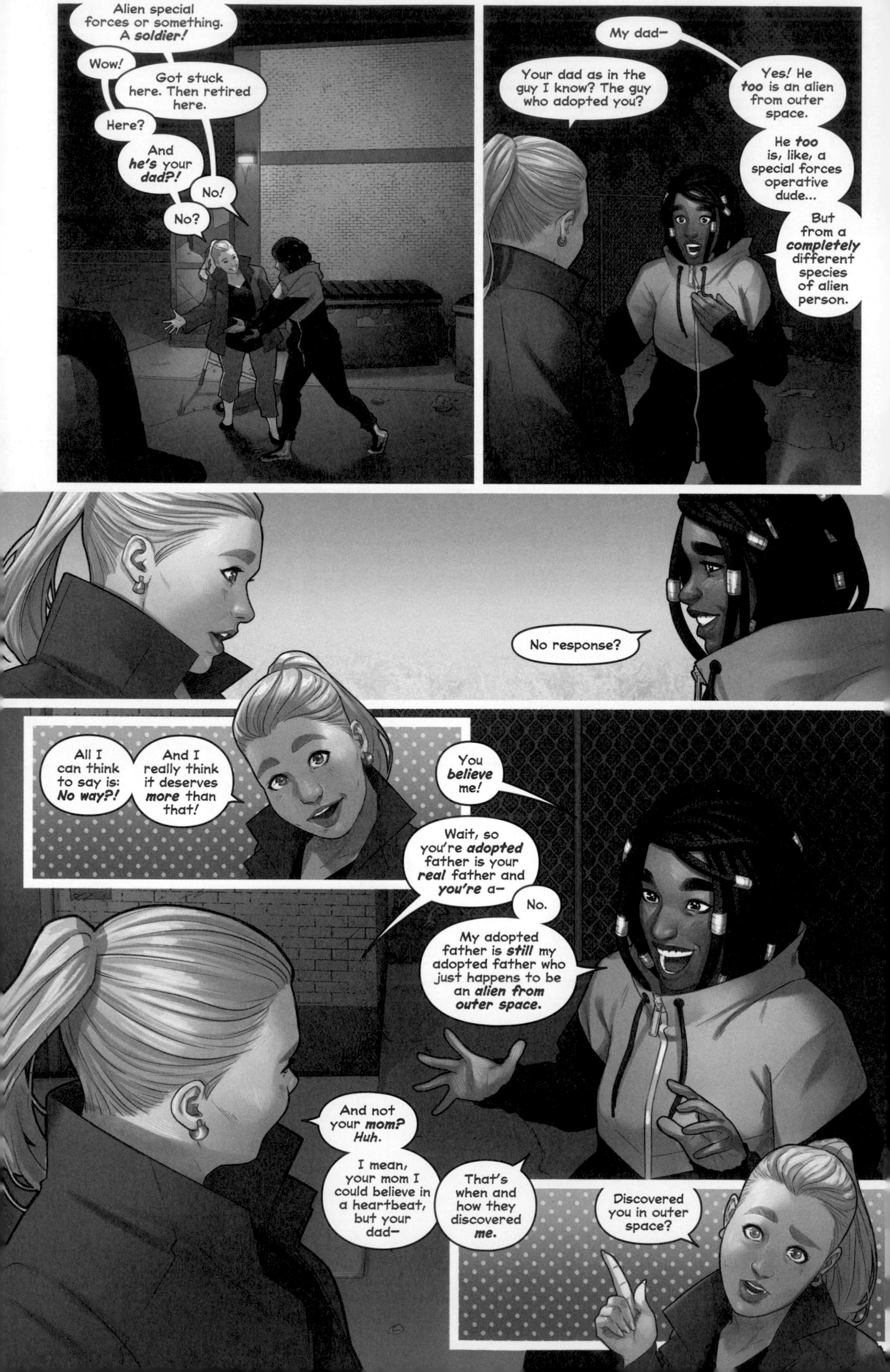
Alien special forces or something. A *soldier!*
Wow!
Got stuck here. Then retired here.
Here?
And *he's* your *dad?!*
No!
No?
My dad—
Your dad as in the guy I know? The guy who adopted you?
Yes! He *too* is an alien from outer space.
He *too* is, like, a special forces operative dude...
But from a *completely* different species of alien person.
No response?
All I can think to say is: *No way?!*
And I really think it deserves *more* than that!
You *believe* me!
Wait, so you're *adopted* father is your *real* father and *you're* a—
No.
My adopted father is *still* my adopted father who just happens to be an *alien from outer space.*
And not your *mom? Huh.*
I mean, your mom I could believe in a heartbeat, but your dad—
That's when and how they discovered *me.*
Discovered you in outer space?

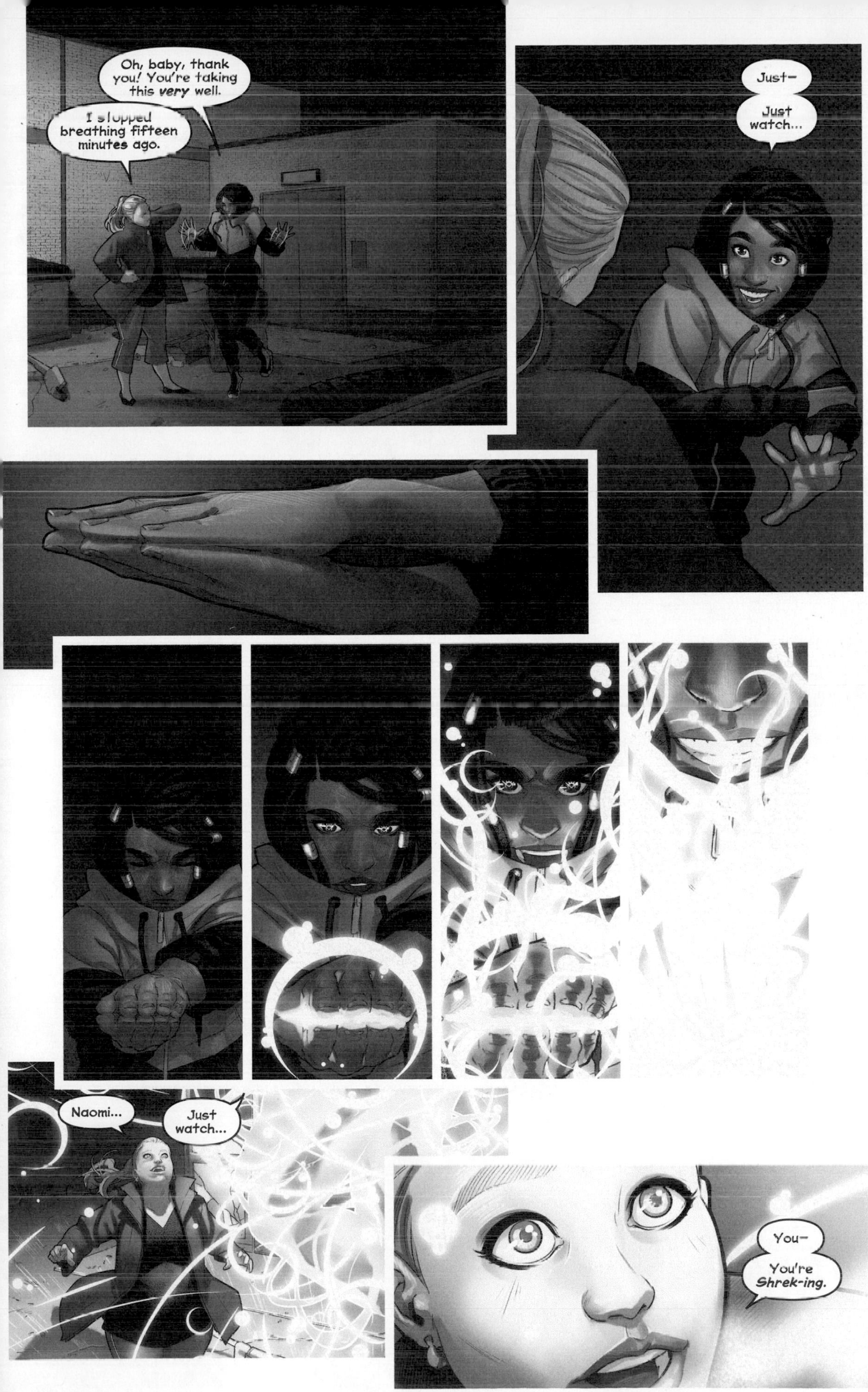
Oh, baby, thank you! You're taking this very well.
I stopped breathing fifteen minutes ago.
Just—
Just watch...
Naomi...
Just watch...
You—
You're Shrek-ing.

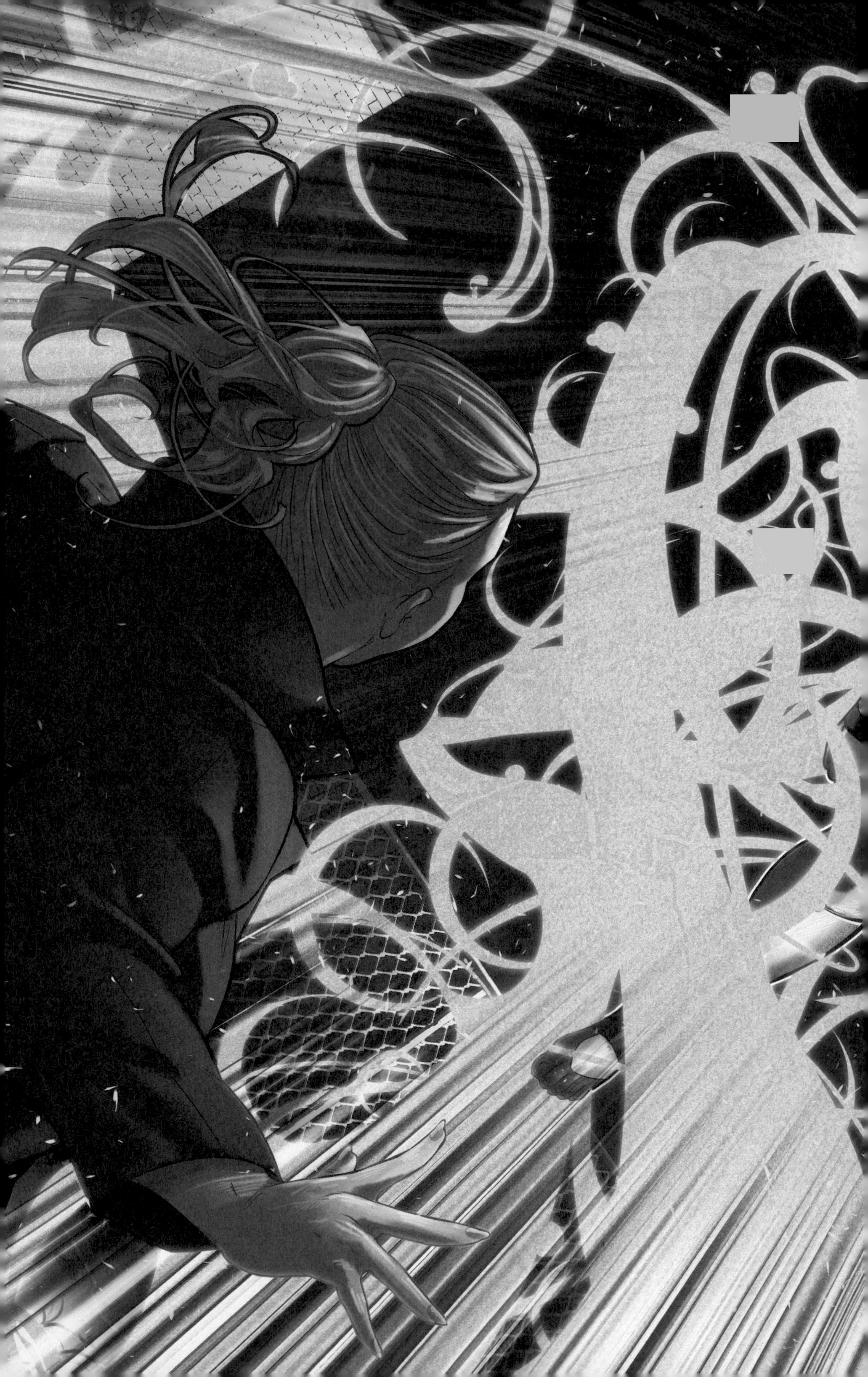

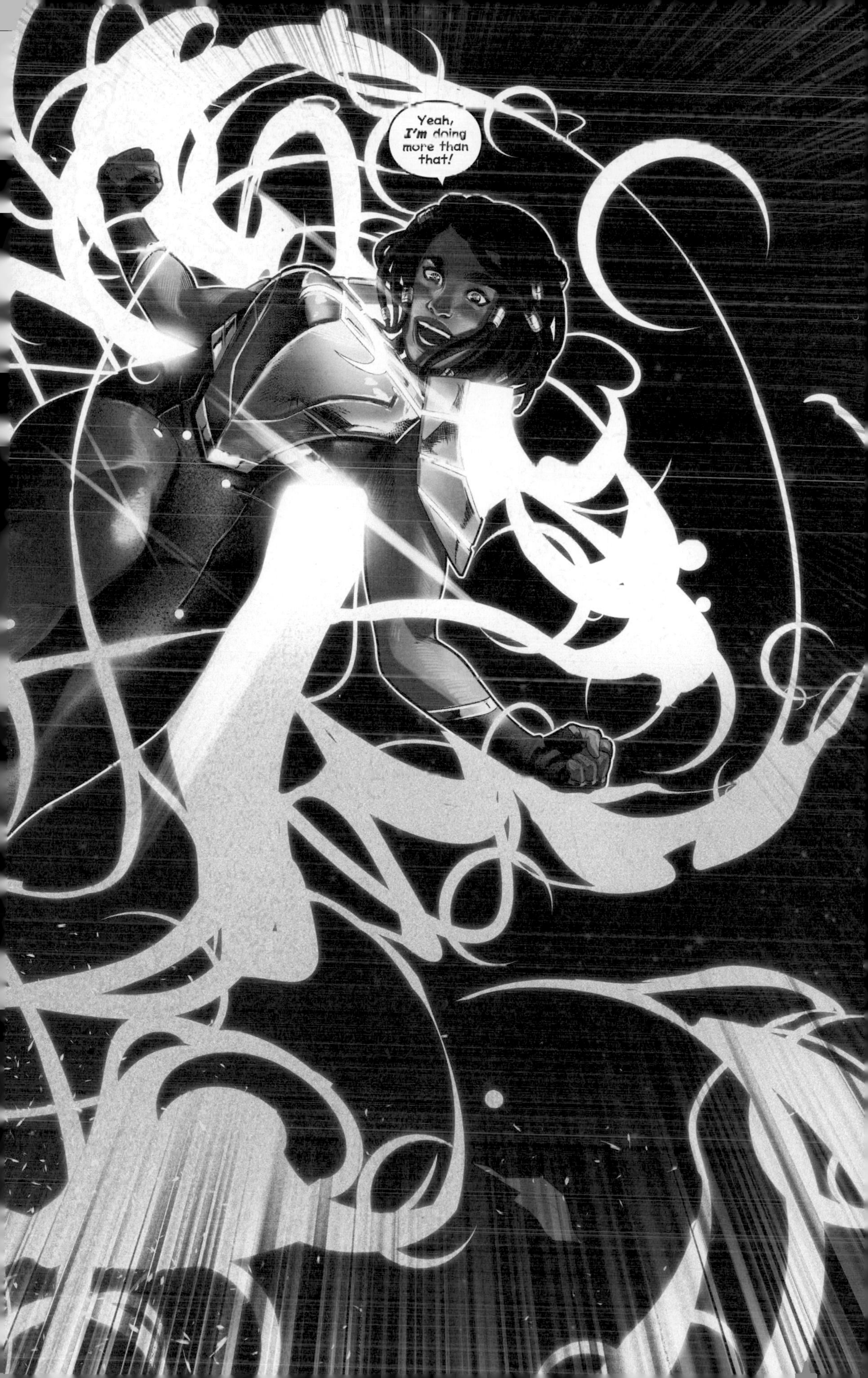
Yeah, *I'm* doing more than that!

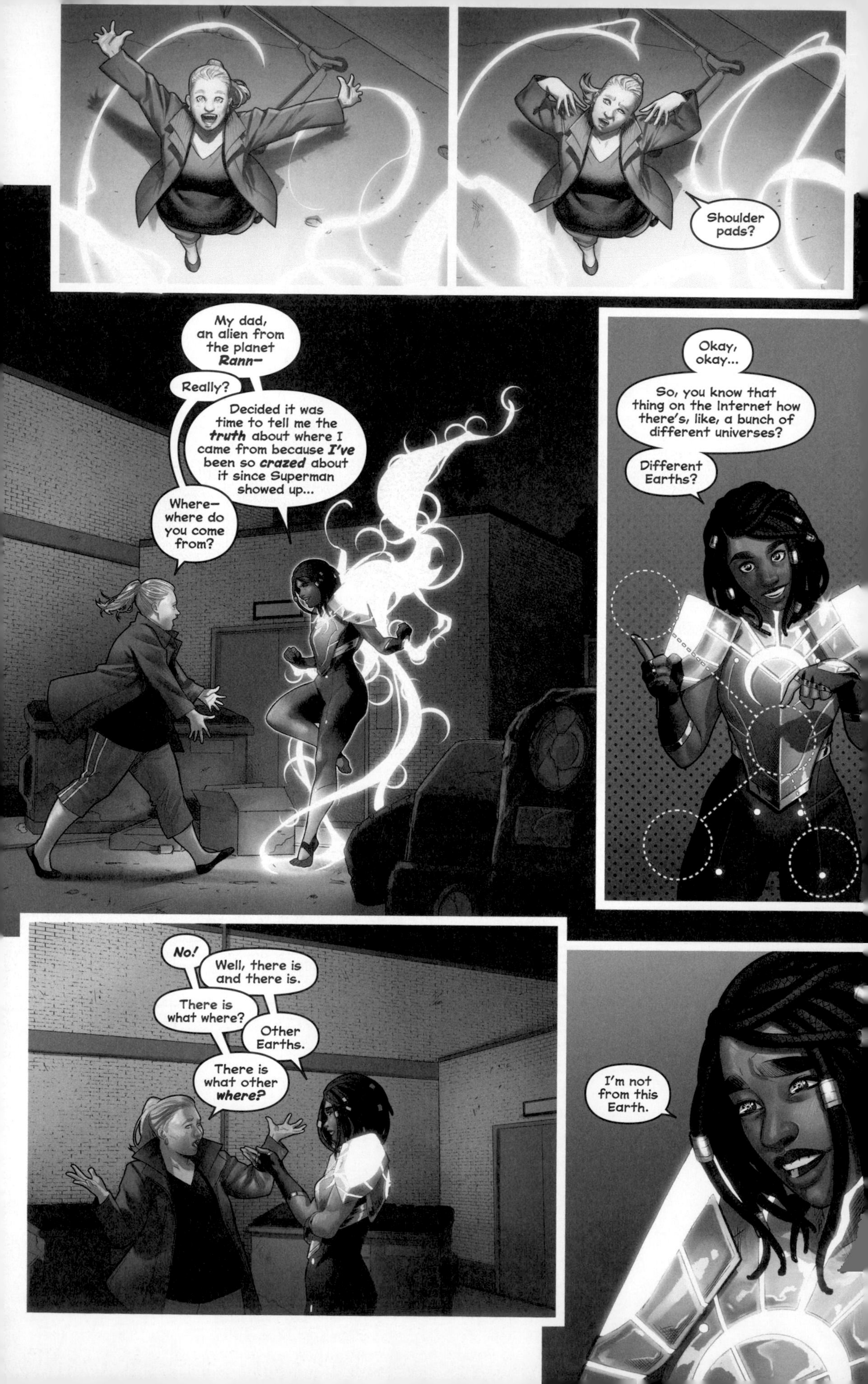
Shoulder pads?
My dad, an alien from the planet Rann–
Really?
Decided it was time to tell me the truth about where I came from because I've been so crazed about it since Superman showed up...
Where– where do you come from?
Okay, okay...
So, you know that thing on the Internet how there's, like, a bunch of different universes?
Different Earths?
No!
Well, there is and there is.
There is what where?
Other Earths.
There is what other where?
I'm not from this Earth.

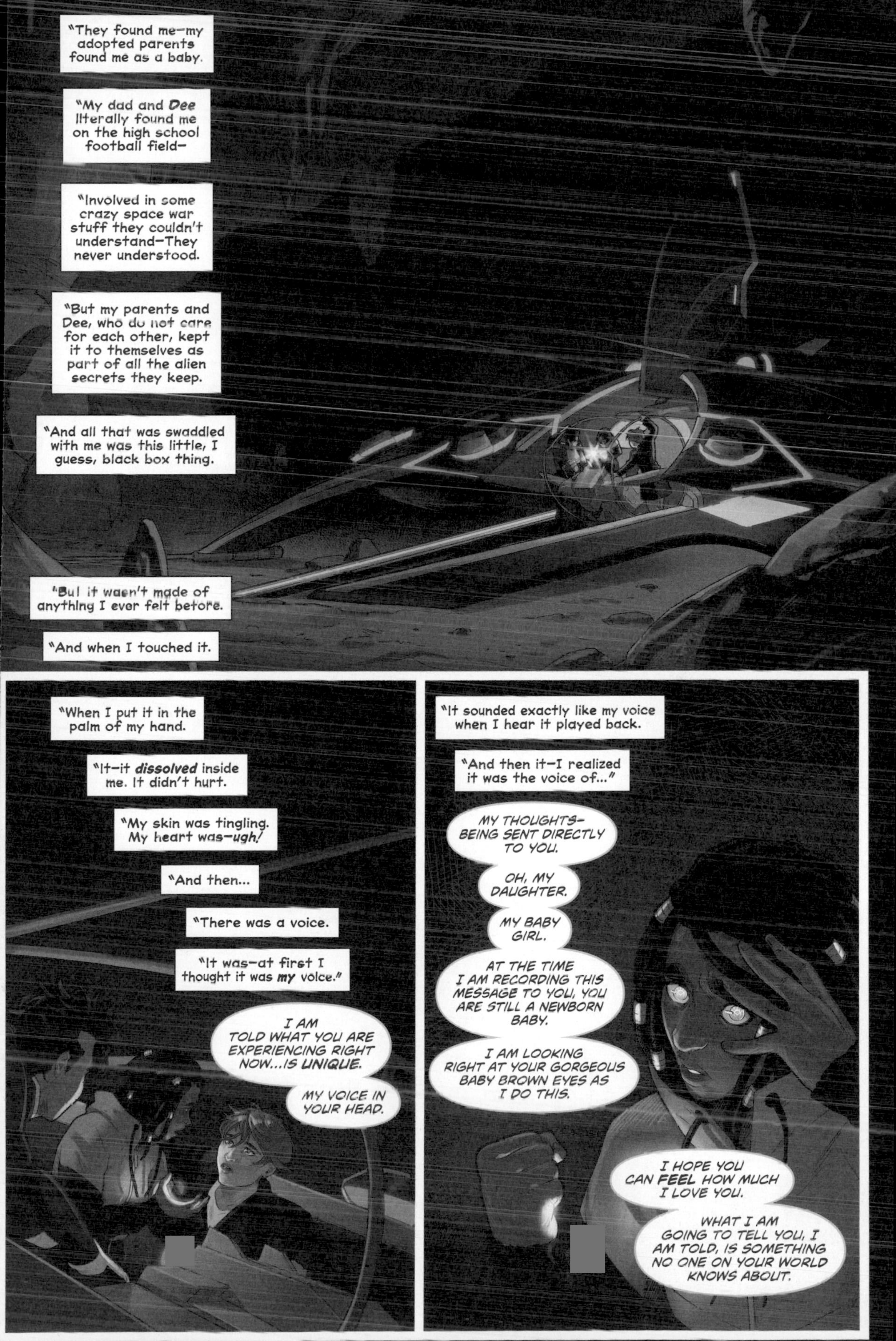
"They found me—my adopted parents found me as a baby.
"My dad and Dee literally found me on the high school football field—
"Involved in some crazy space war stuff they couldn't understand—They never understood.
"But my parents and Dee, who do not care for each other, kept it to themselves as part of all the alien secrets they keep.
"And all that was swaddled with me was this little, I guess, black box thing.
"But it wasn't made of anything I ever felt before.
"And when I touched it.
"When I put it in the palm of my hand.
"It—it dissolved inside me. It didn't hurt.
"My skin was tingling. My heart was—ugh!
"And then...
"There was a voice.
"It was—at first I thought it was my voice."
I AM TOLD WHAT YOU ARE EXPERIENCING RIGHT NOW...IS UNIQUE.
MY VOICE IN YOUR HEAD.
"It sounded exactly like my voice when I hear it played back.
"And then it—I realized it was the voice of..."
MY THOUGHTS—BEING SENT DIRECTLY TO YOU.
OH, MY DAUGHTER.
MY BABY GIRL.
AT THE TIME I AM RECORDING THIS MESSAGE TO YOU, YOU ARE STILL A NEWBORN BABY.
I AM LOOKING RIGHT AT YOUR GORGEOUS BABY BROWN EYES AS I DO THIS.
I HOPE YOU CAN FEEL HOW MUCH I LOVE YOU.
WHAT I AM GOING TO TELL YOU, I AM TOLD, IS SOMETHING NO ONE ON YOUR WORLD KNOWS ABOUT.

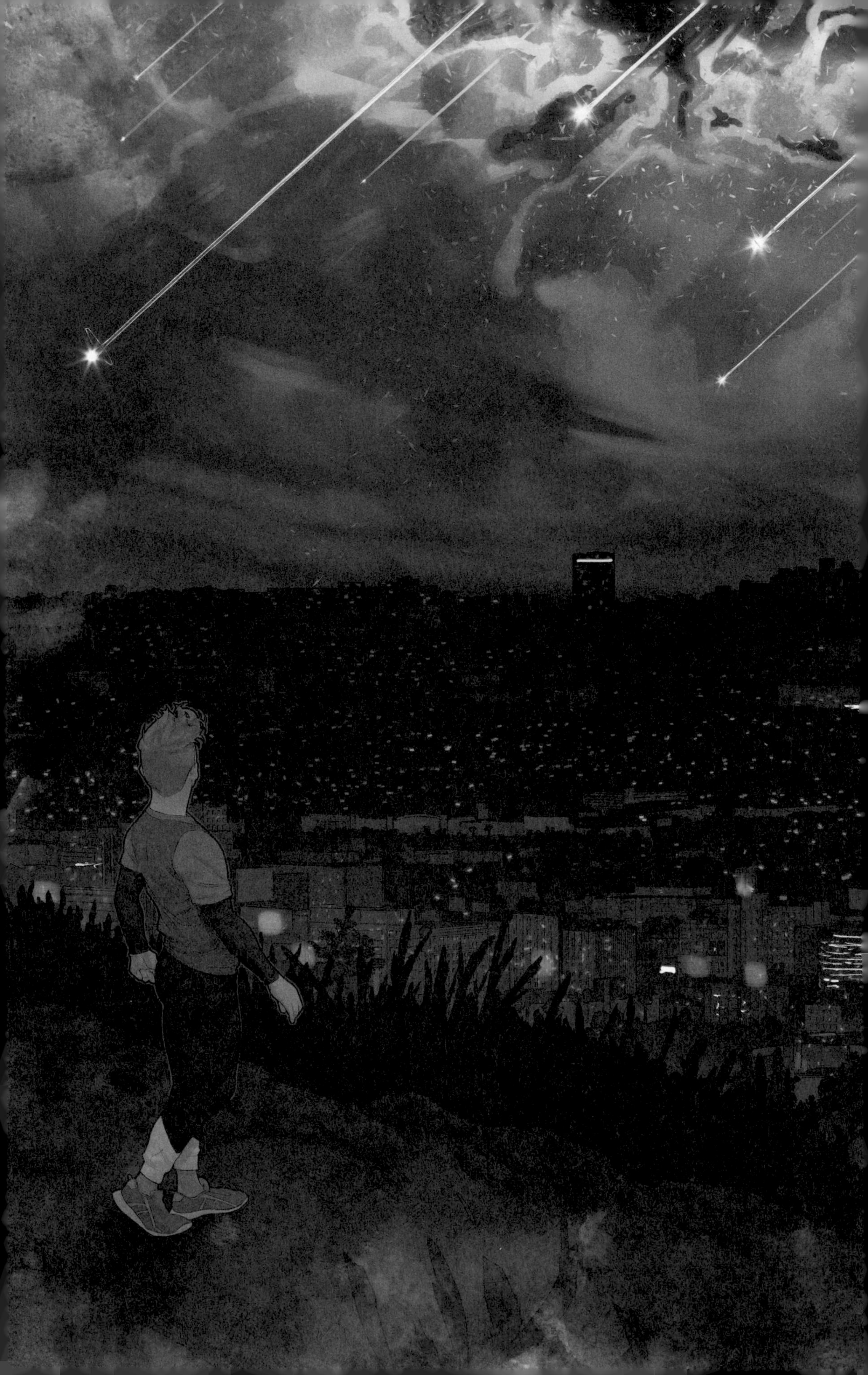

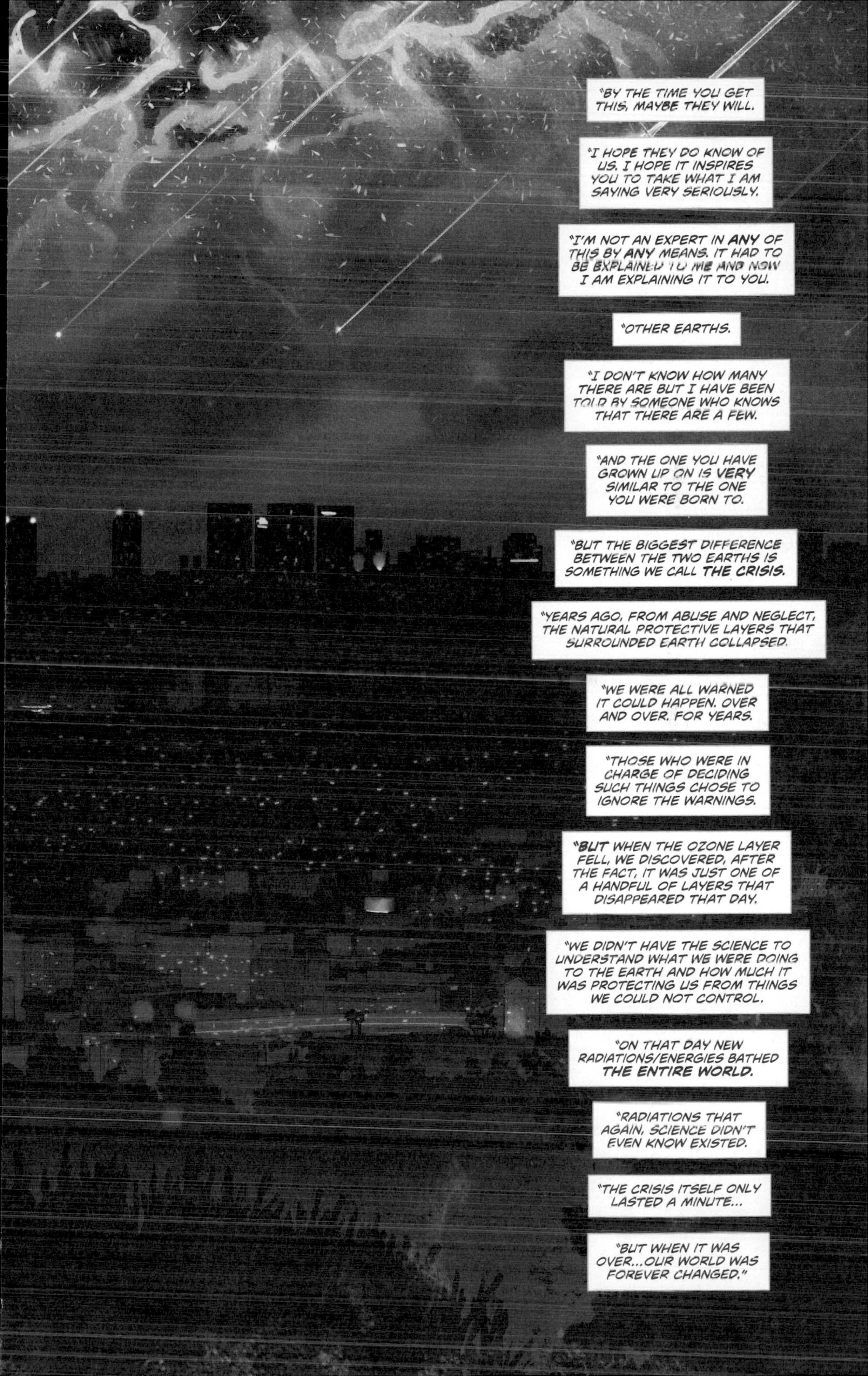
"BY THE TIME YOU GET THIS, MAYBE THEY WILL.
"I HOPE THEY DO KNOW OF US. I HOPE IT INSPIRES YOU TO TAKE WHAT I AM SAYING VERY SERIOUSLY.
"I'M NOT AN EXPERT IN ANY OF THIS BY ANY MEANS. IT HAD TO BE EXPLAINED TO ME AND NOW I AM EXPLAINING IT TO YOU.
"OTHER EARTHS.
"I DON'T KNOW HOW MANY THERE ARE BUT I HAVE BEEN TOLD BY SOMEONE WHO KNOWS THAT THERE ARE A FEW.
"AND THE ONE YOU HAVE GROWN UP ON IS VERY SIMILAR TO THE ONE YOU WERE BORN TO.
"BUT THE BIGGEST DIFFERENCE BETWEEN THE TWO EARTHS IS SOMETHING WE CALL THE CRISIS.
"YEARS AGO, FROM ABUSE AND NEGLECT, THE NATURAL PROTECTIVE LAYERS THAT SURROUNDED EARTH COLLAPSED.
"WE WERE ALL WARNED IT COULD HAPPEN. OVER AND OVER. FOR YEARS.
"THOSE WHO WERE IN CHARGE OF DECIDING SUCH THINGS CHOSE TO IGNORE THE WARNINGS.
"BUT WHEN THE OZONE LAYER FELL, WE DISCOVERED, AFTER THE FACT, IT WAS JUST ONE OF A HANDFUL OF LAYERS THAT DISAPPEARED THAT DAY.
"WE DIDN'T HAVE THE SCIENCE TO UNDERSTAND WHAT WE WERE DOING TO THE EARTH AND HOW MUCH IT WAS PROTECTING US FROM THINGS WE COULD NOT CONTROL.
"ON THAT DAY NEW RADIATIONS/ENERGIES BATHED THE ENTIRE WORLD.
"RADIATIONS THAT AGAIN, SCIENCE DIDN'T EVEN KNOW EXISTED.
"THE CRISIS ITSELF ONLY LASTED A MINUTE...
"BUT WHEN IT WAS OVER...OUR WORLD WAS FOREVER CHANGED."

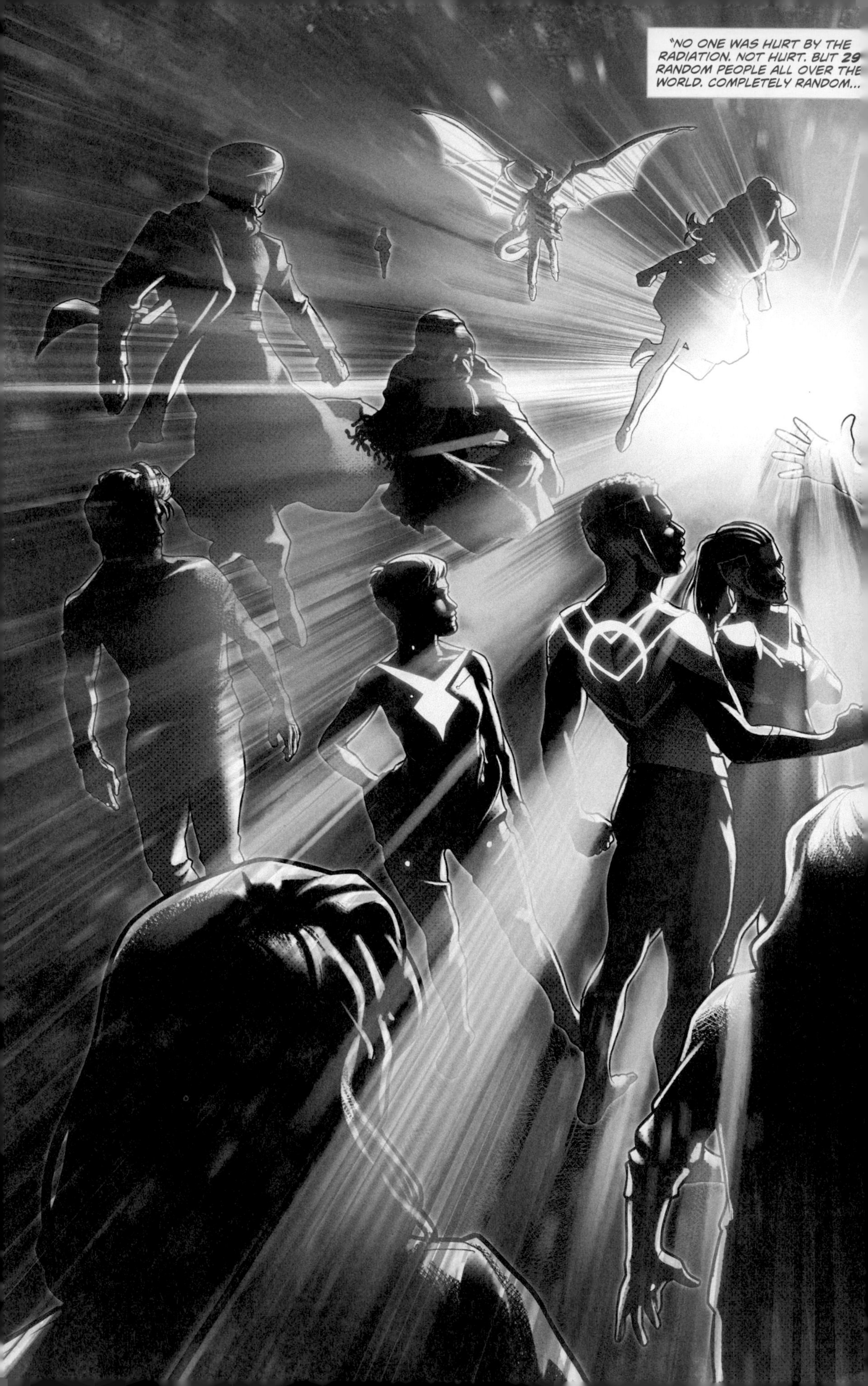
"NO ONE WAS HURT BY THE RADIATION. NOT HURT. BUT 29 RANDOM PEOPLE ALL OVER THE WORLD. COMPLETELY RANDOM...

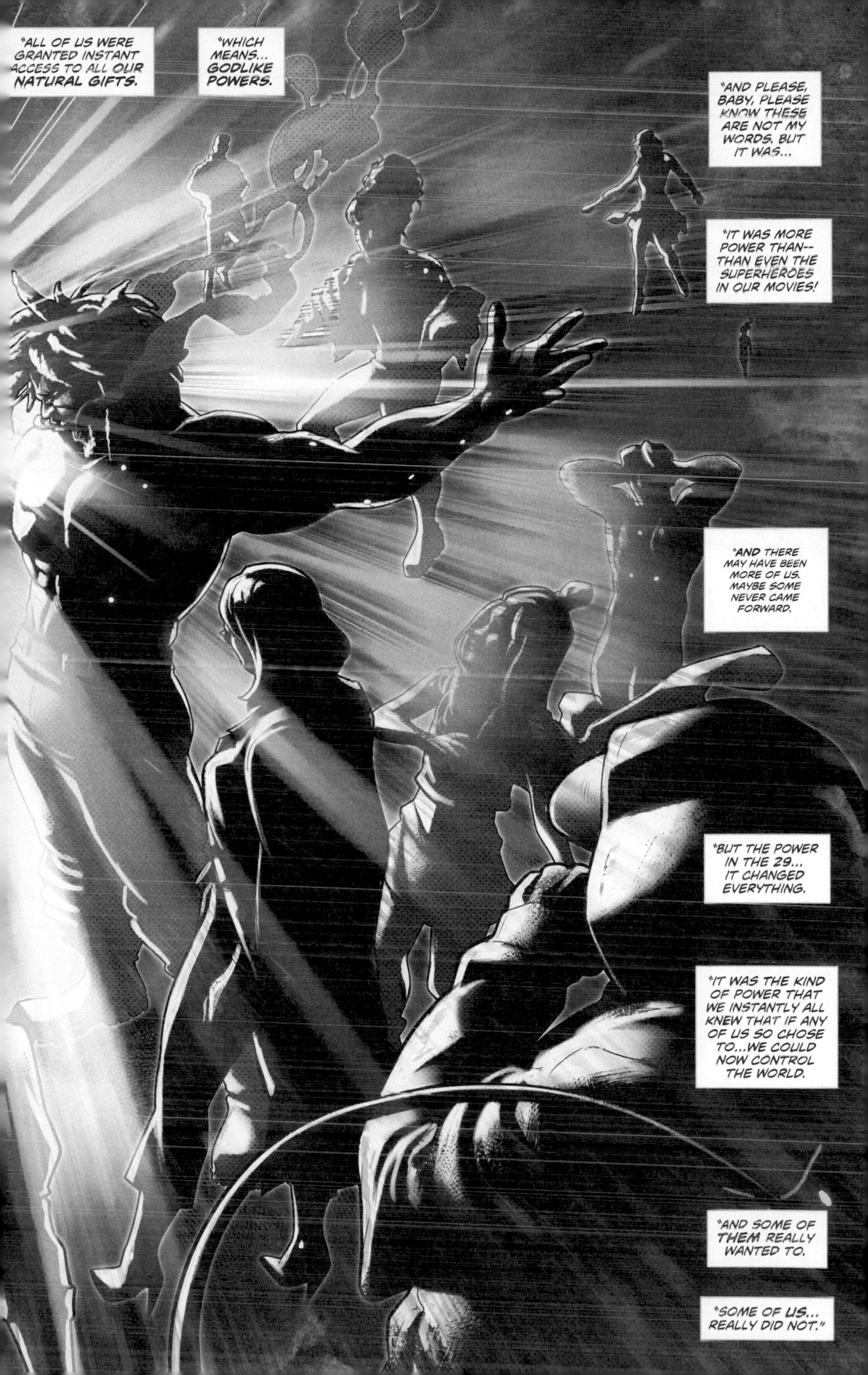
"ALL OF US WERE GRANTED INSTANT ACCESS TO ALL OUR NATURAL GIFTS.
"WHICH MEANS... GODLIKE POWERS.
"AND PLEASE, BABY, PLEASE KNOW THESE ARE NOT MY WORDS, BUT IT WAS...
"IT WAS MORE POWER THAN-- THAN EVEN THE SUPERHEROES IN OUR MOVIES!
"AND THERE MAY HAVE BEEN MORE OF US. MAYBE SOME NEVER CAME FORWARD.
"BUT THE POWER IN THE 29... IT CHANGED EVERYTHING.
"IT WAS THE KIND OF POWER THAT WE INSTANTLY ALL KNEW THAT IF ANY OF US SO CHOSE TO...WE COULD NOW CONTROL THE WORLD.
"AND SOME OF THEM REALLY WANTED TO.
"SOME OF US... REALLY DID NOT."

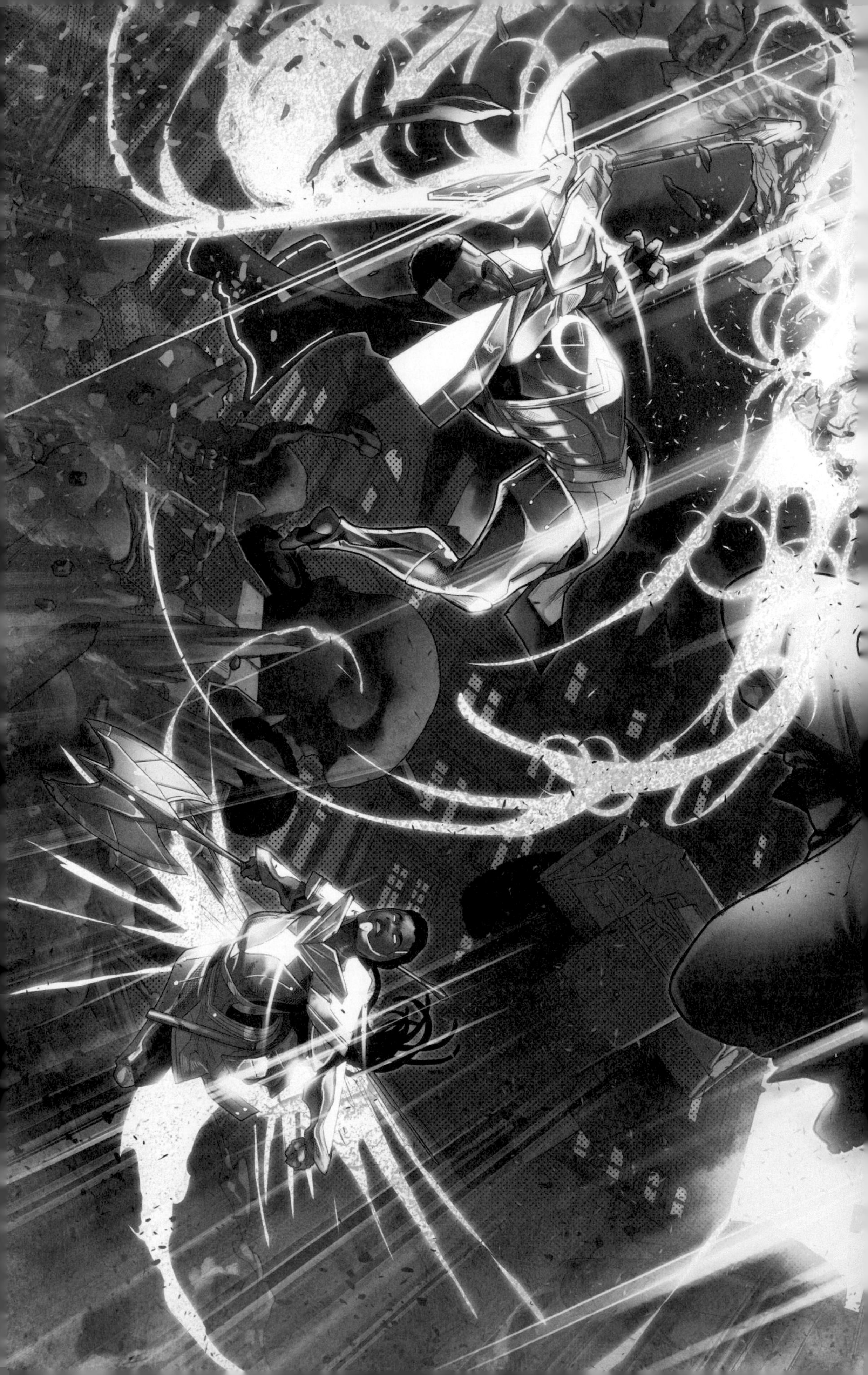

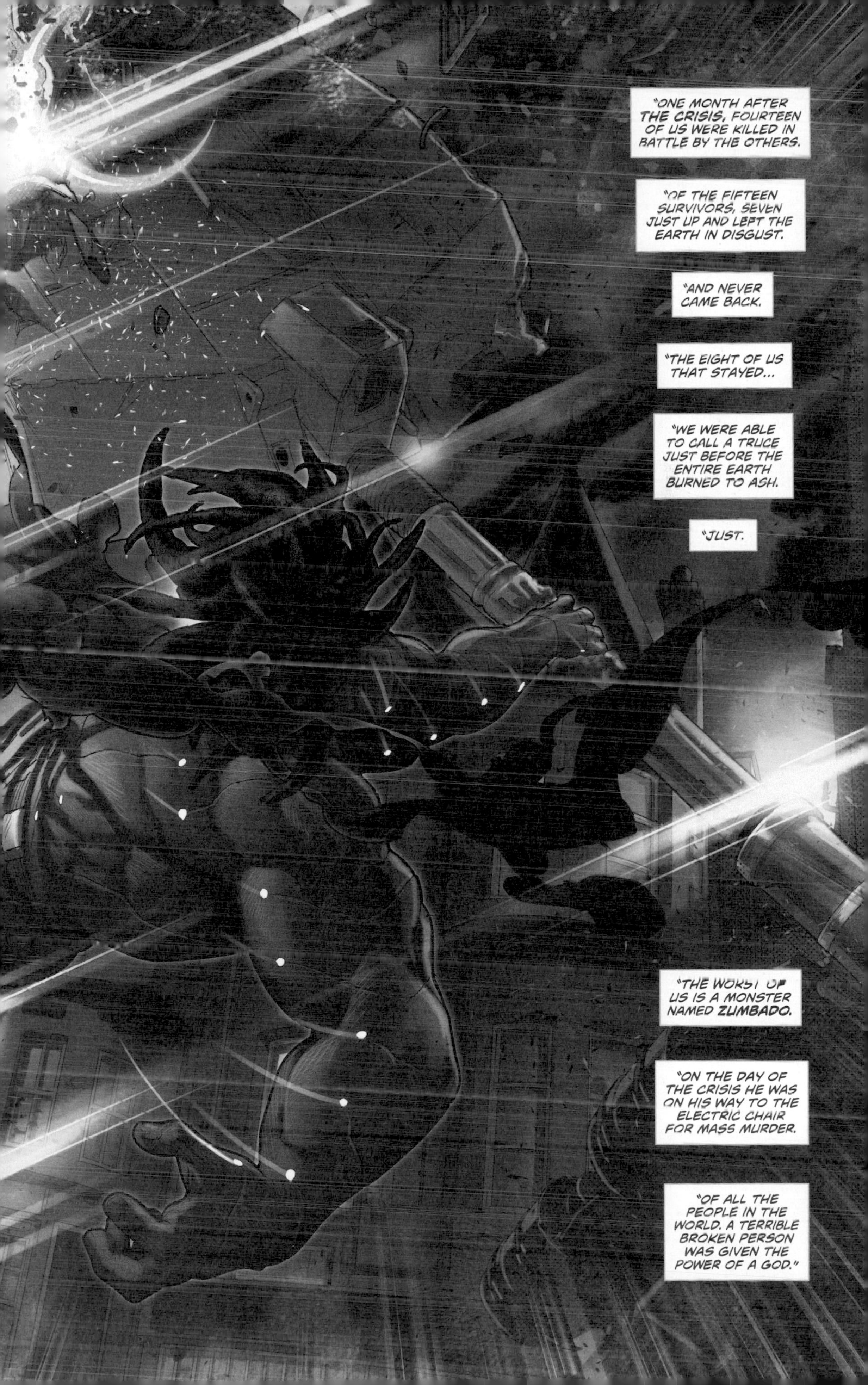
"ONE MONTH AFTER THE CRISIS, FOURTEEN OF US WERE KILLED IN BATTLE BY THE OTHERS.
"OF THE FIFTEEN SURVIVORS, SEVEN JUST UP AND LEFT THE EARTH IN DISGUST.
"AND NEVER CAME BACK.
"THE EIGHT OF US THAT STAYED...
"WE WERE ABLE TO CALL A TRUCE JUST BEFORE THE ENTIRE EARTH BURNED TO ASH.
"JUST.
"THE WORST OF US IS A MONSTER NAMED ZUMBADO.
"ON THE DAY OF THE CRISIS HE WAS ON HIS WAY TO THE ELECTRIC CHAIR FOR MASS MURDER.
"OF ALL THE PEOPLE IN THE WORLD. A TERRIBLE BROKEN PERSON WAS GIVEN THE POWER OF A GOD."

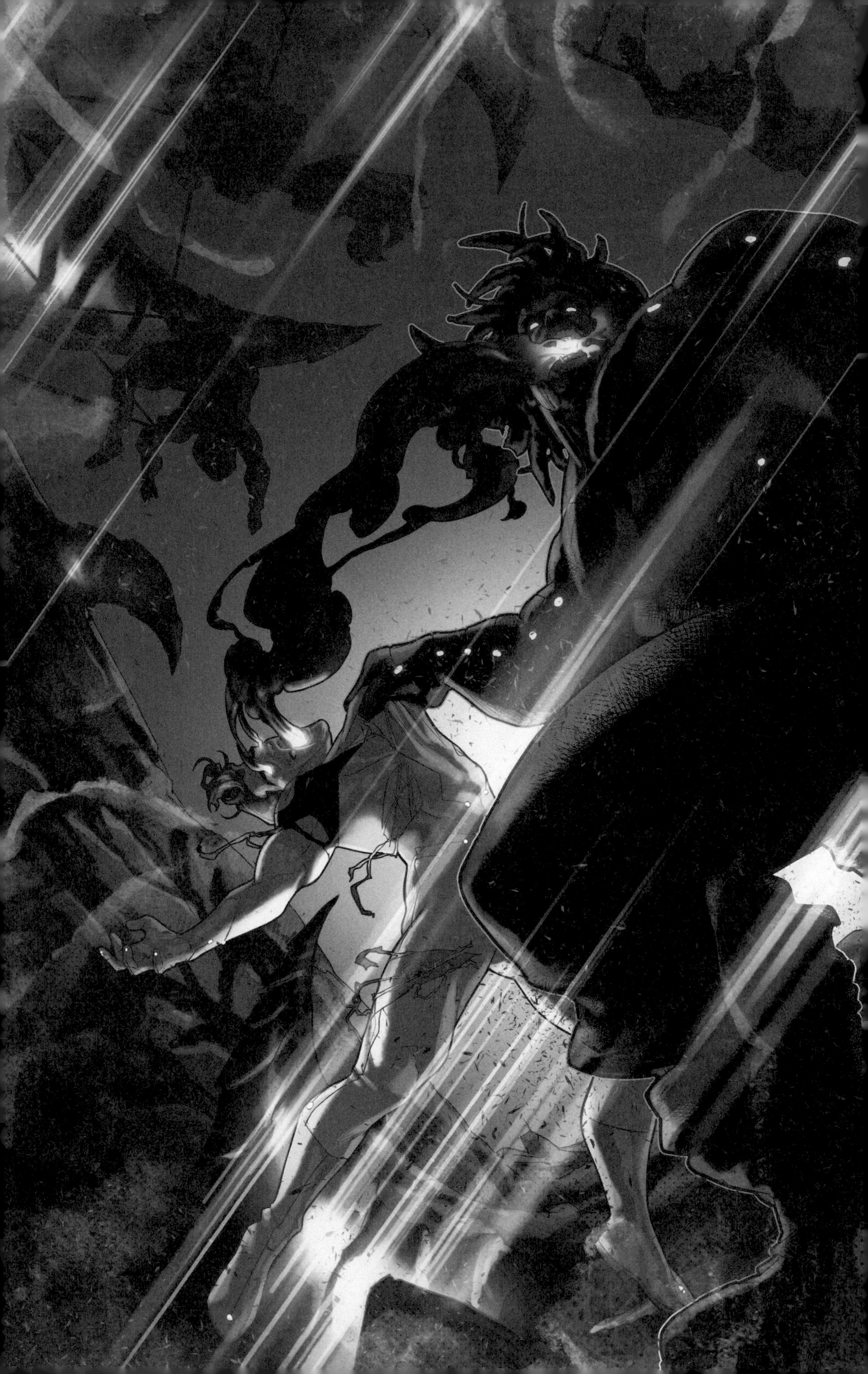

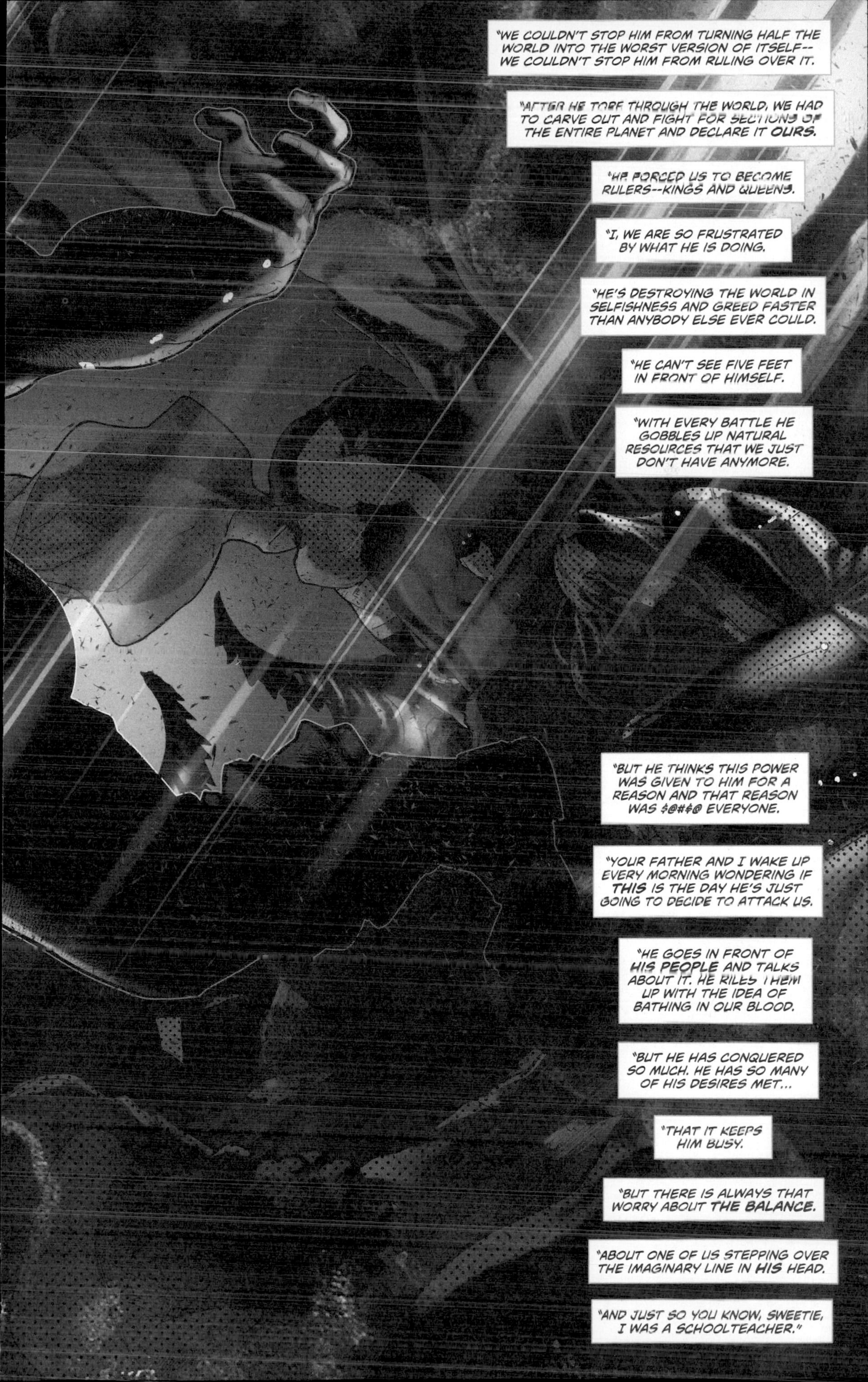
"WE COULDN'T STOP HIM FROM TURNING HALF THE WORLD INTO THE WORST VERSION OF ITSELF-- WE COULDN'T STOP HIM FROM RULING OVER IT.
"AFTER HE TORE THROUGH THE WORLD, WE HAD TO CARVE OUT AND FIGHT FOR SECTIONS OF THE ENTIRE PLANET AND DECLARE IT OURS.
"HE FORCED US TO BECOME RULERS--KINGS AND QUEENS.
"I, WE ARE SO FRUSTRATED BY WHAT HE IS DOING.
"HE'S DESTROYING THE WORLD IN SELFISHNESS AND GREED FASTER THAN ANYBODY ELSE EVER COULD.
"HE CAN'T SEE FIVE FEET IN FRONT OF HIMSELF.
"WITH EVERY BATTLE HE GOBBLES UP NATURAL RESOURCES THAT WE JUST DON'T HAVE ANYMORE.
"BUT HE THINKS THIS POWER WAS GIVEN TO HIM FOR A REASON AND THAT REASON WAS $@#$@ EVERYONE.
"YOUR FATHER AND I WAKE UP EVERY MORNING WONDERING IF THIS IS THE DAY HE'S JUST GOING TO DECIDE TO ATTACK US.
"HE GOES IN FRONT OF HIS PEOPLE AND TALKS ABOUT IT. HE RILES THEM UP WITH THE IDEA OF BATHING IN OUR BLOOD.
"BUT HE HAS CONQUERED SO MUCH. HE HAS SO MANY OF HIS DESIRES MET...
"THAT IT KEEPS HIM BUSY.
"BUT THERE IS ALWAYS THAT WORRY ABOUT THE BALANCE.
"ABOUT ONE OF US STEPPING OVER THE IMAGINARY LINE IN HIS HEAD.
"AND JUST SO YOU KNOW, SWEETIE, I WAS A SCHOOLTEACHER."

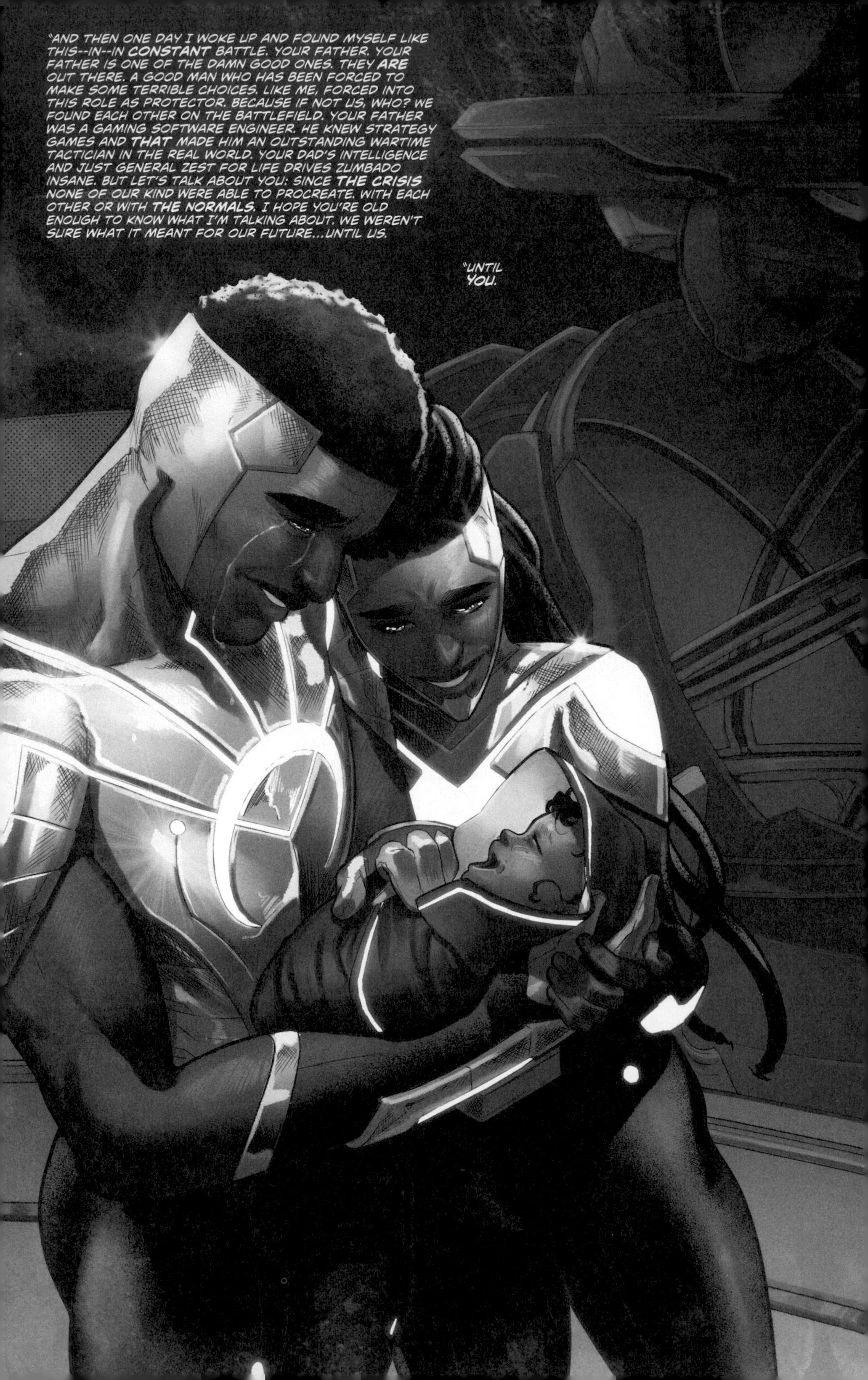
"AND THEN ONE DAY I WOKE UP AND FOUND MYSELF LIKE THIS--IN--IN CONSTANT BATTLE. YOUR FATHER. YOUR FATHER IS ONE OF THE DAMN GOOD ONES. THEY ARE OUT THERE. A GOOD MAN WHO HAS BEEN FORCED TO MAKE SOME TERRIBLE CHOICES. LIKE ME, FORCED INTO THIS ROLE AS PROTECTOR. BECAUSE IF NOT US, WHO? WE FOUND EACH OTHER ON THE BATTLEFIELD. YOUR FATHER WAS A GAMING SOFTWARE ENGINEER. HE KNEW STRATEGY GAMES AND THAT MADE HIM AN OUTSTANDING WARTIME TACTICIAN IN THE REAL WORLD. YOUR DAD'S INTELLIGENCE AND JUST GENERAL ZEST FOR LIFE DRIVES ZUMBADO INSANE. BUT LET'S TALK ABOUT YOU: SINCE THE CRISIS NONE OF OUR KIND WERE ABLE TO PROCREATE. WITH EACH OTHER OR WITH THE NORMALS. I HOPE YOU'RE OLD ENOUGH TO KNOW WHAT I'M TALKING ABOUT. WE WEREN'T SURE WHAT IT MEANT FOR OUR FUTURE...UNTIL US.
"UNTIL YOU.

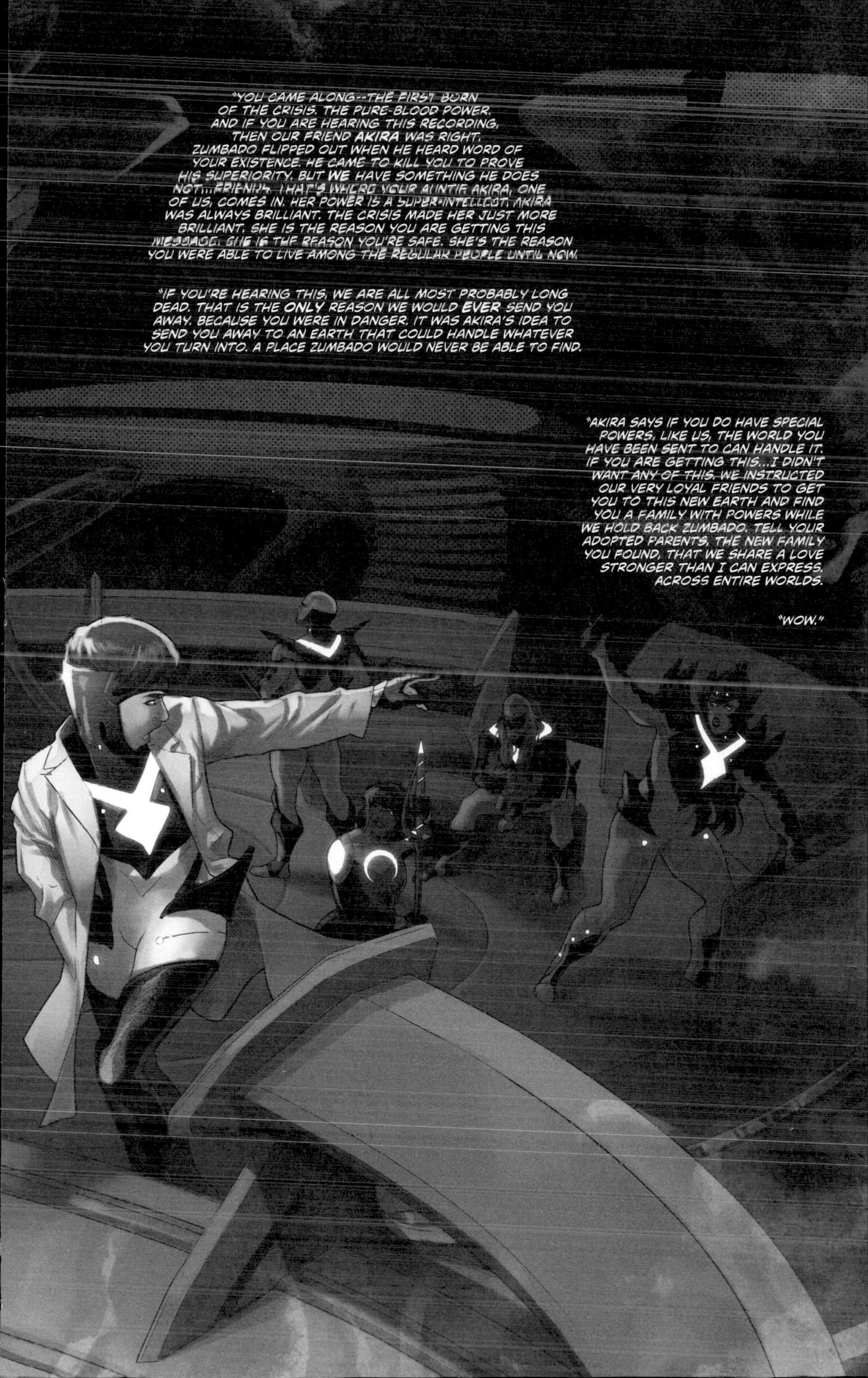
"YOU CAME ALONG--THE FIRST BORN OF THE CRISIS. THE PURE-BLOOD POWER. AND IF YOU ARE HEARING THIS RECORDING, THEN OUR FRIEND AKIRA WAS RIGHT. ZUMBADO FLIPPED OUT WHEN HE HEARD WORD OF YOUR EXISTENCE. HE CAME TO KILL YOU TO PROVE HIS SUPERIORITY. BUT WE HAVE SOMETHING HE DOES NOT...FRIENDS. THAT'S WHERE YOUR AUNTIE AKIRA, ONE OF US, COMES IN. HER POWER IS A SUPER-INTELLECT. AKIRA WAS ALWAYS BRILLIANT. THE CRISIS MADE HER JUST MORE BRILLIANT. SHE IS THE REASON YOU ARE GETTING THIS MESSAGE. SHE IS THE REASON YOU'RE SAFE. SHE'S THE REASON YOU WERE ABLE TO LIVE AMONG THE REGULAR PEOPLE UNTIL NOW.
"IF YOU'RE HEARING THIS, WE ARE ALL MOST PROBABLY LONG DEAD. THAT IS THE ONLY REASON WE WOULD EVER SEND YOU AWAY. BECAUSE YOU WERE IN DANGER. IT WAS AKIRA'S IDEA TO SEND YOU AWAY TO AN EARTH THAT COULD HANDLE WHATEVER YOU TURN INTO. A PLACE ZUMBADO WOULD NEVER BE ABLE TO FIND.
"AKIRA SAYS IF YOU DO HAVE SPECIAL POWERS, LIKE US, THE WORLD YOU HAVE BEEN SENT TO CAN HANDLE IT. IF YOU ARE GETTING THIS...I DIDN'T WANT ANY OF THIS. WE INSTRUCTED OUR VERY LOYAL FRIENDS TO GET YOU TO THIS NEW EARTH AND FIND YOU A FAMILY WITH POWERS WHILE WE HOLD BACK ZUMBADO. TELL YOUR ADOPTED PARENTS, THE NEW FAMILY YOU FOUND, THAT WE SHARE A LOVE STRONGER THAN I CAN EXPRESS. ACROSS ENTIRE WORLDS.
"WOW."

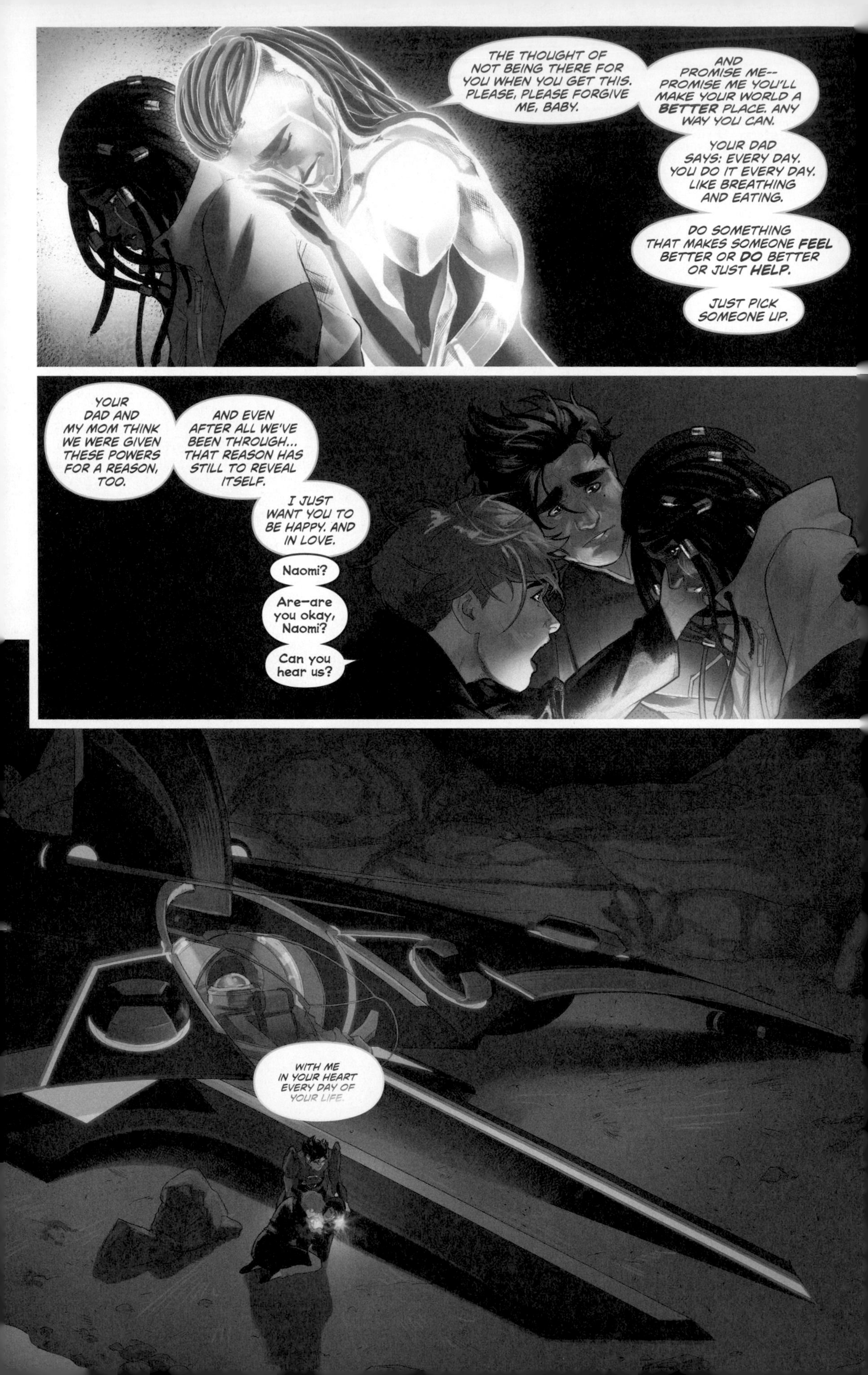
THE THOUGHT OF NOT BEING THERE FOR YOU WHEN YOU GET THIS. PLEASE, PLEASE FORGIVE ME, BABY.
AND PROMISE ME-- PROMISE ME YOU'LL MAKE YOUR WORLD A BETTER PLACE. ANY WAY YOU CAN.
YOUR DAD SAYS: EVERY DAY. YOU DO IT EVERY DAY. LIKE BREATHING AND EATING.
DO SOMETHING THAT MAKES SOMEONE FEEL BETTER OR DO BETTER OR JUST HELP.
JUST PICK SOMEONE UP.
YOUR DAD AND MY MOM THINK WE WERE GIVEN THESE POWERS FOR A REASON, TOO.
AND EVEN AFTER ALL WE'VE BEEN THROUGH... THAT REASON HAS STILL TO REVEAL ITSELF.
I JUST WANT YOU TO BE HAPPY. AND IN LOVE.
Naomi?
Are-are you okay, Naomi?
Can you hear us?
WITH ME IN YOUR HEART EVERY DAY OF YOUR LIFE.

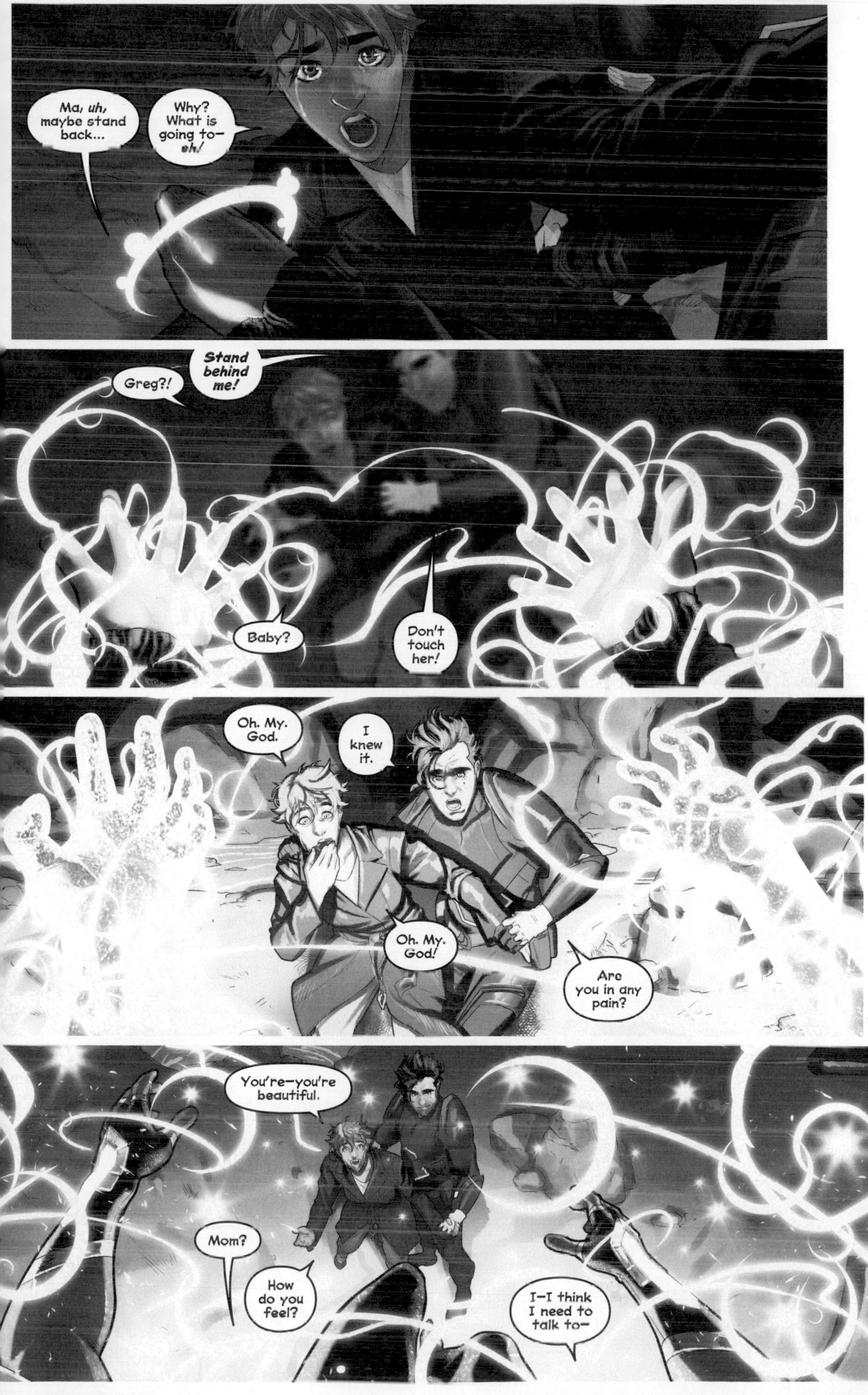
Ma, uh, maybe stand back...
Why? What is going to— oh!
Greg?!
Stand behind me!
Baby?
Don't touch her!
Oh. My. God.
I knew it.
Oh. My. God!
Are you in any pain?
You're—you're beautiful.
Mom?
How do you feel?
I—I think I need to talk to—

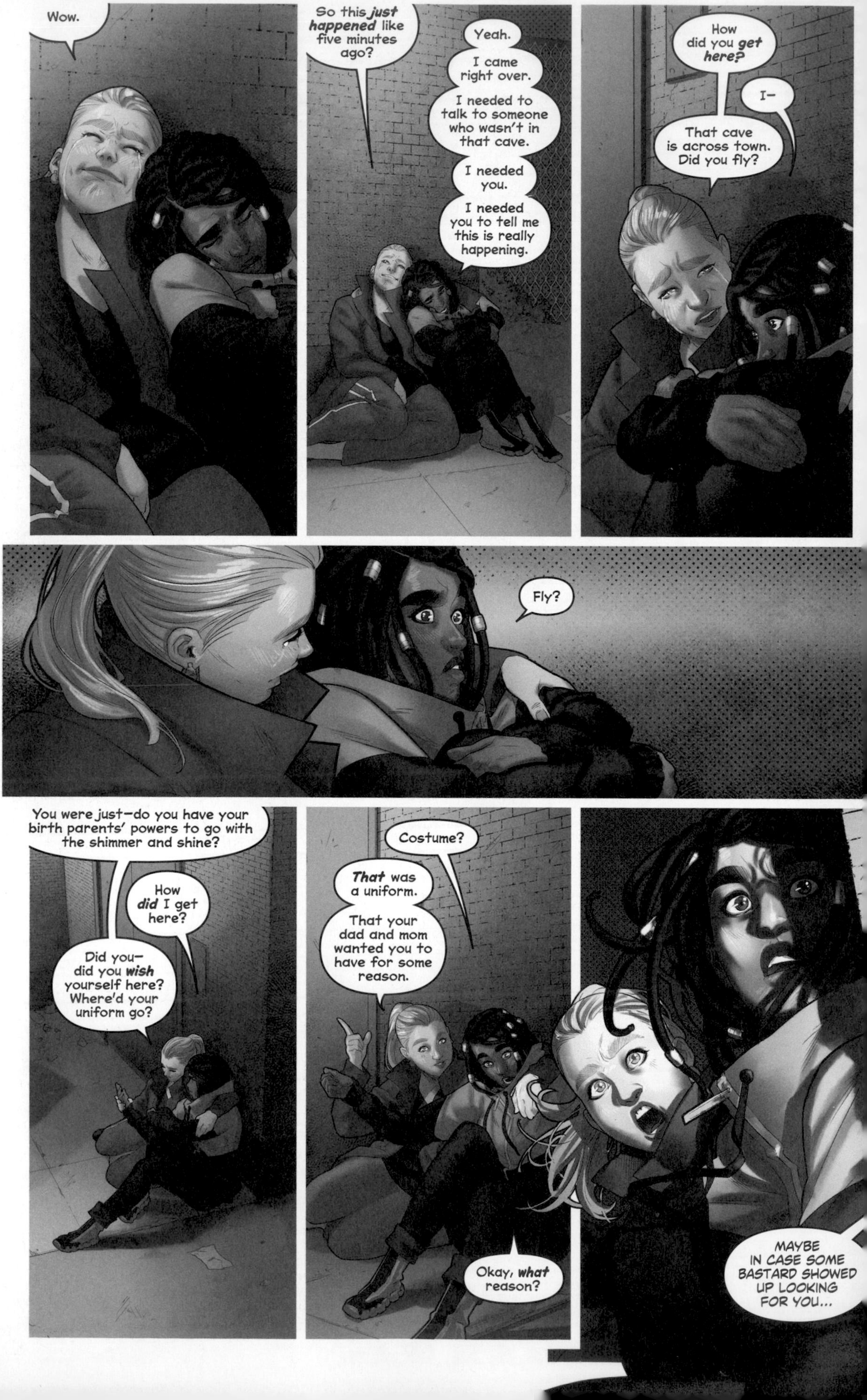
Wow.
So this *just happened* like five minutes ago?
Yeah.
I came right over.
I needed to talk to someone who wasn't in that cave.
I needed you.
I needed you to tell me this is really happening.
How did you *get here?*
I–
That cave is across town. Did you fly?
Fly?
You were just–do you have your birth parents' powers to go with the shimmer and shine?
How *did* I get here?
Did you– did you *wish* yourself here? Where'd your uniform go?
Costume?
That was a uniform.
That your dad and mom wanted you to have for some reason.
Okay, *what* reason?
MAYBE IN CASE SOME BASTARD SHOWED UP LOOKING FOR YOU...

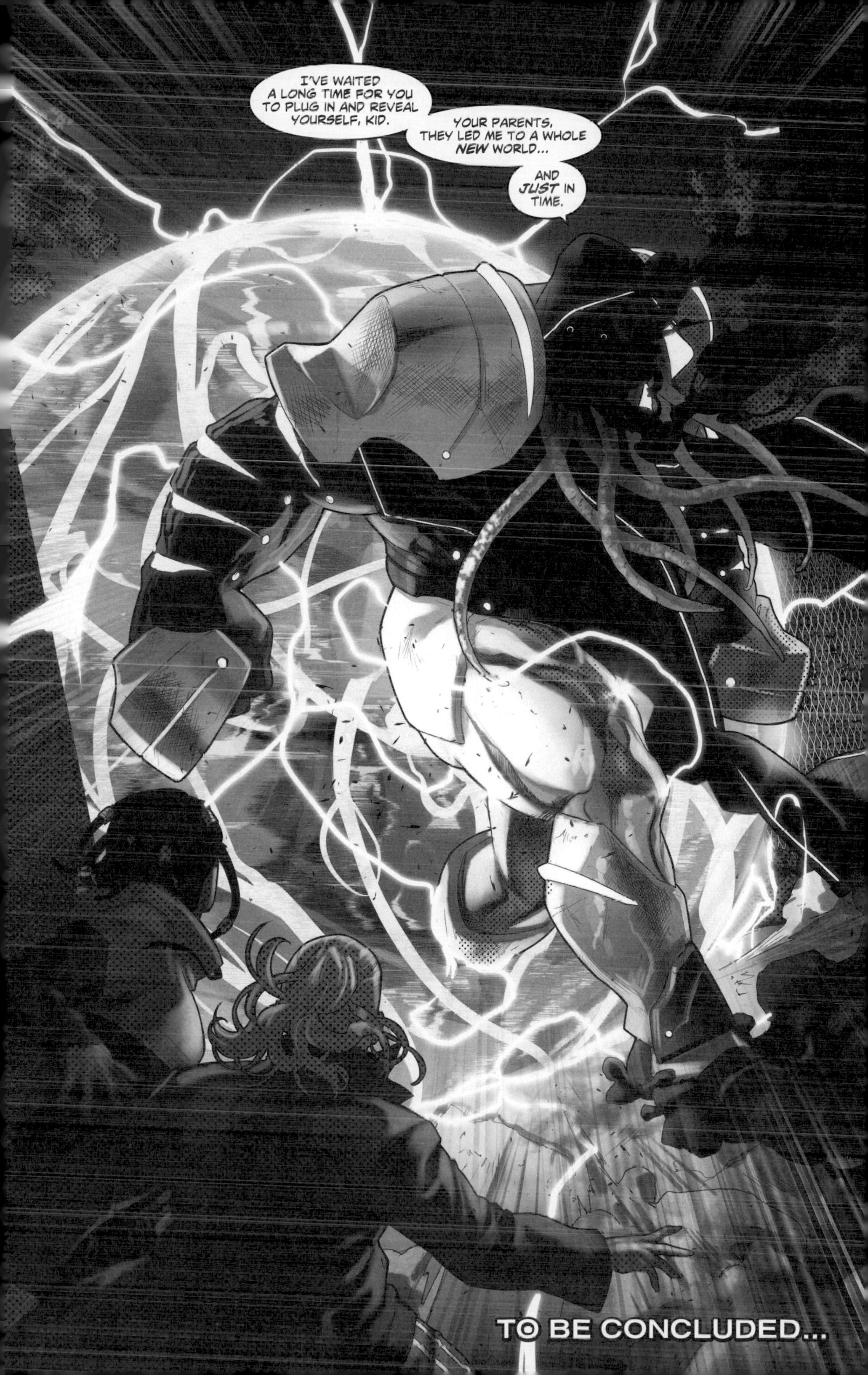
I'VE WAITED A LONG TIME FOR YOU TO PLUG IN AND REVEAL YOURSELF, KID.
YOUR PARENTS, THEY LED ME TO A WHOLE NEW WORLD...
AND JUST IN TIME.
TO BE CONCLUDED...

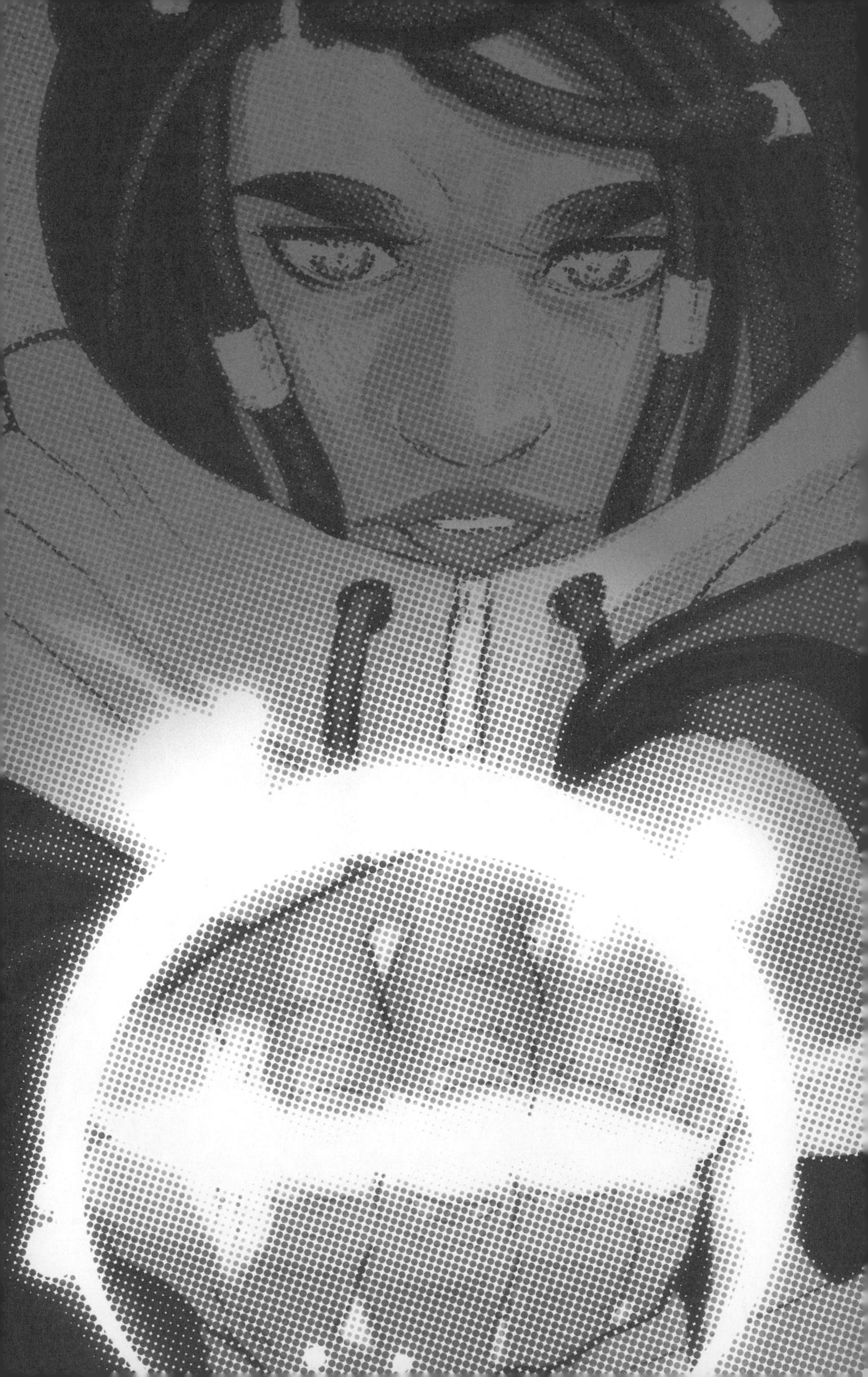

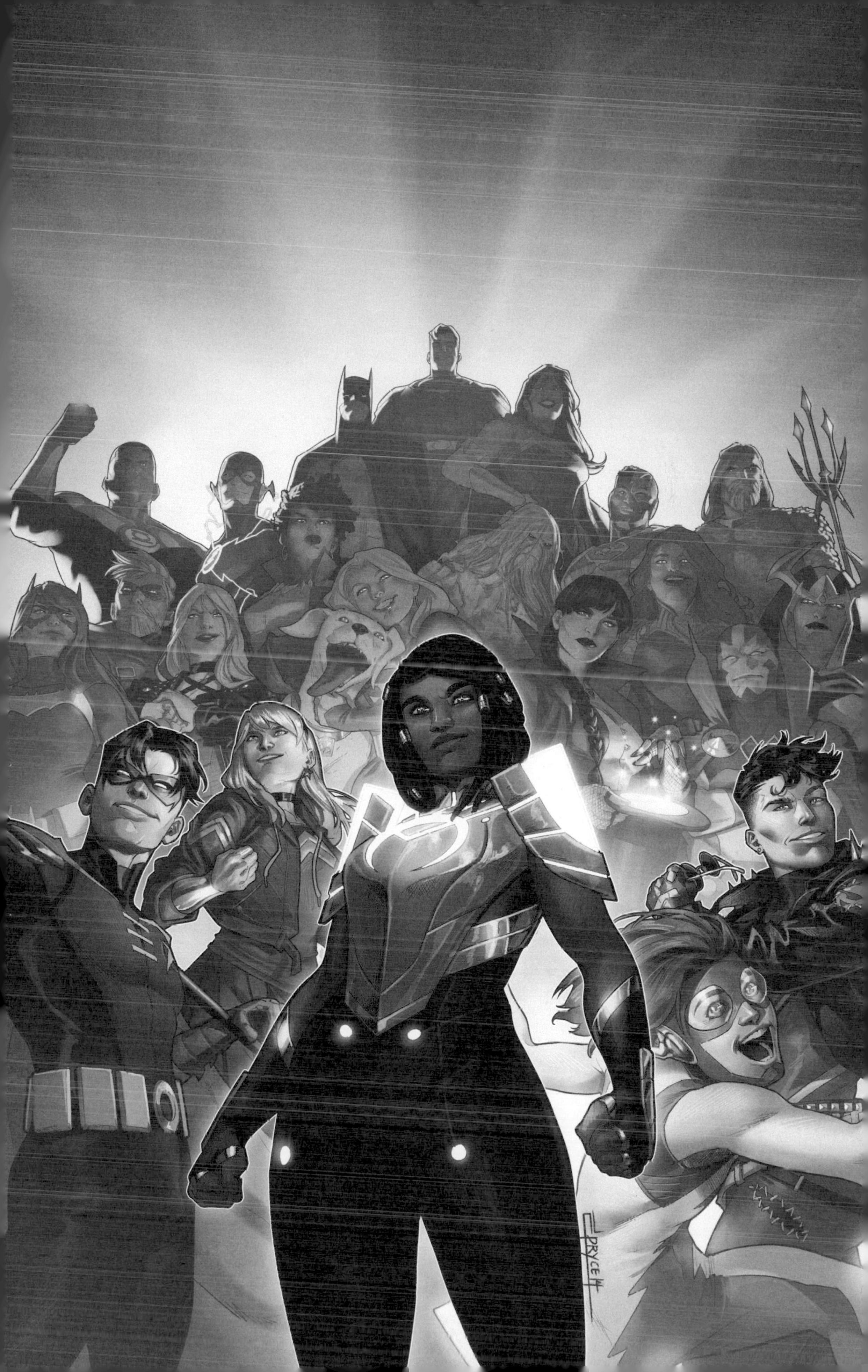

SIX

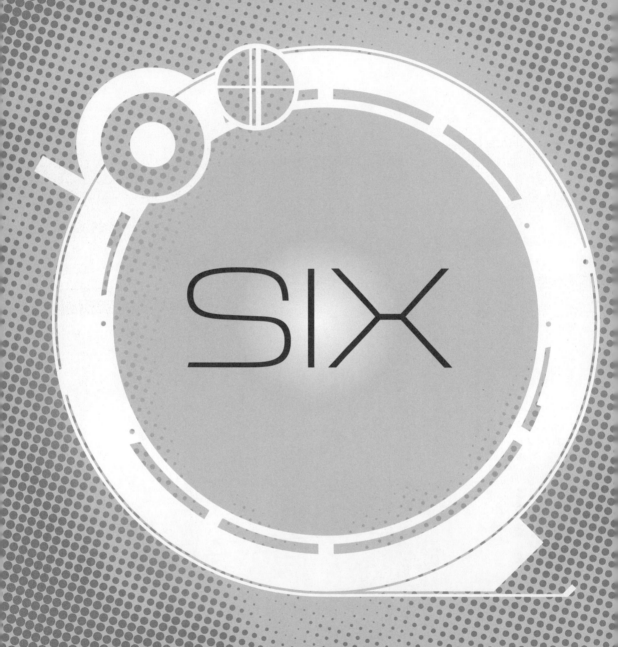

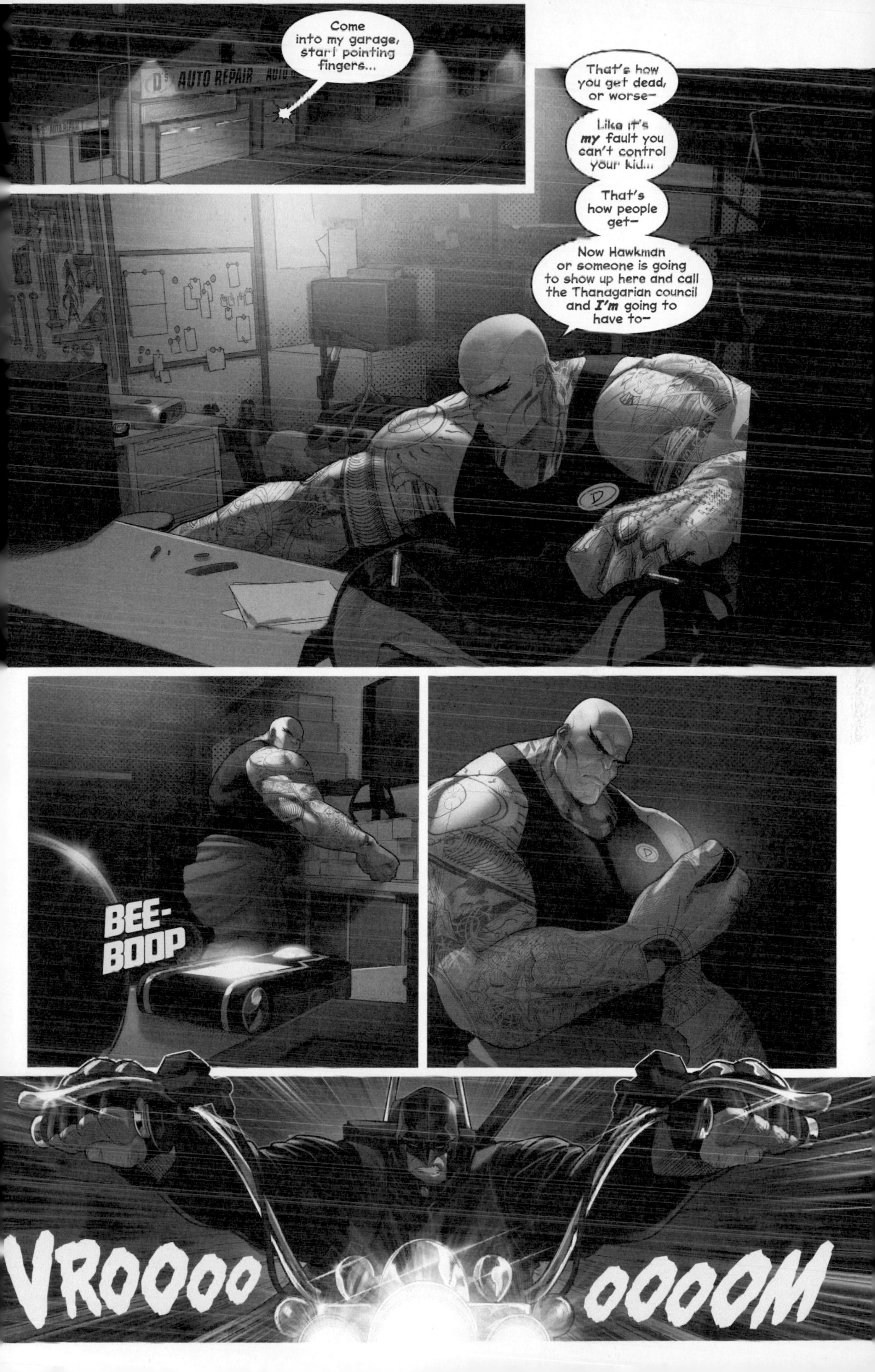
D's AUTO REPAIR
Come into my garage, start pointing fingers...
That's how you get dead, or worse—
Like it's *my* fault you can't control your kid...
That's how people get—
Now Hawkman or someone is going to show up here and call the Thanagarian council and *I'm* going to have to—
BEE-BOOP
VROOOO OOOOM

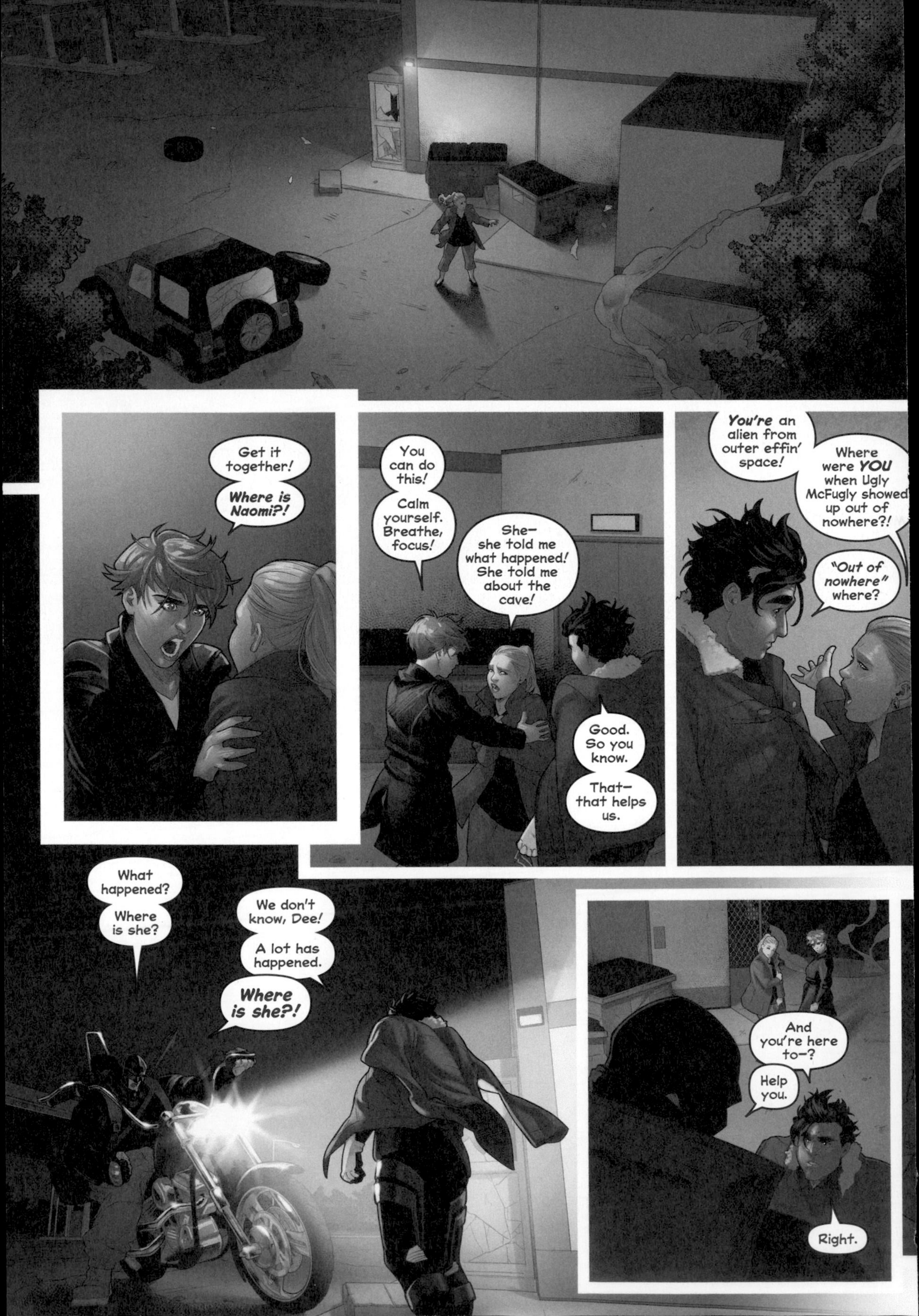

Get it together!
Where is Naomi?!
You can do this!
Calm yourself. Breathe, focus!
She— she told me what happened! She told me about the cave!
Good. So you know.
That— that helps us.
You're an alien from outer effin' space!
Where were YOU when Ugly McFugly showed up out of nowhere?!
"Out of nowhere" where?
What happened?
Where is she?
We don't know, Dee!
A lot has happened.
Where is she?!
And you're here to—?
Help you.
Right.

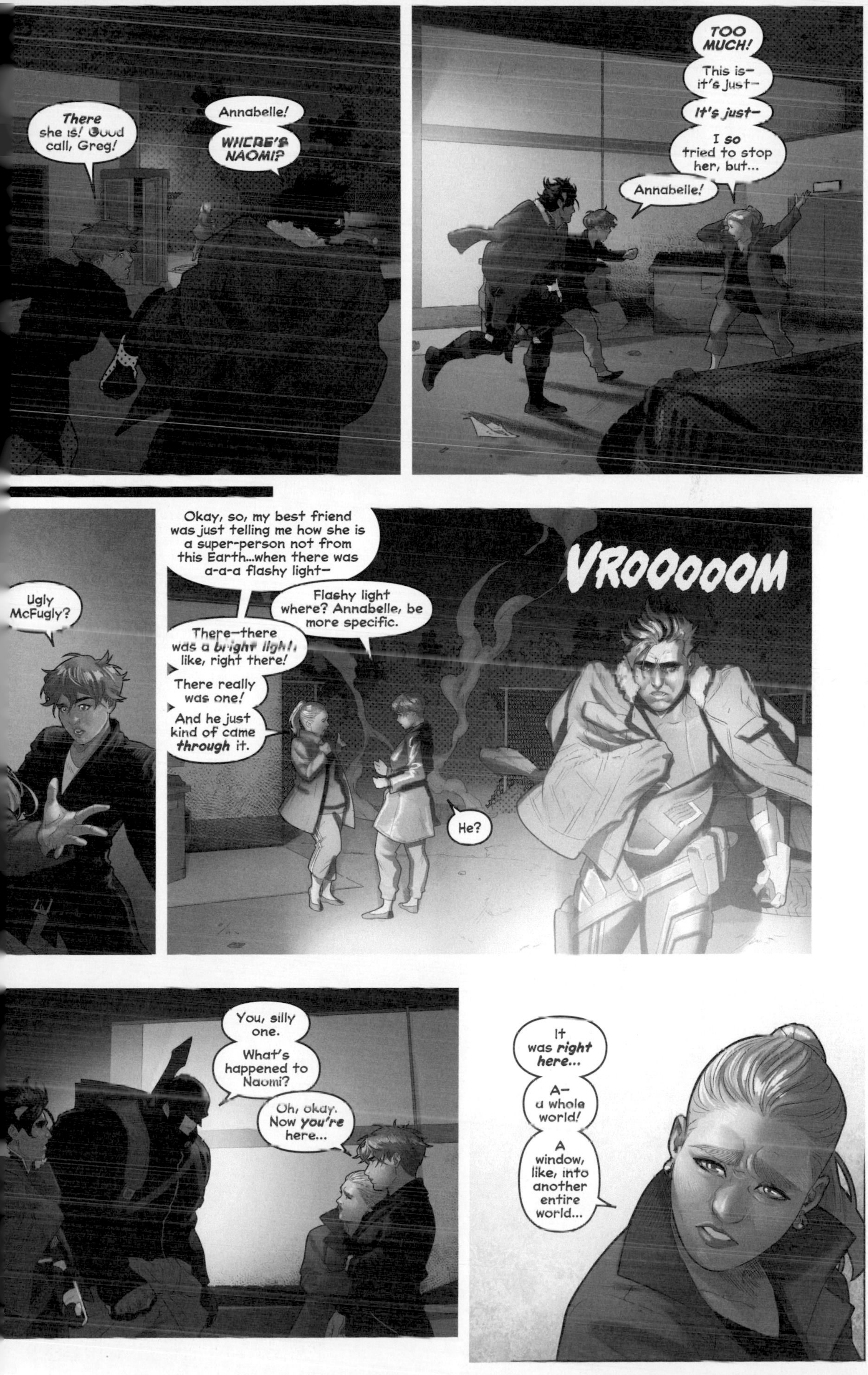

There she is! Good call, Greg!
Annabelle!
WHERE'S NAOMI?
TOO MUCH!
This is— it's just—
It's just—
I so tried to stop her, but...
Annabelle!
Okay, so, my best friend was just telling me how she is a super-person not from this Earth...when there was a-a-a flashy light—
Flashy light where? Annabelle, be more specific.
Ugly McFugly?
There—there was a bright light! like, right there!
There really was one!
And he just kind of came through it.
He?
VROOOOOM
You, silly one.
What's happened to Naomi?
Oh, okay. Now you're here...
It was right here...
A— a whole world!
A window, like, into another entire world...

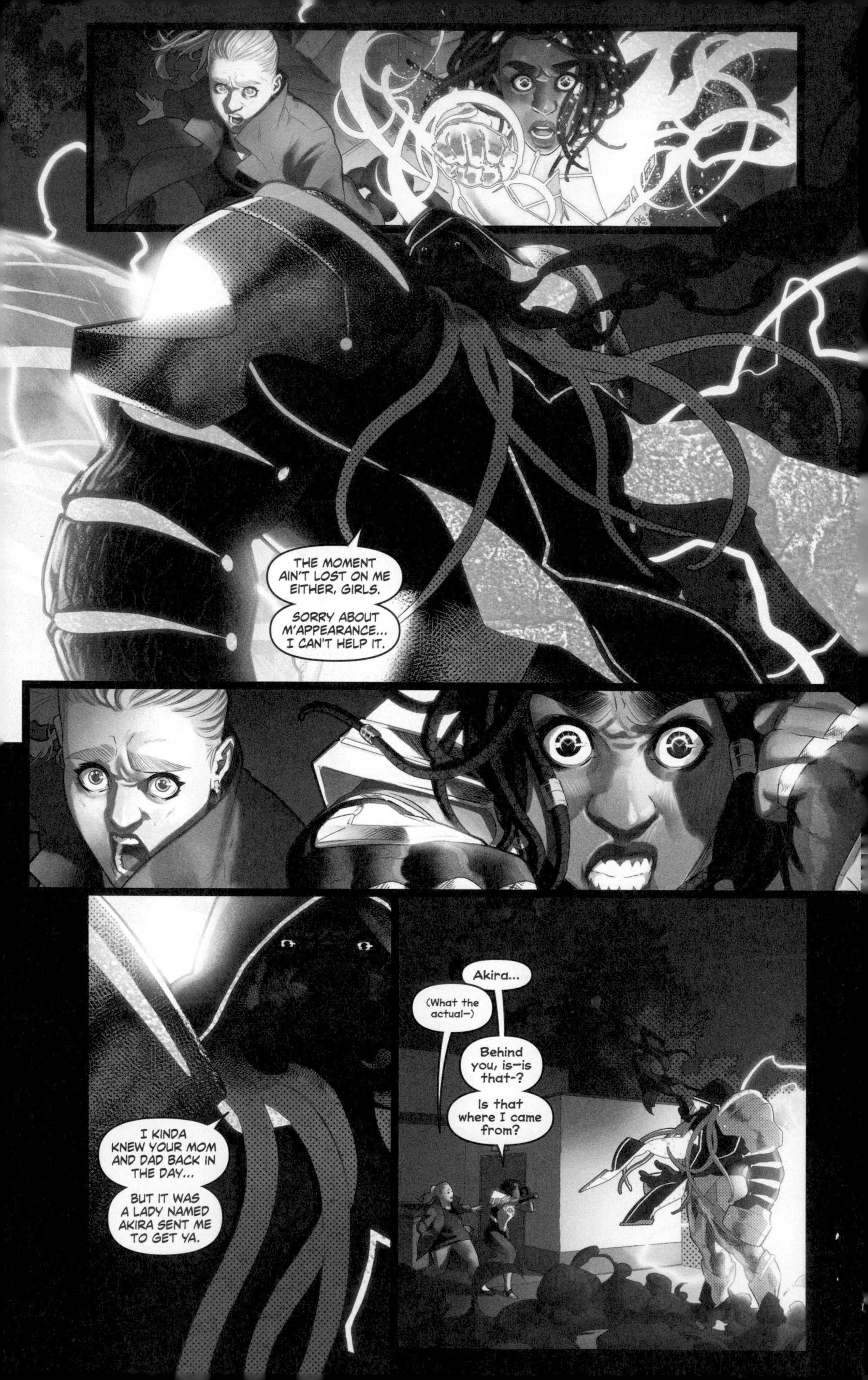
THE MOMENT AIN'T LOST ON ME EITHER, GIRLS.
SORRY ABOUT M'APPEARANCE... I CAN'T HELP IT.
I KINDA KNEW YOUR MOM AND DAD BACK IN THE DAY...
BUT IT WAS A LADY NAMED AKIRA SENT ME TO GET YA.
Akira...
(What the actual—)
Behind you, is—is that-?
Is that where I came from?

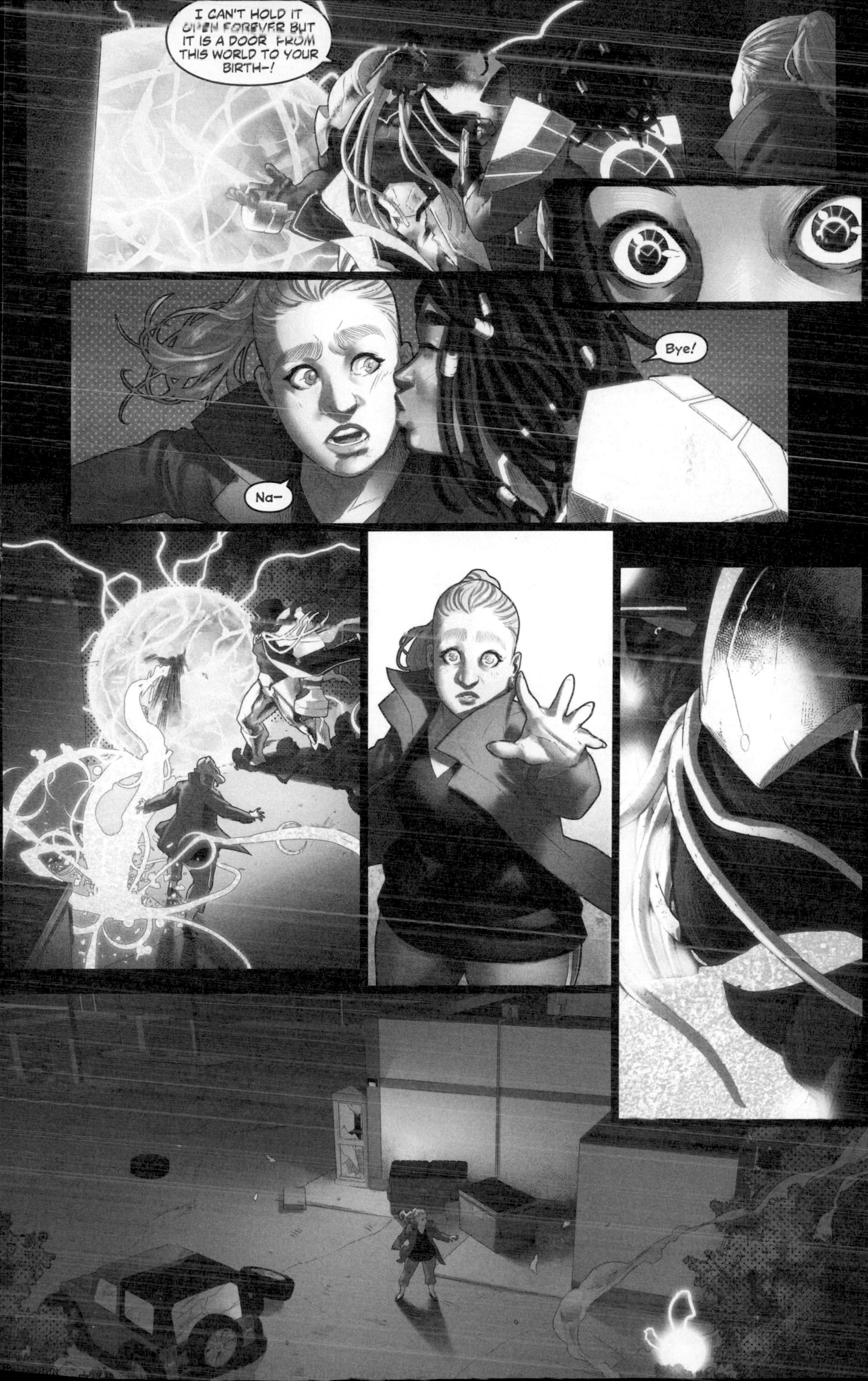
I CAN'T HOLD IT OPEN FOREVER BUT IT IS A DOOR FROM THIS WORLD TO YOUR BIRTH-!
Bye!
Na-

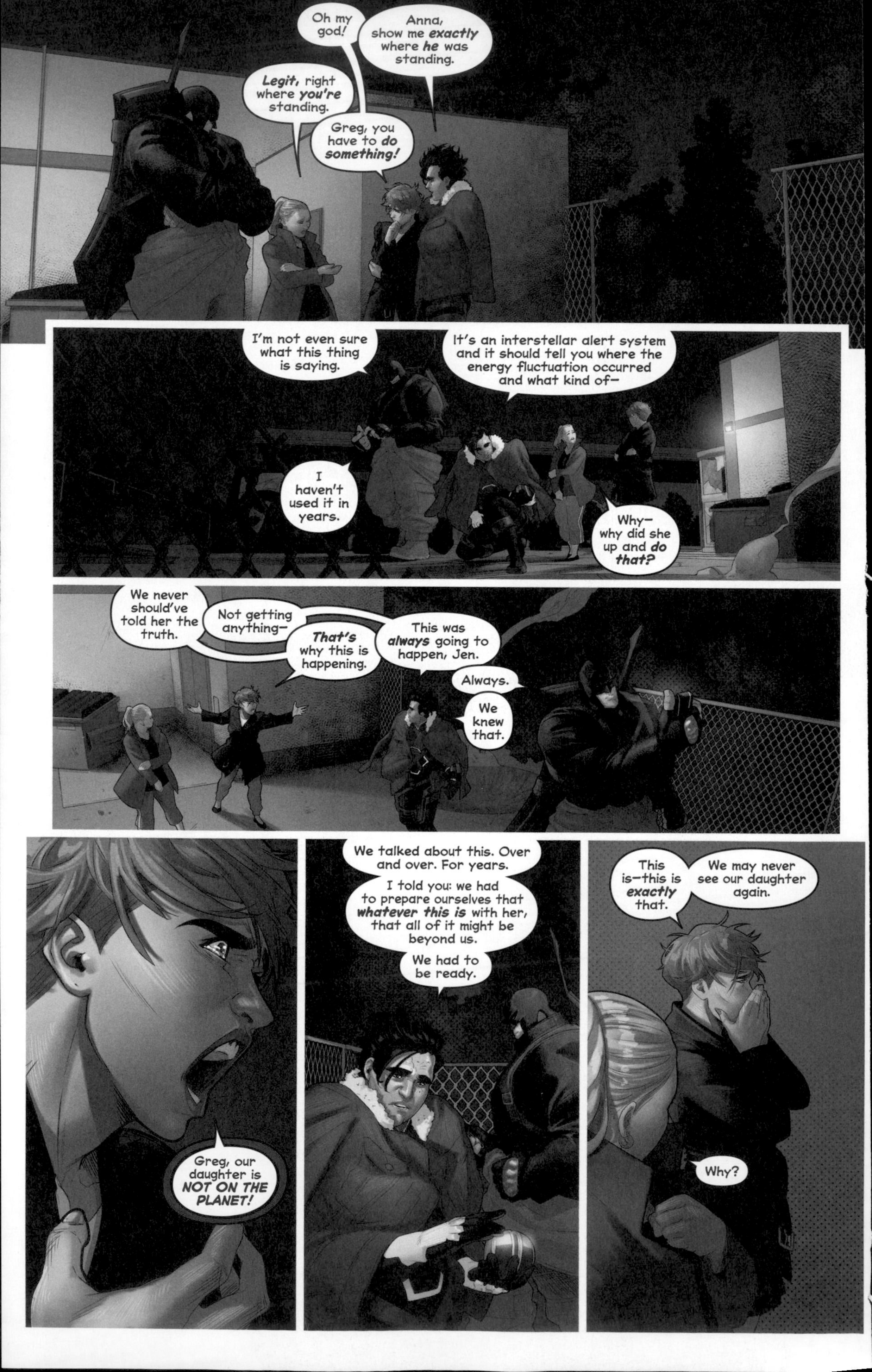
Oh my god!
Anna, show me exactly where he was standing.
Legit, right where you're standing.
Greg, you have to do something!
I'm not even sure what this thing is saying.
It's an interstellar alert system and it should tell you where the energy fluctuation occurred and what kind of—
I haven't used it in years.
Why— why did she up and do that?
We never should've told her the truth.
Not getting anything—
That's why this is happening.
This was always going to happen, Jen.
Always.
We knew that.
Greg, our daughter is NOT ON THE PLANET!
We talked about this. Over and over. For years.
I told you: we had to prepare ourselves that whatever this is with her, that all of it might be beyond us.
We had to be ready.
This is—this is exactly that.
We may never see our daughter again.
Why?

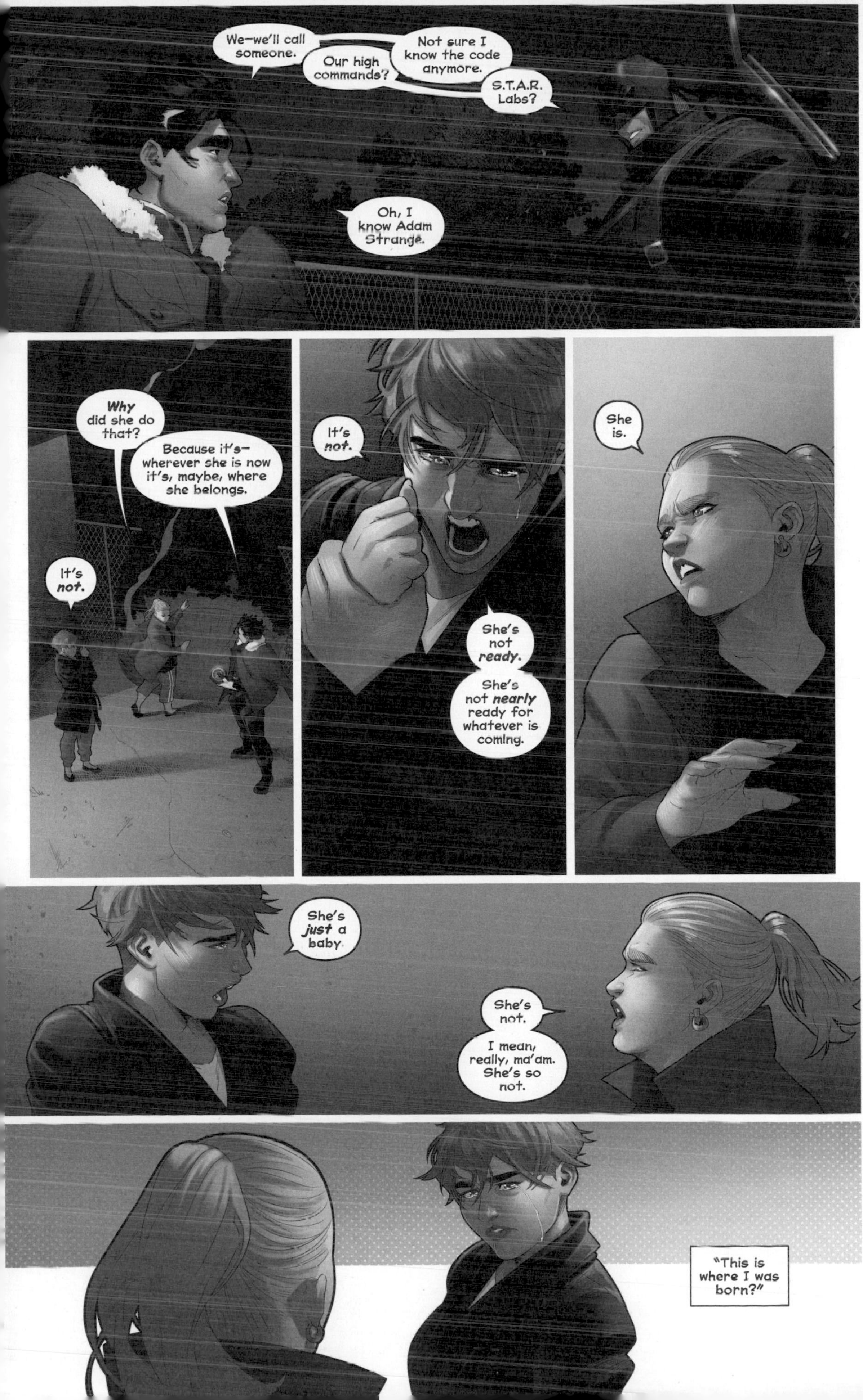
We–we'll call someone.
Our high commands?
Not sure I know the code anymore.
S.T.A.R. Labs?
Oh, I know Adam Strange.
Why did she do that?
Because it's– wherever she is now it's, maybe, where she belongs.
It's not.
It's not.
She's not ready.
She's not nearly ready for whatever is coming.
She is.
She's just a baby.
She's not.
I mean, really, ma'am. She's so not.
"This is where I was born?"

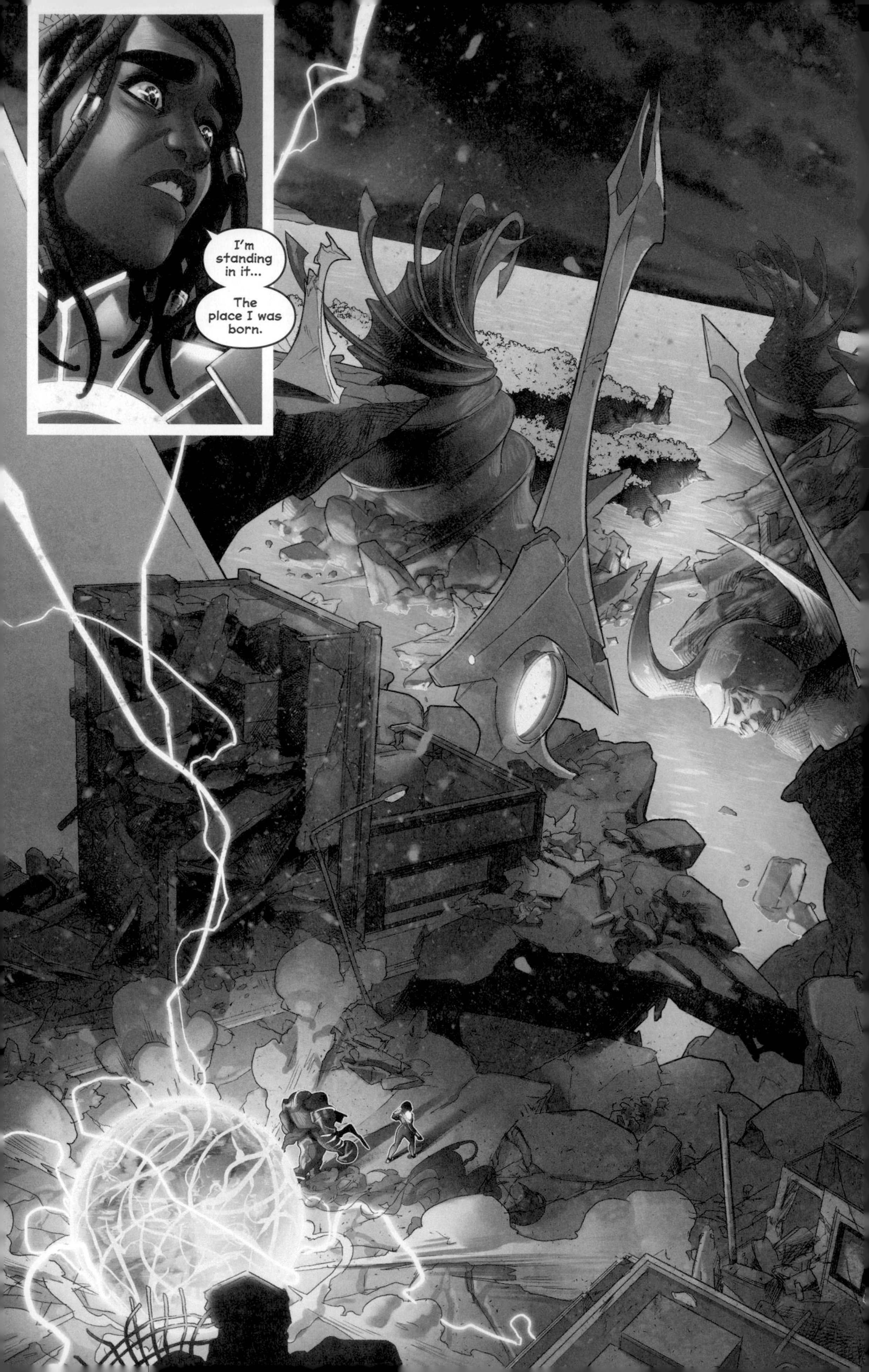
I'm standing in it...
The place I was born.

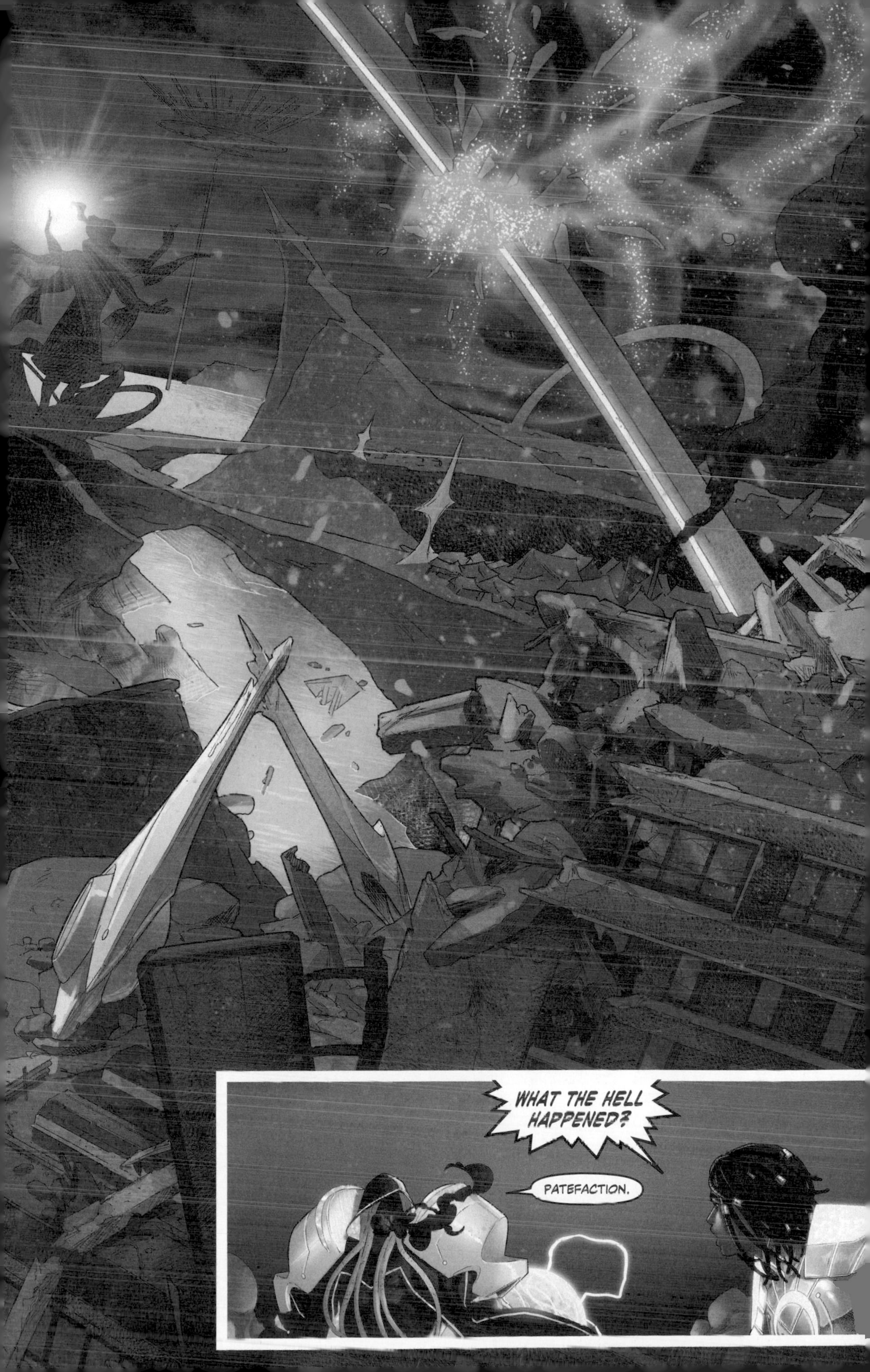
WHAT THE HELL HAPPENED?
PATEFACTION.

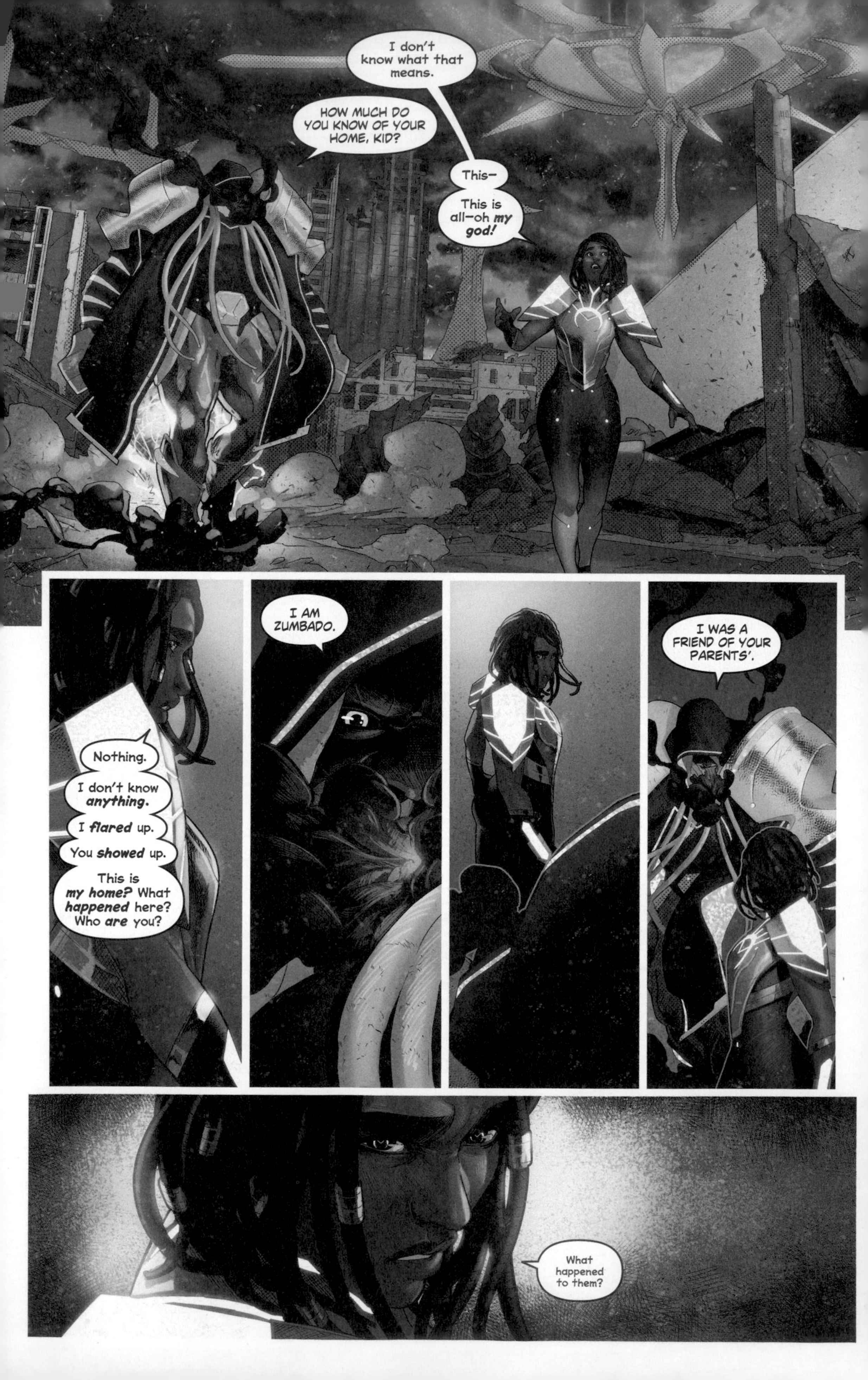

HOW MUCH DO YOU KNOW OF YOUR HOME, KID?
I don't know what that means.
This—
This is all—oh *my god!*
Nothing.
I don't know *anything.*
I *flared* up.
You *showed* up.
This is *my home?* What *happened* here? Who *are* you?
I AM ZUMBADO.
I WAS A FRIEND OF YOUR PARENTS'.
What happened to them?

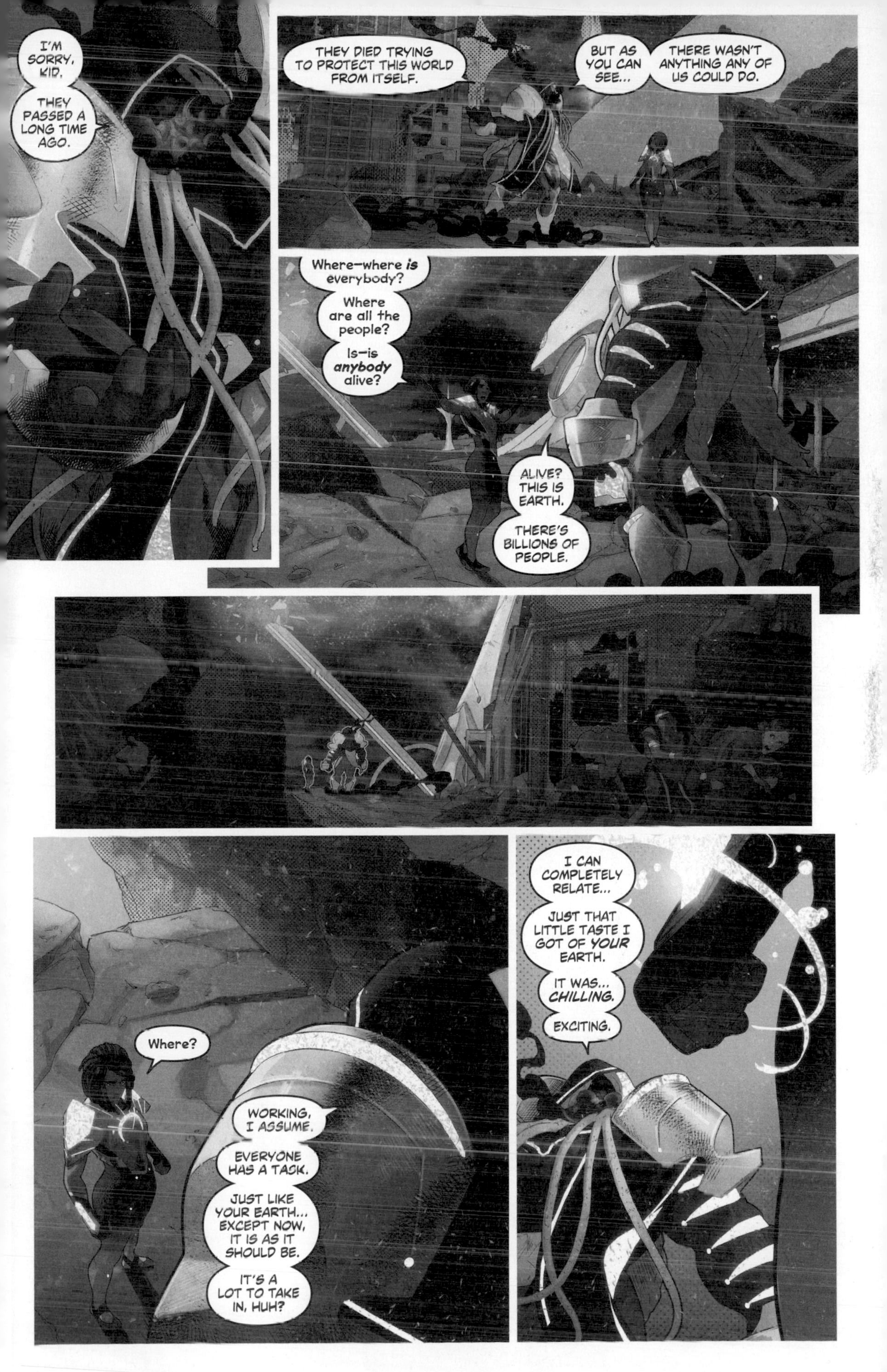
I'M SORRY, KID.
THEY PASSED A LONG TIME AGO.
THEY DIED TRYING TO PROTECT THIS WORLD FROM ITSELF.
BUT AS YOU CAN SEE...
THERE WASN'T ANYTHING ANY OF US COULD DO.
Where—where *is* everybody?
Where are all the people?
Is—is *anybody* alive?
ALIVE? THIS IS EARTH.
THERE'S BILLIONS OF PEOPLE.
Where?
WORKING, I ASSUME.
EVERYONE HAS A TASK.
JUST LIKE YOUR EARTH... EXCEPT NOW, IT IS AS IT SHOULD BE.
IT'S A LOT TO TAKE IN, HUH?
I CAN COMPLETELY RELATE...
JUST THAT LITTLE TASTE I GOT OF *YOUR* EARTH.
IT WAS... *CHILLING*.
EXCITING.

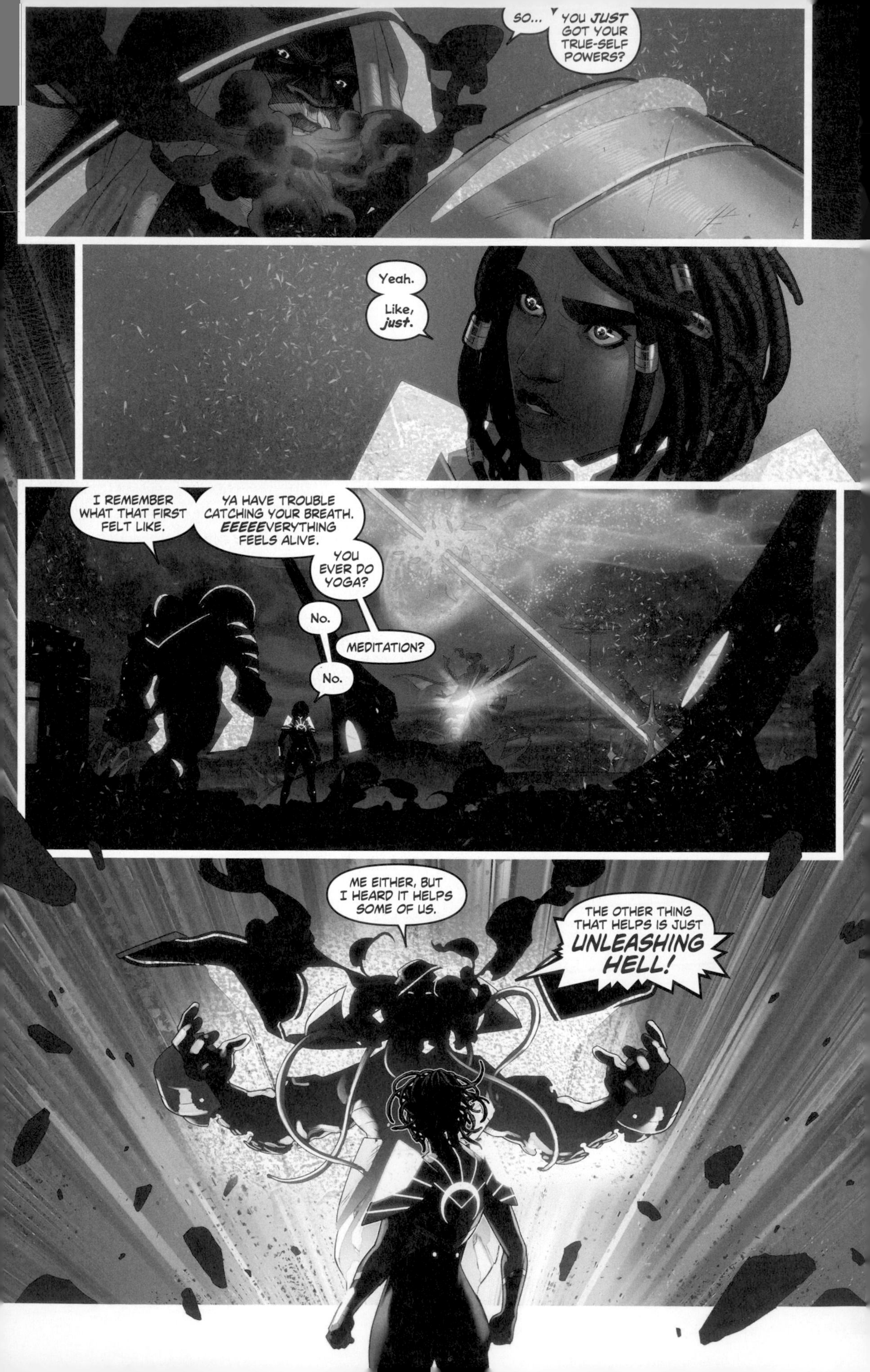
SO...
YOU JUST GOT YOUR TRUE-SELF POWERS?
Yeah.
Like, just.
I REMEMBER WHAT THAT FIRST FELT LIKE.
YA HAVE TROUBLE CATCHING YOUR BREATH. EEEEEVERYTHING FEELS ALIVE.
YOU EVER DO YOGA?
No.
MEDITATION?
No.
ME EITHER, BUT I HEARD IT HELPS SOME OF US.
THE OTHER THING THAT HELPS IS JUST UNLEASHING HELL!

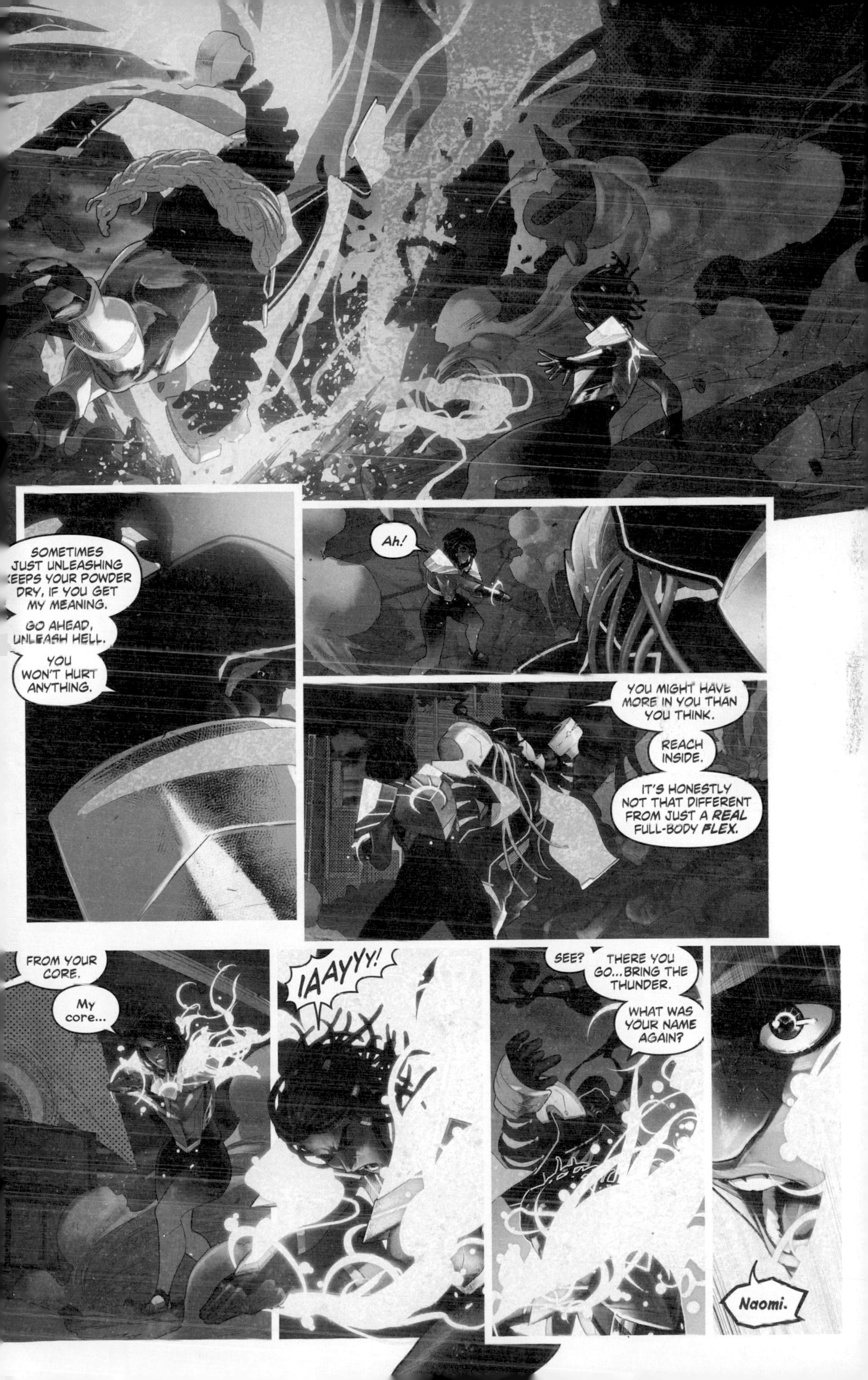
SOMETIMES JUST UNLEASHING KEEPS YOUR POWDER DRY, IF YOU GET MY MEANING.
GO AHEAD, UNLEASH HELL.
YOU WON'T HURT ANYTHING.
Ah!
YOU MIGHT HAVE MORE IN YOU THAN YOU THINK.
REACH INSIDE.
IT'S HONESTLY NOT THAT DIFFERENT FROM JUST A REAL FULL-BODY FLEX.
FROM YOUR CORE.
My core...
IAAYYY!
SEE?
THERE YOU GO...BRING THE THUNDER.
WHAT WAS YOUR NAME AGAIN?
Naomi.

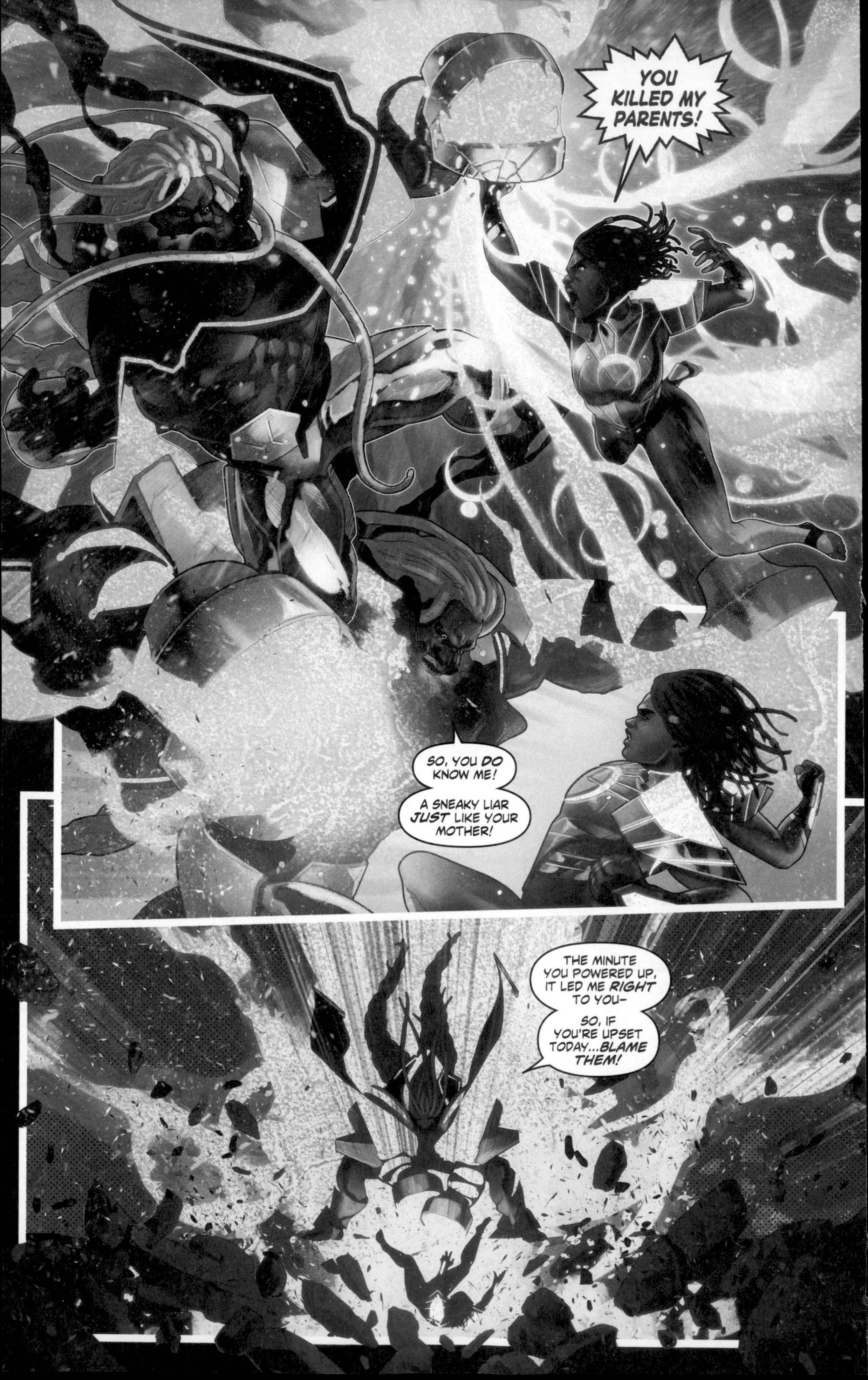
YOU KILLED MY PARENTS!
SO, YOU DO KNOW ME!
A SNEAKY LIAR JUST LIKE YOUR MOTHER!
THE MINUTE YOU POWERED UP, IT LED ME RIGHT TO YOU–
SO, IF YOU'RE UPSET TODAY...BLAME THEM!

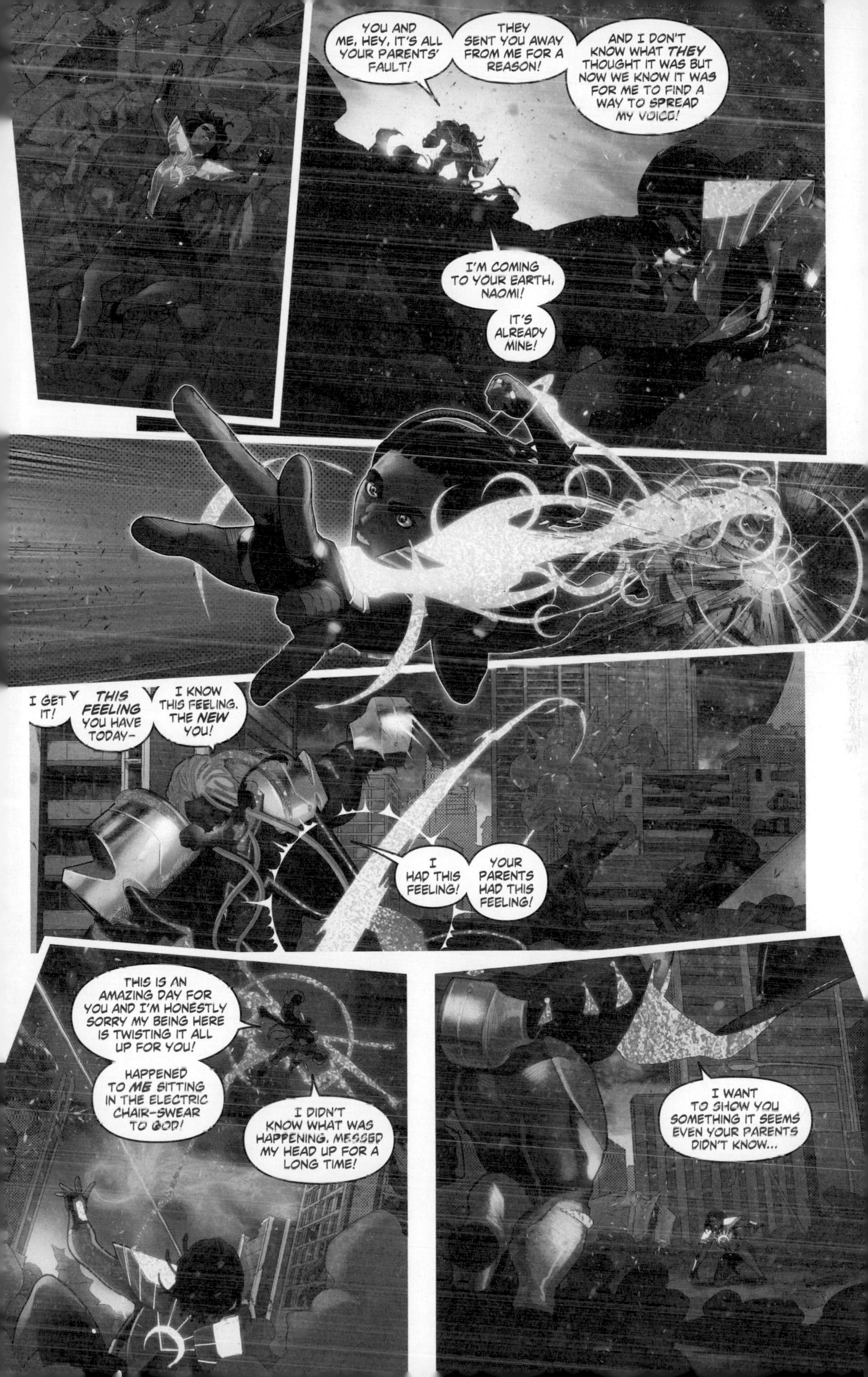
YOU AND ME, HEY, IT'S ALL YOUR PARENTS' FAULT!
THEY SENT YOU AWAY FROM ME FOR A REASON!
AND I DON'T KNOW WHAT THEY THOUGHT IT WAS BUT NOW WE KNOW IT WAS FOR ME TO FIND A WAY TO SPREAD MY VOICE!
I'M COMING TO YOUR EARTH, NAOMI!
IT'S ALREADY MINE!
I GET IT!
THIS FEELING YOU HAVE TODAY–
I KNOW THIS FEELING. THE NEW YOU!
I HAD THIS FEELING!
YOUR PARENTS HAD THIS FEELING!
THIS IS AN AMAZING DAY FOR YOU AND I'M HONESTLY SORRY MY BEING HERE IS TWISTING IT ALL UP FOR YOU!
HAPPENED TO ME SITTING IN THE ELECTRIC CHAIR–SWEAR TO GOD!
I DIDN'T KNOW WHAT WAS HAPPENING. MESSED MY HEAD UP FOR A LONG TIME!
I WANT TO SHOW YOU SOMETHING IT SEEMS EVEN YOUR PARENTS DIDN'T KNOW...

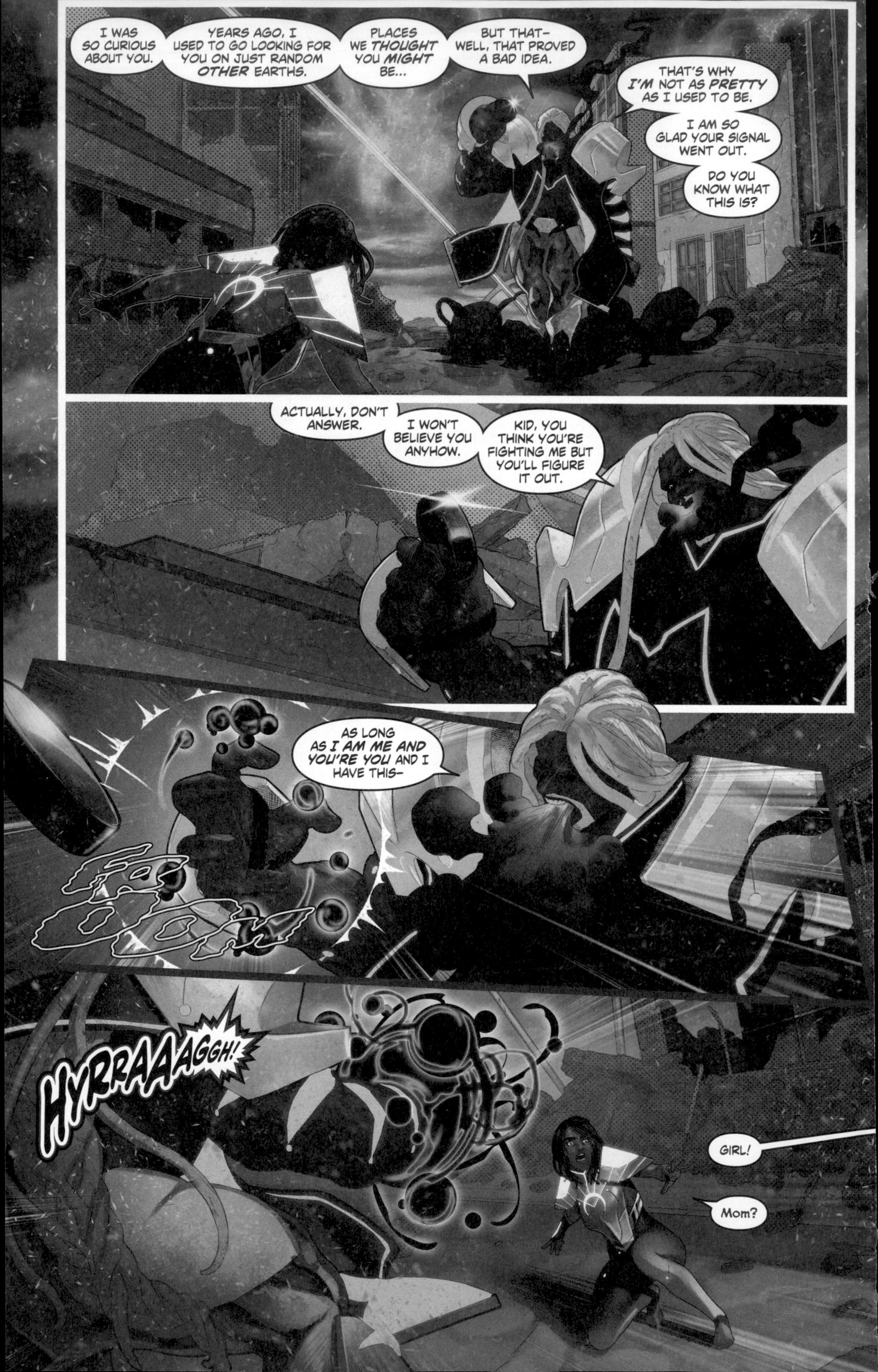
I WAS SO CURIOUS ABOUT YOU.
YEARS AGO, I USED TO GO LOOKING FOR YOU ON JUST RANDOM *OTHER* EARTHS.
PLACES WE *THOUGHT* YOU *MIGHT* BE...
BUT THAT-WELL, THAT PROVED A BAD IDEA.
THAT'S WHY *I'M* NOT AS *PRETTY* AS I USED TO BE.
I AM SO GLAD YOUR SIGNAL WENT OUT.
DO YOU KNOW WHAT THIS IS?
ACTUALLY, DON'T ANSWER.
I WON'T BELIEVE YOU ANYHOW.
KID, YOU THINK YOU'RE FIGHTING ME BUT YOU'LL FIGURE IT OUT.
AS LONG AS *I AM ME AND YOU'RE YOU* AND I HAVE THIS-
HYRRAAAAGGH!
GIRL!
Mom?

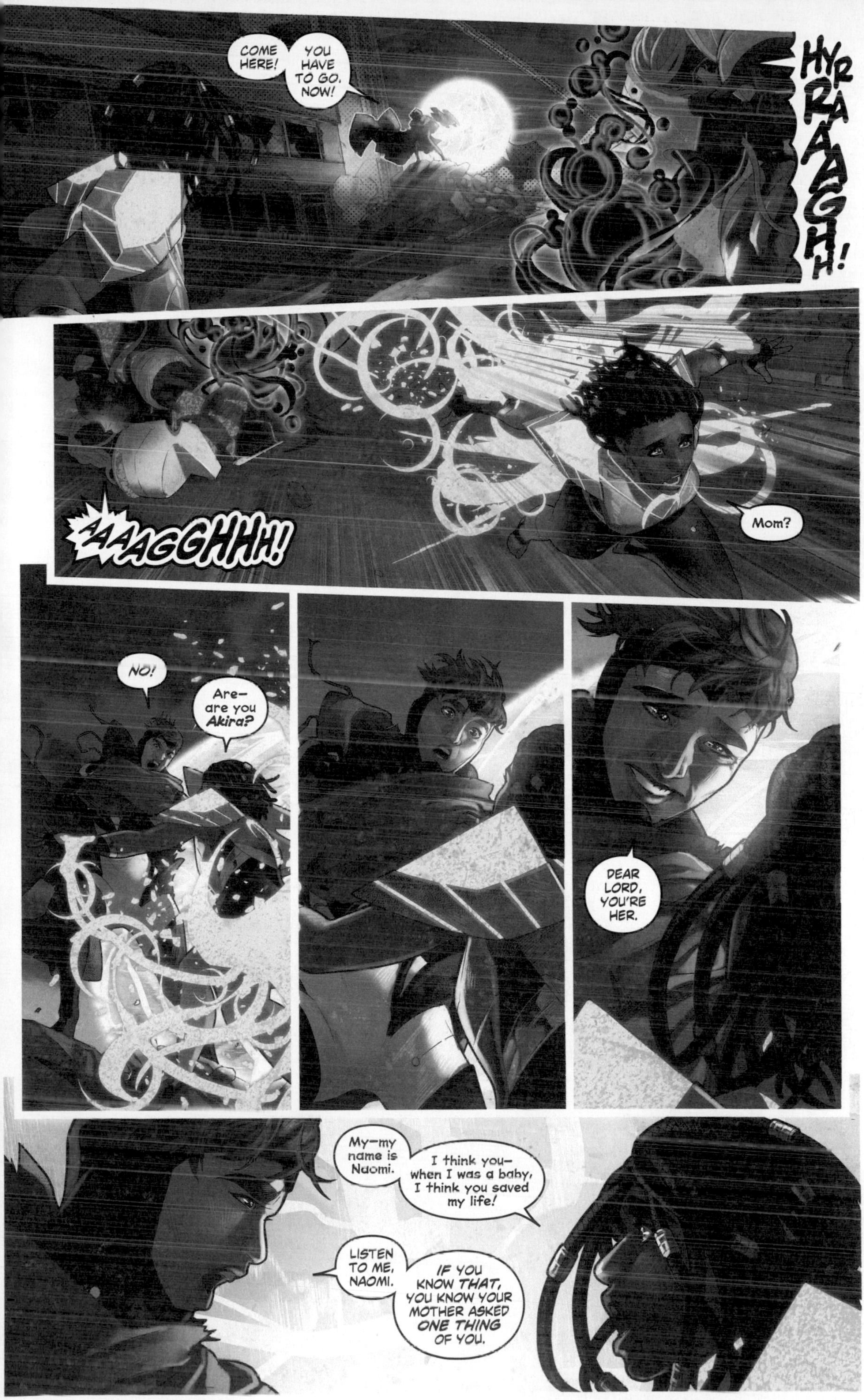
COME HERE!
YOU HAVE TO GO. NOW!
HYRRAAAGHH!
AAAAGGHHH!
Mom?
NO!
Are— are you Akira?
DEAR LORD, YOU'RE HER.
My—my name is Naomi.
I think you— when I was a baby, I think you saved my life!
LISTEN TO ME, NAOMI.
IF YOU KNOW THAT, YOU KNOW YOUR MOTHER ASKED ONE THING OF YOU.

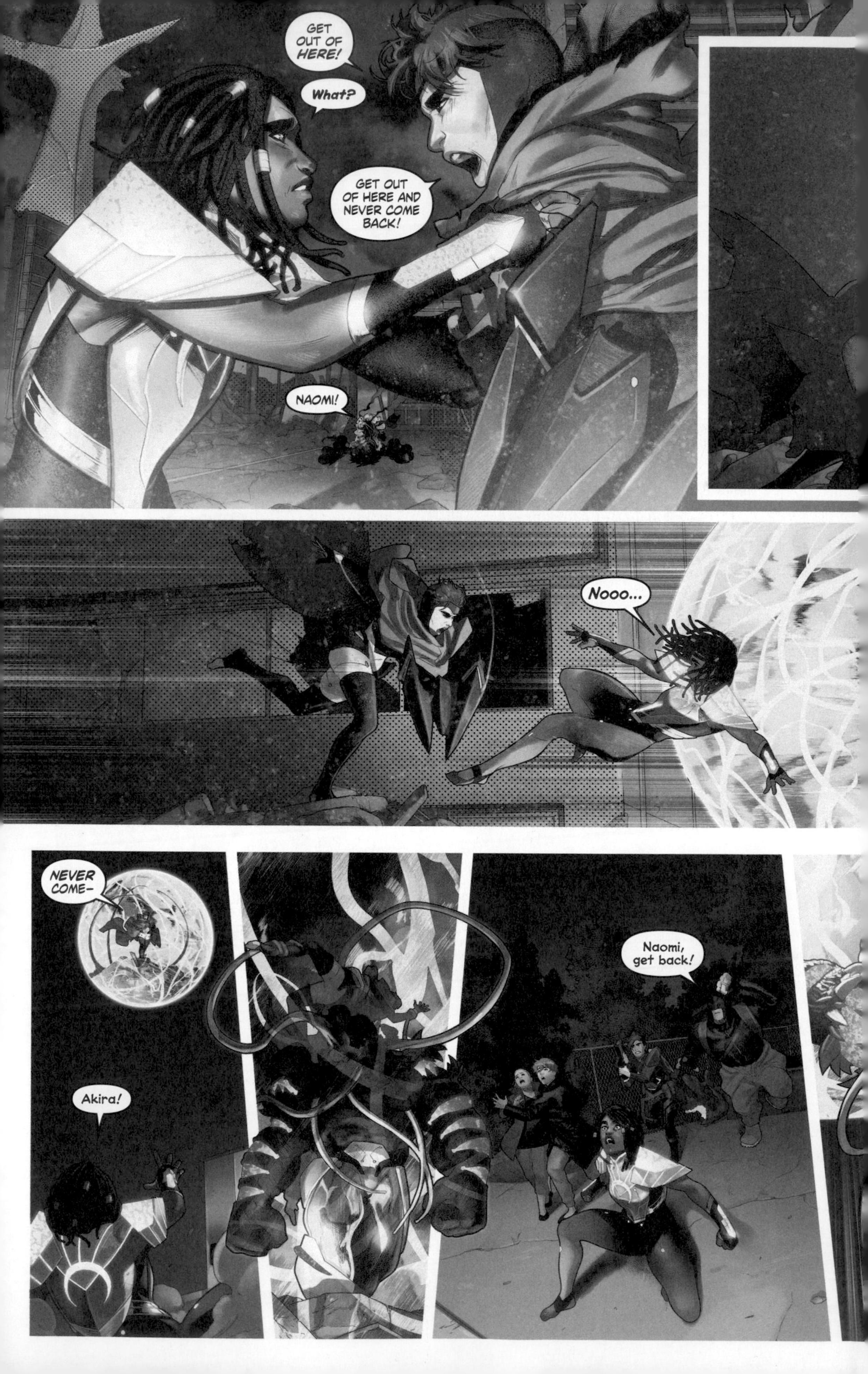
GET OUT OF HERE!
What?
GET OUT OF HERE AND NEVER COME BACK!
NAOMI!
Nooo...
NEVER COME-
Akira!
Naomi, get back!

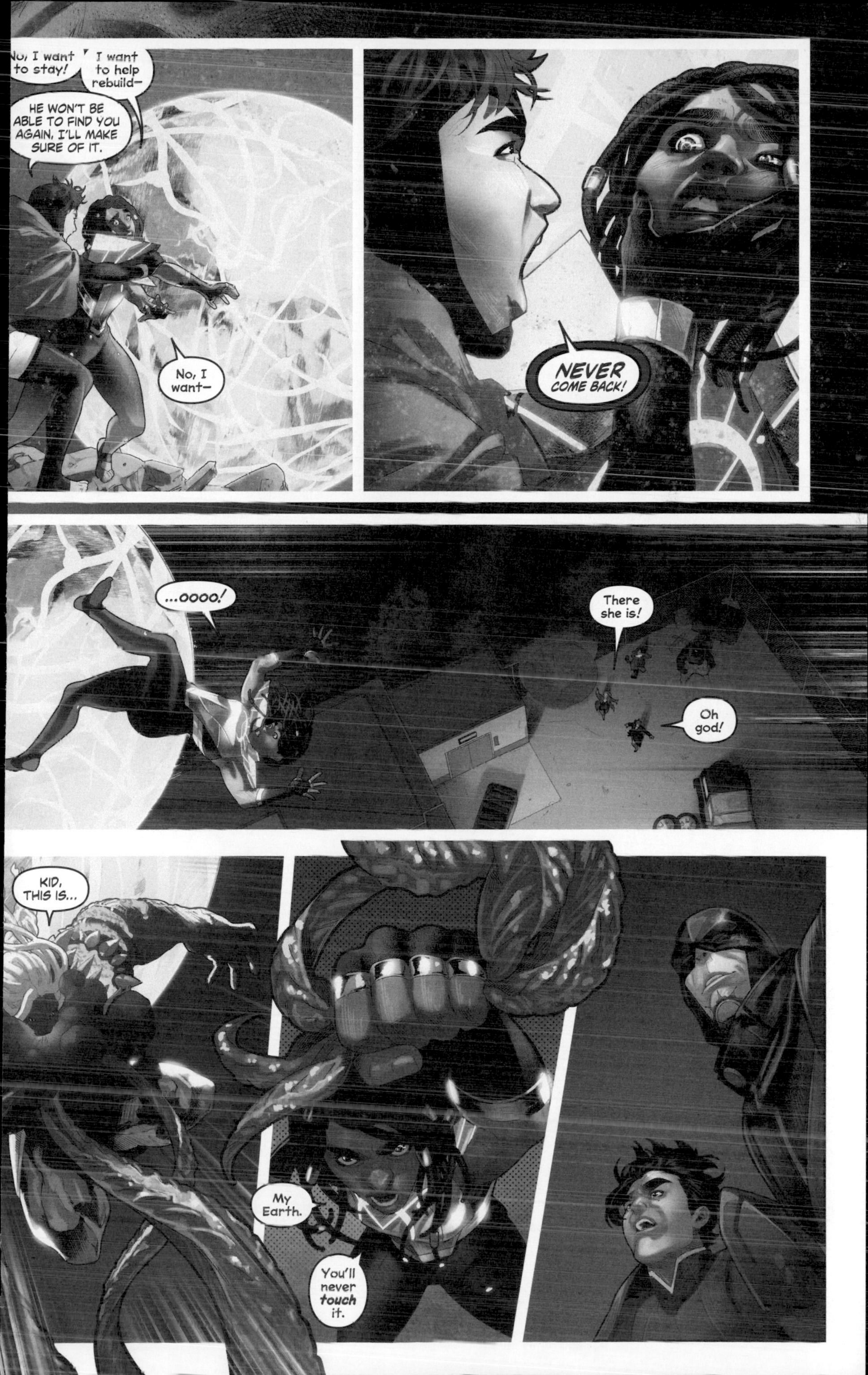
No, I want to stay!
I want to help rebuild—
HE WON'T BE ABLE TO FIND YOU AGAIN, I'LL MAKE SURE OF IT.
No, I want—
NEVER COME BACK!
...oooo!
There she is!
Oh god!
KID, THIS IS...
My Earth.
You'll never touch it.

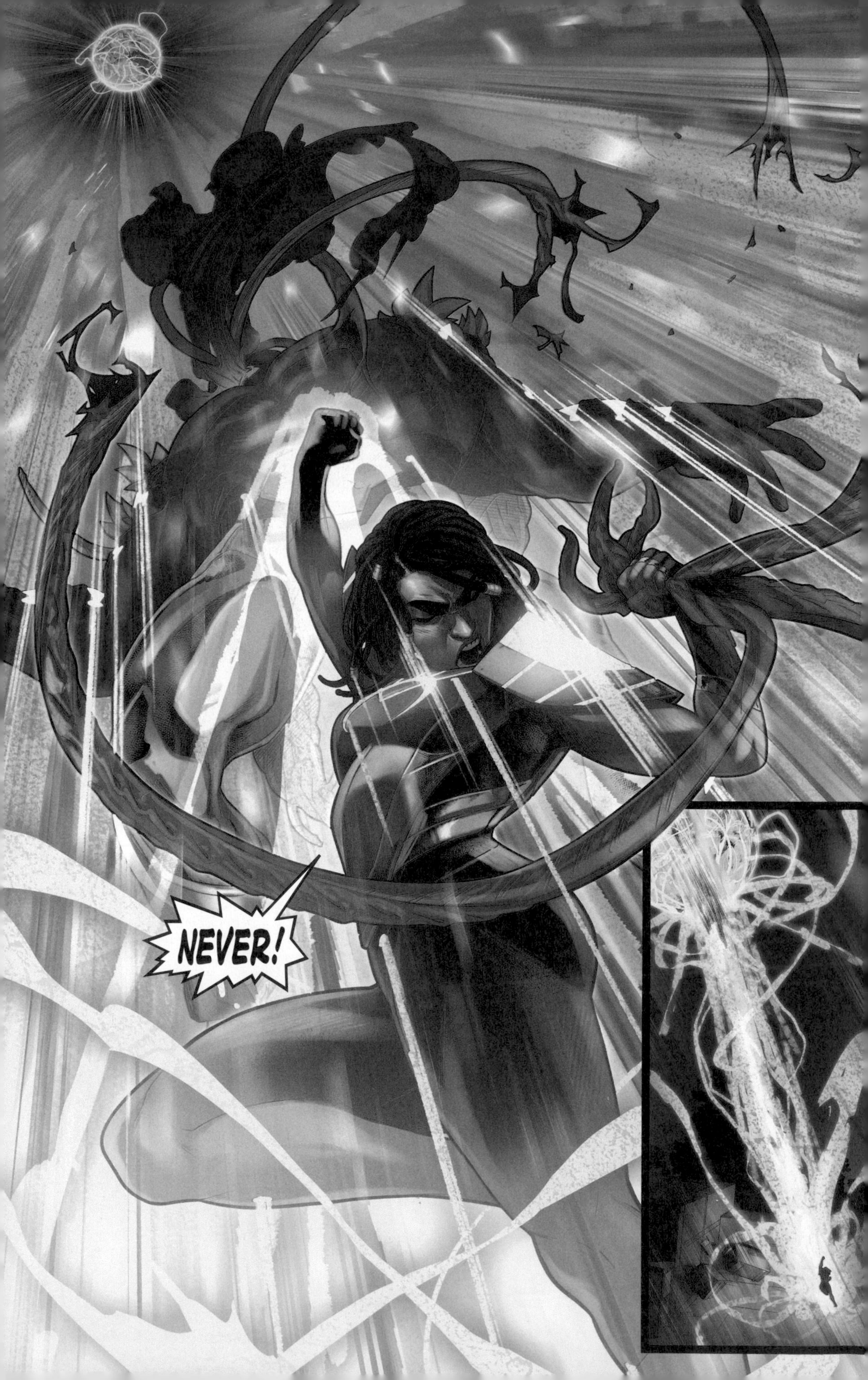
NEVER!

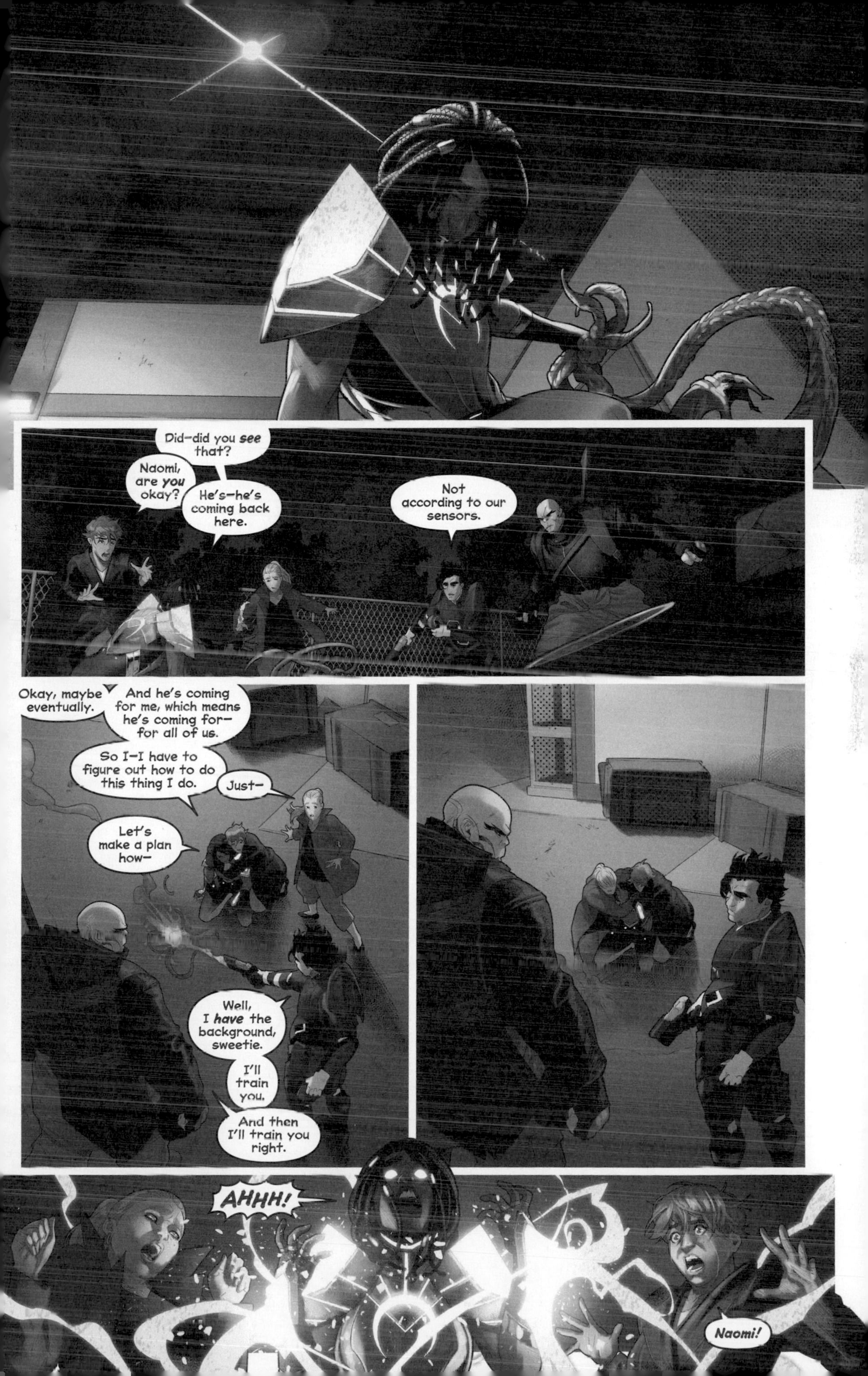

Did-did you *see* that?
Naomi, are *you* okay?
He's—he's coming back here.
Not according to our sensors.
Okay, maybe eventually.
And he's coming for me, which means he's coming for—for all of us.
So I—I have to figure out how to do this thing I do.
Just—
Let's make a plan how—
Well, I *have* the background, sweetie.
I'll train you.
And then I'll train you right.
AHHH!
Naomi!

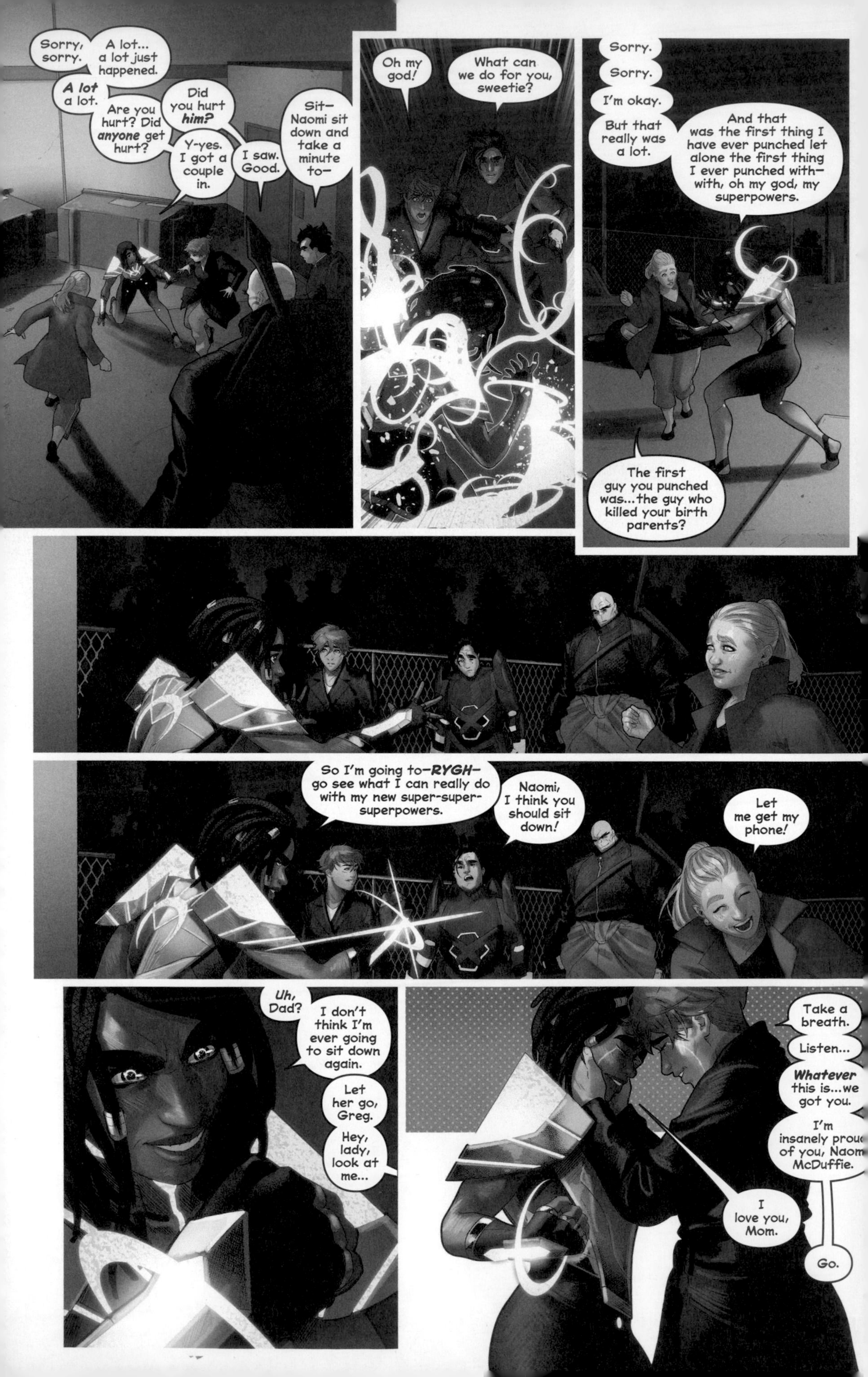

Sorry, sorry.
A lot... a lot just happened.
A lot a lot.
Are you hurt? Did anyone get hurt?
Y-yes. I got a couple in.
Did you hurt him?
I saw. Good.
Sit— Naomi sit down and take a minute to—
Oh my god!
What can we do for you, sweetie?
Sorry.
Sorry.
I'm okay.
But that really was a lot.
And that was the first thing I have ever punched let alone the first thing I ever punched with— with, oh my god, my superpowers.
The first guy you punched was...the guy who killed your birth parents?
So I'm going to—RYGH—go see what I can really do with my new super-super-superpowers.
Naomi, I think you should sit down!
Let me get my phone!
Uh, Dad?
I don't think I'm ever going to sit down again.
Let her go, Greg.
Hey, lady, look at me...
Take a breath.
Listen...
Whatever this is...we got you.
I'm insanely proud of you, Naomi McDuffie.
I love you, Mom.
Go.

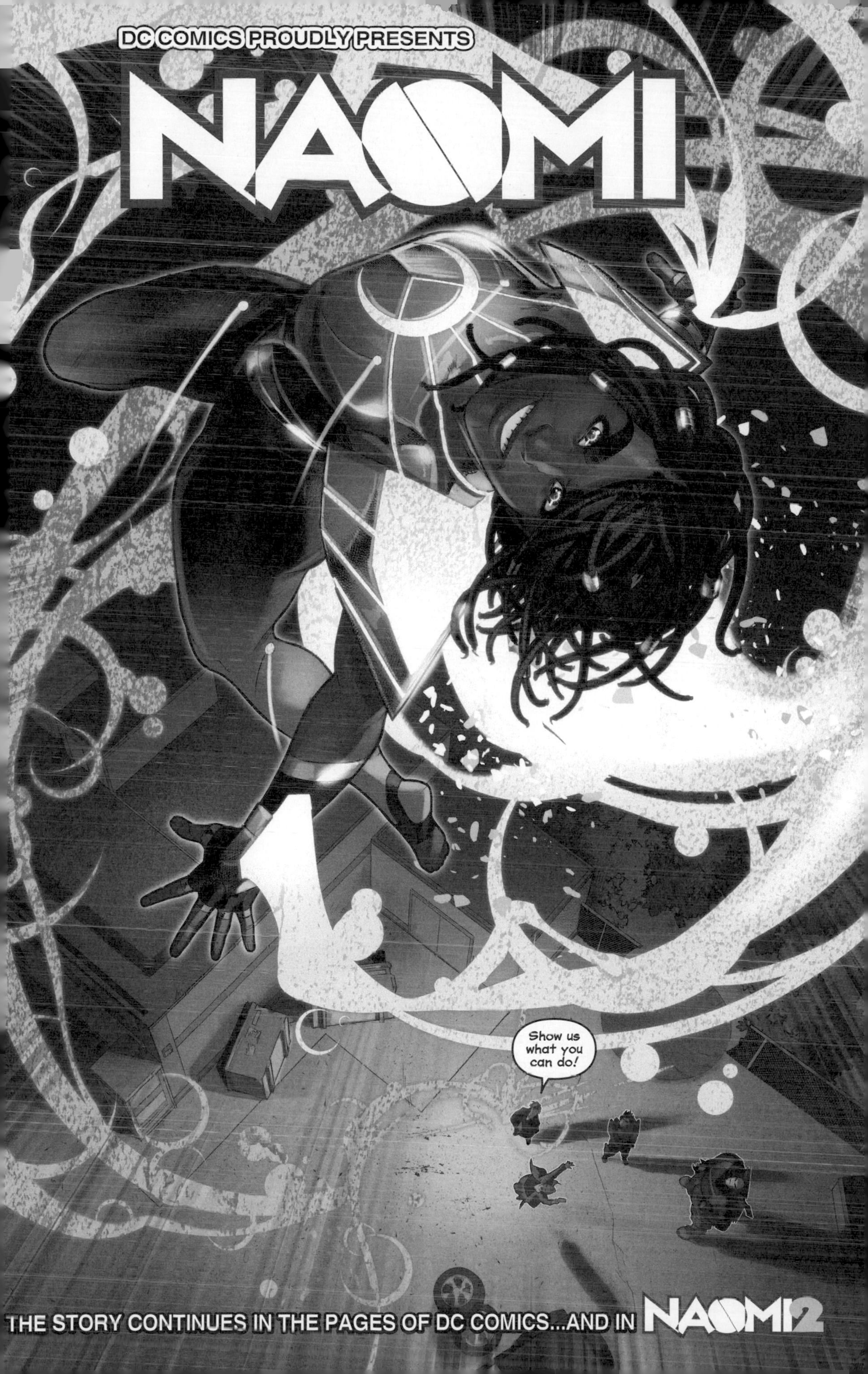
DC COMICS PROUDLY PRESENTS
NAOMI
Show us what you can do!
THE STORY CONTINUES IN THE PAGES OF DC COMICS...AND IN NAOMI 2

AFTERWORD

Hi! I'm Brian Bendis. I'm one of the co-creators of *Naomi*, and I am writing this afterword behind my fellow co-creators' backs. As I type, neither David nor Jamal know that I'm writing this. I just wanted a little me-and-you time to talk about...them.

So David and I have been friends for a long time. When the Bendi first moved to Portland in the early 2000s, David and I met and quickly became friends. I was already reading his often-awesome underground blaxploitation zine *BodAzz MoFo*, as it had made its way to a record store that I frequented back in Cleveland. (In the '90s there were record stores that you could frequent. Check out the movie *High Fidelity*. It was just like that.)

In Portland, David was the local movie reviewer for the free rock 'n' roll newspaper. David would often invite me to the advance screenings with him. We had a lot of fun, and from there we built our friendship on a shared love of story and craft. I talk about this publicly anywhere I can, but David was a big part of the success of Miles Morales. David was a helping hand and a kind and honest sounding board. The pop culture phenomenon of Miles is because of David's generous help and honesty.

From there, I eventually asked him to come teach with me. I had been teaching college writing for a few years, but with the growing number of children in my house and the shocking developments with some of my comics being turned into TV shows and movies, I was worried I wasn't always going to make it to class. As David and I were so similar in temperament and passion about certain things, I thought he would be an excellent pinch hitter. (Also, writers need to get out of the house.)

As the years passed, the class became less about each of us tag-team teaching and more about two nerdy professors in a classroom holding court together.

It was during these sessions that David and I dug deeper into the structure of the hero's journey and the evolving modern version of it. I would look across the classroom and see David and think to myself, "He and I should be doing this, not just talking about it."

I had warned him that we were going to create something together.

Then I got this sweet deal at DC. And then I got real sick and almost went away. I don't love discussing this next part, but it's true, and it's a big part of the emotions on the pages you JUST read. Over a year ago I got really sick and I was told I wasn't gonna get better. David, like my other best friends, was right there. Right there.

It was during these hospital visits that we had the earliest discussions about what *Naomi* would be. David and I were going to create a character together that would reflect a lot of the truth of his growing up in Portland while at the same time speaking to the DC Universe in a new and exciting way. We didn't know her name or her powers, but we knew...*why*. Creating new things is REALLY hard, but knowing *why* early on is really...special. I sat in the hospital with the knowledge that I was never going to meet Naomi, and David was at my bedside as often as humanly possible.

But hey! Things kind of miraculously went the other way, and the very next week *Naomi* was born.

What I'm saying is, this book came out of...a lot of emotions. This book came out of a newfound lease on life and a newfound level of friendship and partnership that we didn't even know we had. And a lot of feelings about family!

Sorry to get so personal and emotional, but everything about creating *Naomi* was personal and emotional.

BUT! As well as I personally know David, that's as *little* as I still know Jamal—I know absolutely nothing about him other than there is nothing you can't throw at him. There is no panel or page he won't bring truth to. Jamal had some amazing choices in front of him, and he chose *Naomi*. In return, we did everything we could to make Naomi's journey something worth Jamal's immense talent. Thank you, Jamal!

Some of you might know that I have two adopted daughters. *Naomi* is not a direct reflection of them. Like other subjects in life, when you have something like adoption in your family, you might find yourself lucky enough to be surrounded by other families with their own similar but different stories and energies. Almost everyone involved in this book has a very special type of family.

So no, this story is not my daughters' story in disguise. My daughters know their stories and they can tell their stories one day in whatever shape or form they want. But the truth of adoption, the universal shared truth, has been such a big part of all of our lives that we wanted *Naomi* to be able to reflect it in a fun, true way. Of course, there have been so many orphans in comics. (What do Bruce Wayne, Clark Kent, and Peter Parker all have in common?) Naomi fits into a long tradition, but from her own unique family and perspective.

My daughter Sabrina did double-check about my human upbringing. It was a fair ask.

Although this is not the story of my daughters, they have spent a great deal of time discussing and building *Naomi* with us. They feel their connection to her. It was my daughter Tabatha who, having seen Jamal's first images of Naomi, pointed to me and said, "Thor!" I said, "What does that mean?" She replied, "How people feel when Thor walks in the room is how they should feel about Naomi." The end.

The fact is, *Naomi* became a major DC powerhouse because...yeah. Tabatha was right.

By now, David, Jamal, and I have had quite a few months of this book's runaway success to deal with, and we still haven't been able to process it. Multiple printings? Wow! We will never fully understand it other than realizing that we've had that great experience of loving something while doing it and then having the audience respond accordingly.

What an amazing experience this has been. I'm so glad we got to share this with you on numerous levels.

Please share this book with somebody who needs to spend some time with Naomi. That's why we made her. That's why she's here.

Thank you.

And hey, you know what's better than saying, "Welcome to *Naomi*!"?

Saying, "See you for Season Two!"

BENDIS!
Portland, Oregon | 2019

DRAWING FIRE

Character designs by Jamal Campbell

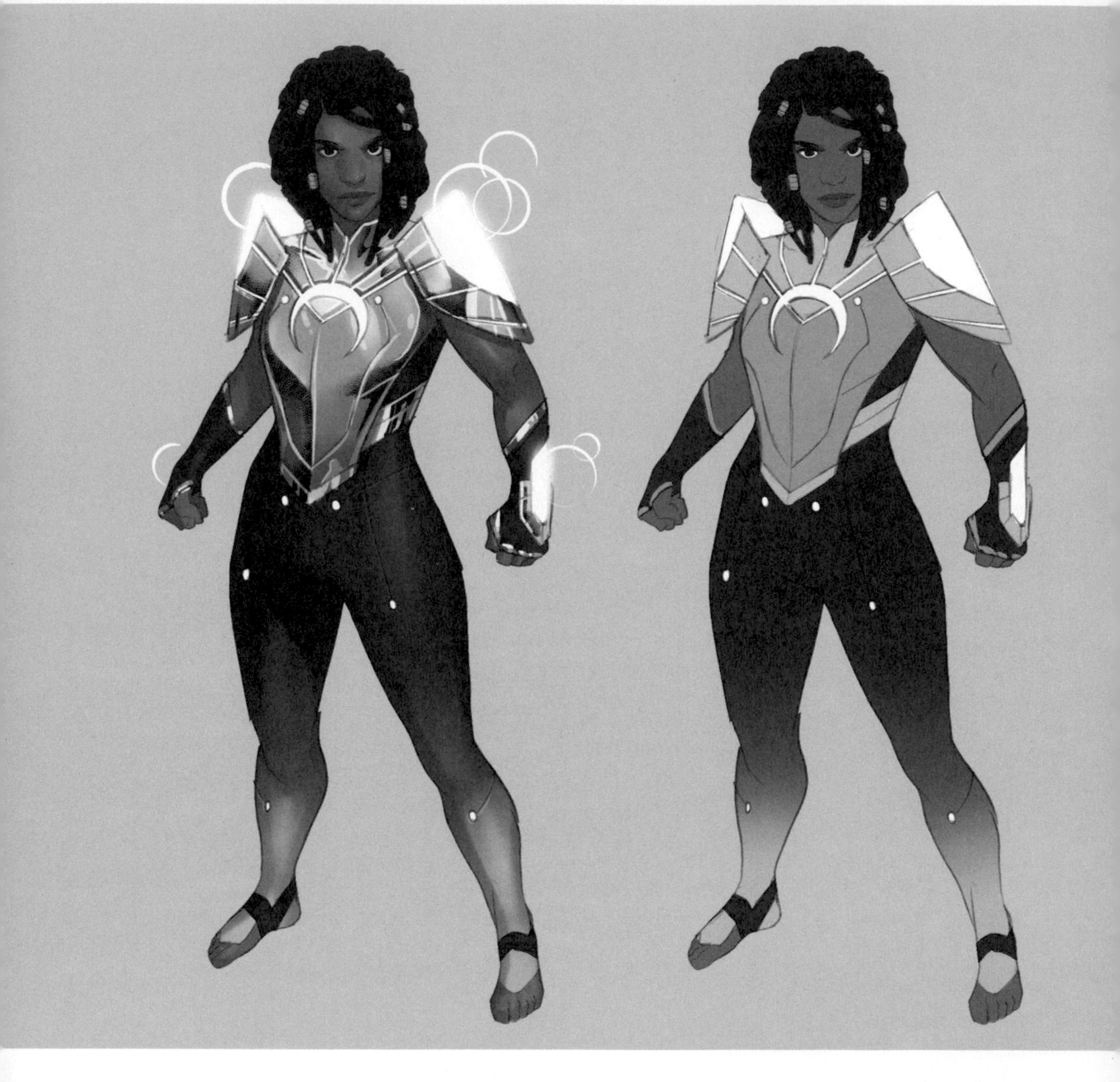

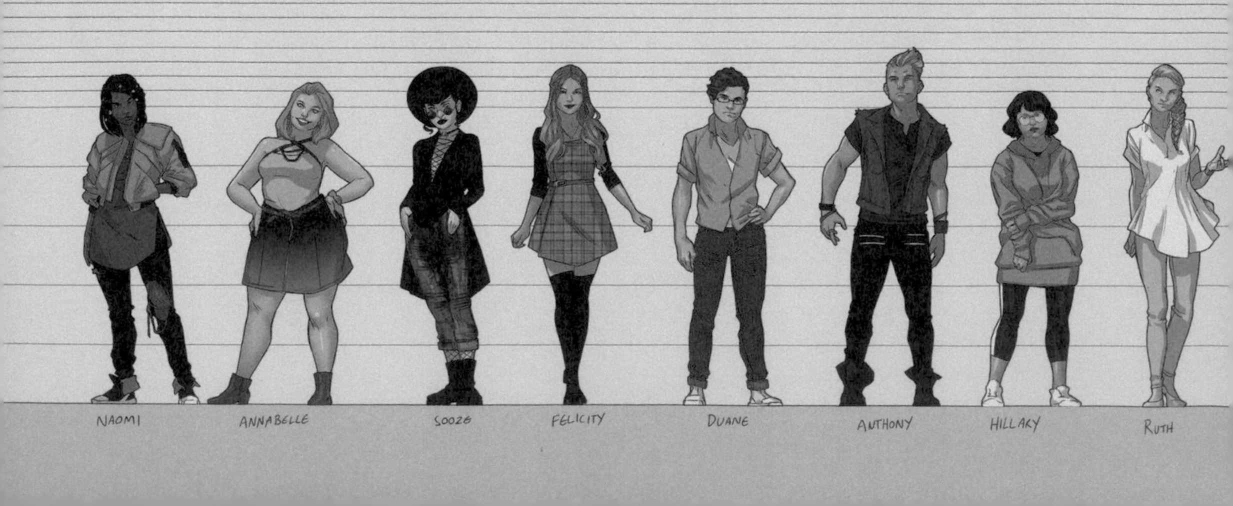
NAOMI
ANNABELLE
SOOZE
FELICITY
DUANE
ANTHONY
HILLARY
RUTH

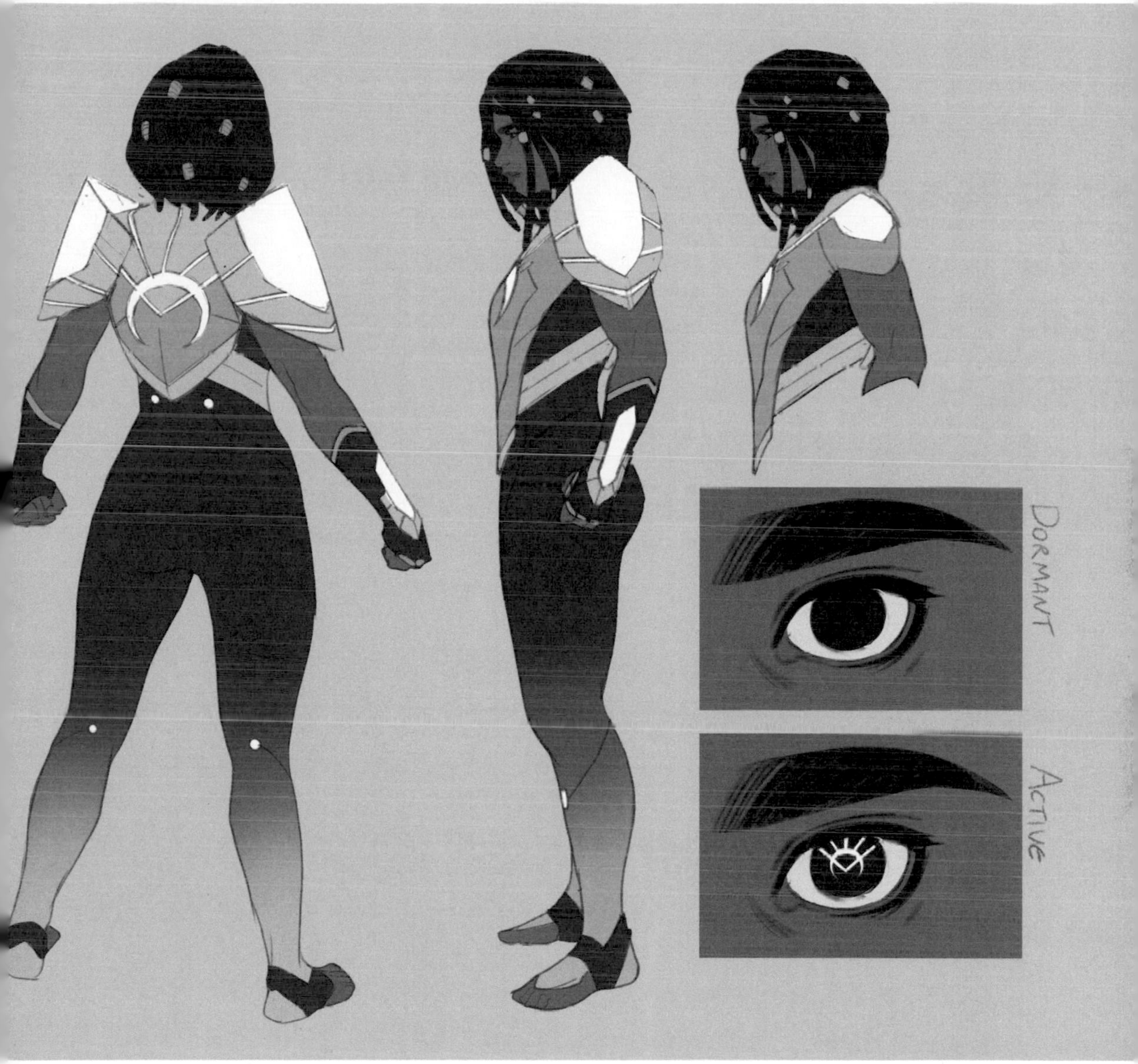
DORMANT
ACTIVE

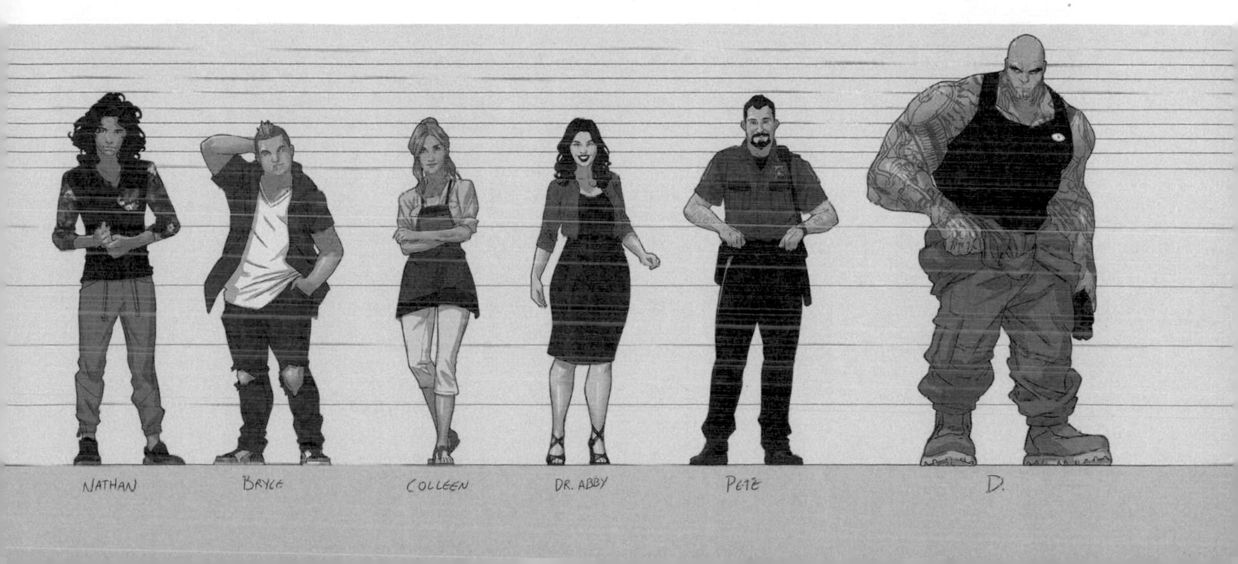
NATHAN
BRYCE
COLLEEN
DR. ABBY
PETE
D.

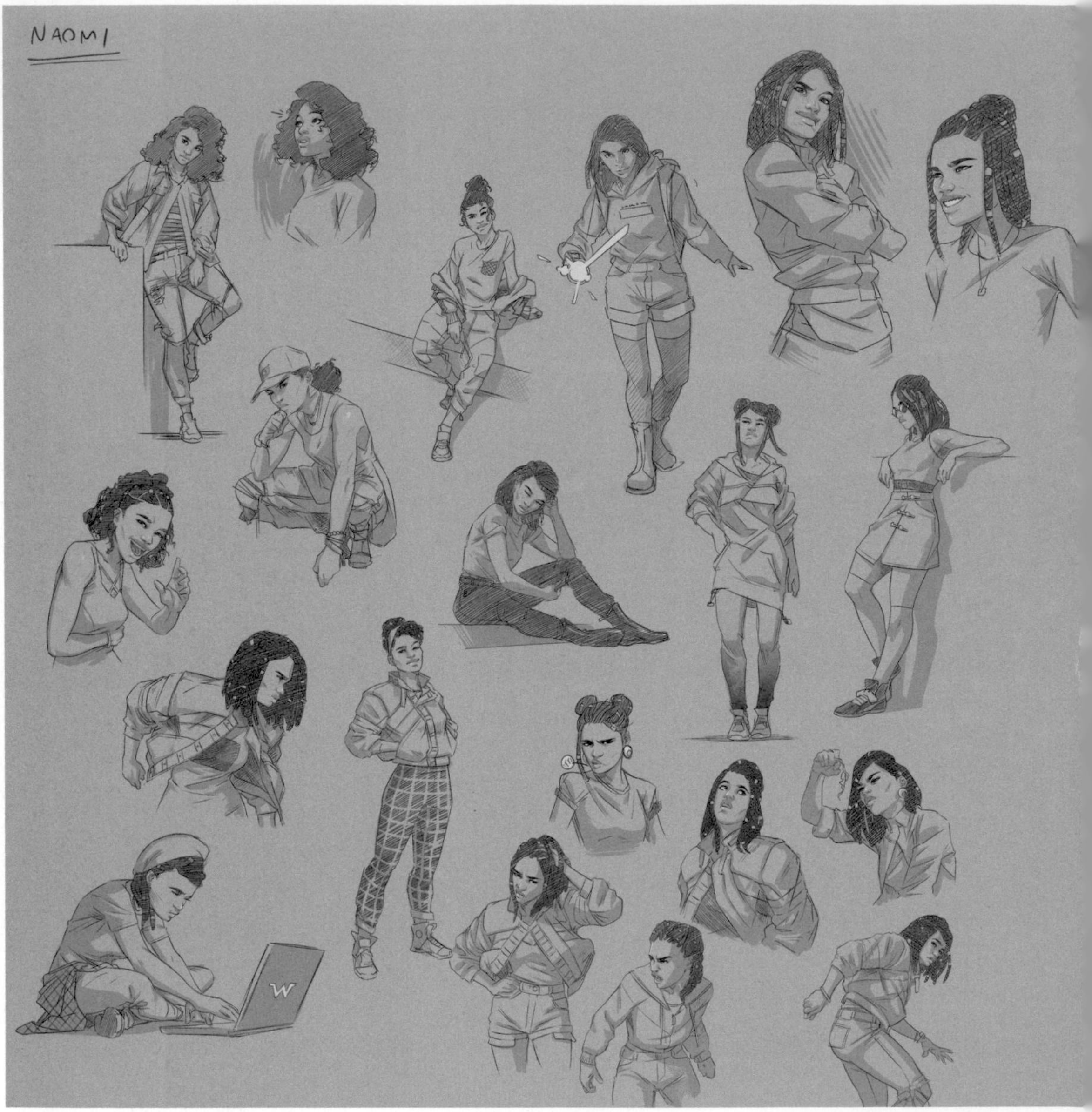
NAOMI

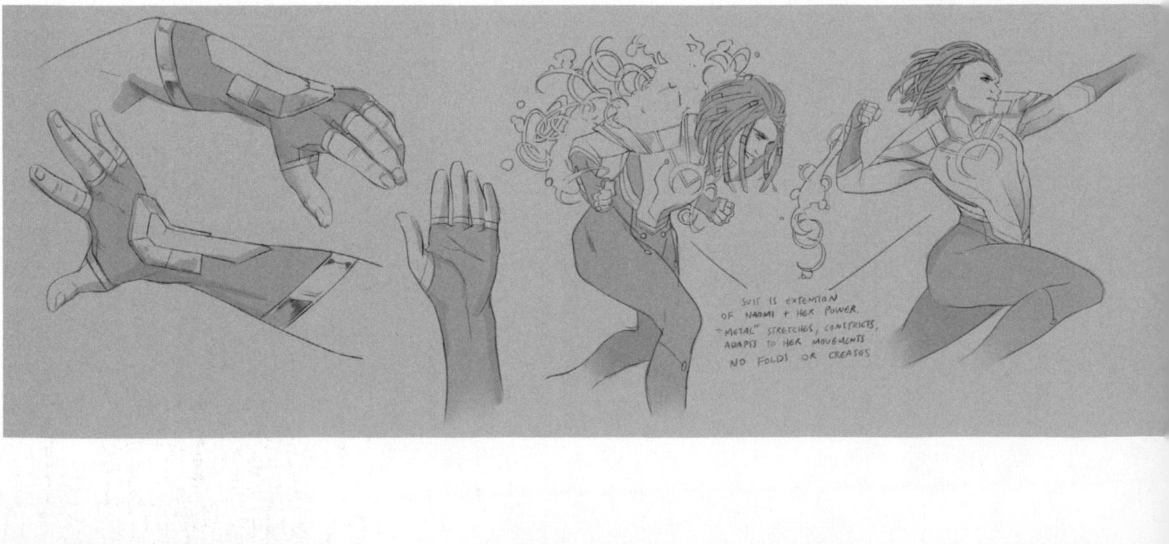
SUIT IS EXTENSION
OF NAOMI + HER POWER.
"METAL" STRETCHES, CONSTRICTS,
ADAPTS TO HER MOVEMENTS
NO FOLDS OR CREASES